A Leap of Faith

Audrey and Tony Walter

Published by New Generation Publishing in 2012

Copyright © Audrey and Tony Walter 2012

First Edition

The author asserts the moral right under the Copyright, Designs and Patents Act 1988 to be identified as the author of this work.

All Rights reserved. No part of this publication may be reproduced, stored in a retrieval system or transmitted, in any form or by any means without the prior consent of the author, nor be otherwise circulated in any form of binding or cover other than that which it is published and without a similar condition being imposed on the subsequent purchaser.

www.newgeneration-publishing.com

 New Generation **Publishing**

Acknowledgements

We would like to take this opportunity to thank all those who helped and assisted in this circumnavigation, of particular mention has to be the Blue Water Rally Organisation without whose guidance and experience this voyage may never have happened. Also Adrian Matthews and his team at Silverwood Yacht Services, Port Solent Marina, Portsmouth; their combined expertise and professionalism during three long years of preparation prior to the voyage was above and beyond the call of duty.

A special mention must be made of all the people who wish to remain anonymous including rally members, family and friends for their extra support and assistance before during and after the voyage, it would have been far more difficult and perhaps impossible without them.

None of us are really independent, we all rely on others to some degree, thank you all for helping us "Sail our Dream".

In the interests of privacy some names in this book have been changed

Dedication

I would like to dedicate this book to my wife for her unrequited believe and faith, even at my lowest ebb it helped ensure a life time's dream come true.

In reality, we should dedicate it to our family, sons Ian and Philip, their wives Becky and Liza and our grandsons, Daniel, Samuel and Jack, even if the grownups thought we were mad, their enthusiasm and encouragement kept us going, the young ones just thought we were TV sized people from the computer messaging and got a shock when they eventually saw us.

My sailing friend of over 40 years Sid, (known colloquially as Hissing Sid), repeated these enduring words before we left,

"If you don't do it, you'll always regret it." Amen to that!

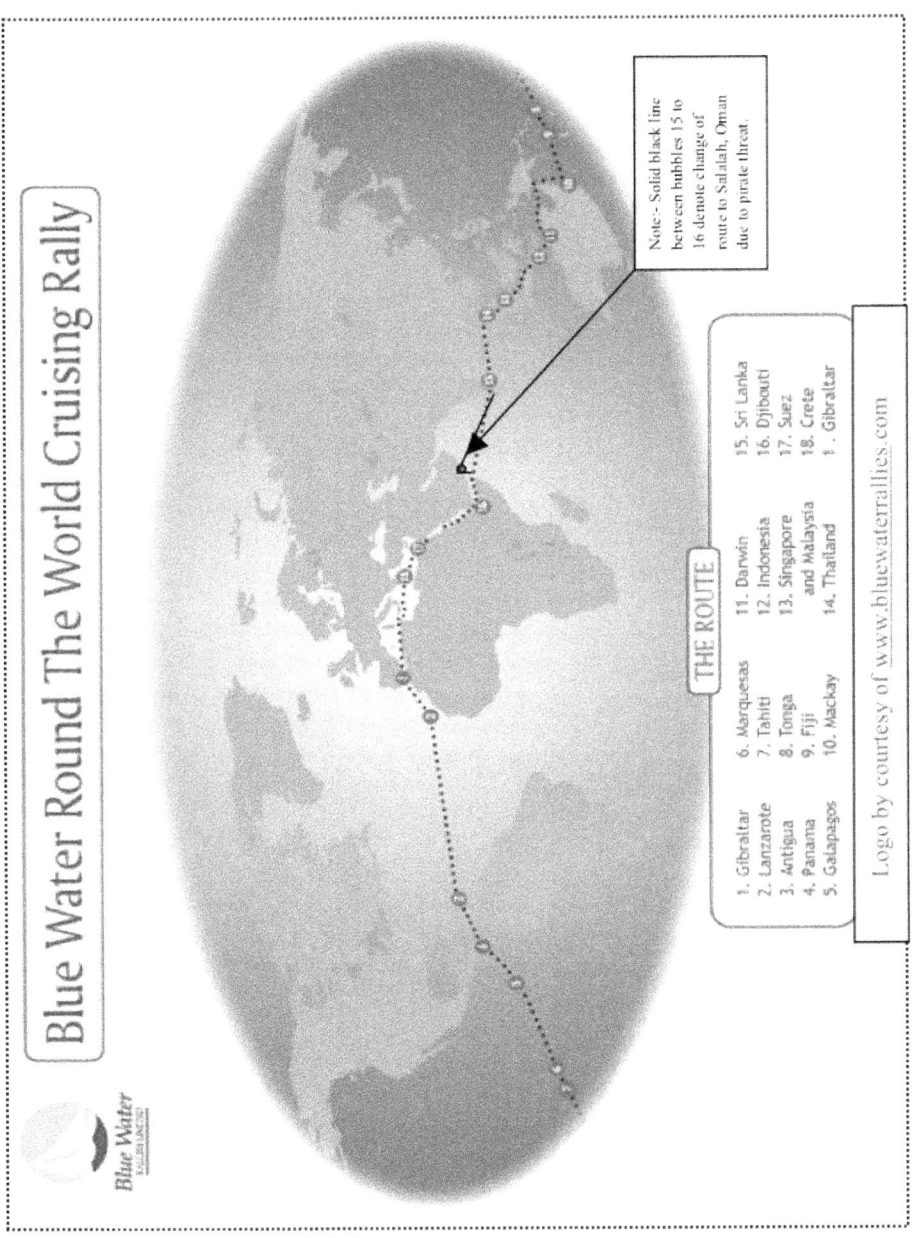

Bio of Audrey and Tony Walter

Audrey

I was born of parents who after surviving the Second World War were happy with the quiet life; my father had served three years in the Burma jungle with the army, my mother became a WREN and survived the Portsmouth Blitz. We lived in a prefabricated council house on the outskirts of Portsmouth and all they wanted afterwards was a safe haven for their growing family.

I have never been a natural sailor and initially found venturing out in the Solent, our local sailing area, an uncomfortable and somewhat fraught experience. I could never see the point in getting cold and wet, rafting up with a load of other boats or taking a dinghy ashore to sit all evening in a pub with a damp bum. OK, I agree, it could be fun and exhilarating when the conditions were right and there was nothing like drifting along with just the wind to propel you, but let's face it, in UK, just how many times does this actually happen?

What became the major turning point was when we took over the running of a 62-foot Northwind sailing yacht in Turkey, I finally appreciated this sailing lark!

One of the things I have to thank my husband for during our marriage is how he has encouraged me to "stretch", i.e. take on ventures I would not normally have contemplated, it was down to him that I grew an appetite for "another world out there".

Tony

On a rainy day when I was 12 years old in the local secondary school, we were allowed to go to the library, I found a copy of Joshua Slocomb's book "Sailing Alone Round the World", the damage was done, I determined that one day I would sail round the world in my own boat.

Life faded the dream, but one day it came back with a vengeance, as soon as I saw "Cayuco" the seed was sown, she was a 1971 Salar 40, designed by Laurent Giles and renowned for their comfortable extended sailing qualities. We bought her in

Greece in 2002, cruised around the Greek Islands and the Turkish coast then sailed her back to England in 2004.

In my mind I kept thinking "this life is not a rehearsal", and, "we only get one chance at it", I was nearly 60 years old and time was running out.

My wife was not enamoured with the idea but humoured me while working on an ambitious fitting out project, the turning point came when both daughters-in-law gave birth to our new grandsons within a month of each other.

"This," she said, "gives us two years to do it, I don't mind being away while they are too young to remember us, but I'm not going for more than two years."

Hence the Blue Water Rally, a two-year circumnavigation using the trade wind route, when we set off from UK, however, my wife had only committed herself as far as the Caribbean.

For Further Information:

www.aleapoffaith.org.uk

Chapters	Title	Page
Prologue:	A Near Disaster Before We Even Left the UK	11
Chapter 1	The Start	28
Chapter 2	The Atlantic Ocean, Canaries to Antigua	50
Chapter 3	Repair Bills, Antigua and the Caribbean	64
Chapter 4	The Panama Canal	76
Chapter 5:	Panama to the Galapagos Islands	98
Chapter 6:	Galapagos Islands to the Marquesas	112
Chapter 7:	Polynesia	143
Chapter 8	Bora Bora to Raratonga and Tonga	159
Chapter 9	Tonga to Fiji	172
Chapter 10	Fiji to Australia	192
Chapter 11	The Great Barrier Reef and over the Top	216
Chapter 12	Darwin and on to Indonesia	199
Chapter 13	Singapore and Malaysia	237
Chapter 14	Thailand	250
Chapter 15	On to Sri Lanka	264
Chapter 16	To the Maldives and Oman	280
Chapter 17	Pirates Ahoy, Salalah to Djibouti	295
Chapter 18	North up the Red Sea	318
Chapter 19	Egypt and through the Suez Canal to Crete	342
Epilogue	Tying the Knot	367

Prologue

A near disaster even before we left UK

Tony

The cockpit drain system had just been renewed today complete with a new 24 volt automatically sensed bilge pump. After dinner that evening, we sat relaxing below in the saloon, my wife, legs lying lazily along the cushion, moved to do the washing up and dropped her bare feet into cold sea water. It's difficult to describe your feelings; there wasn't time to consider that we were literally sinking on the marina while still at our berth and everything happened very quickly. We had to get the water back where it belonged as soon as possible and there was an element of panic. I switched the new pump on, fitted the handle into the manual system and started to pump the considerable amount of sea water back overboard as fast as possible. We never did discover why the automatic switch had been left in the "off" position. Audrey made an emergency call to our friend Adrian to ask for help, he agreed, drove quickly to the marina and relieved me at the pump.

My wife, who was understandingly feeling devastated, wondered about the sanity of all this, said she'd see me in a while and walked away. I knew she was upset and didn't argue; sometimes it's best to say nothing. This was a serious setback; here we were preparing to set off round the world in a small sailing boat and we can't even keep the damn thing afloat at our mooring, I dreaded Audrey's return, this incident could scupper the whole idea.

Adrian and I bailed out Cayuco, traced the problem to a faulty one way valve and closed off the leak. We then stripped out and salvaged everything we could, taking it all up to his workshop for a drying out session.

Adrian and I were still working in the stern cabin mopping up the dregs when Audrey returned, this was our sleeping cabin and it had suffered worse than the two forward ones.

"Hey," she began, there was a pregnant pause, Adrian and I looked at each other and waited for the worse.

Audrey - Reflections on a Certain Fitting Out Cock Up while on Port Solent Marina

We were onboard enjoying a cosy evening, feet up in front of the telly, sounds familiar, very ordinary, much like us at home, I hear you say. We'd eaten our evening meal and felt quite mellow after a glass of wine; well, nothing much was happening. I got up reluctantly to do the washing up and found myself ankle deep in water, "Hells Bells" or words to that affect. Tony jumped up making similar proclamations. The carpets throughout the saloon were under water but more to the point we were slowly sinking and destined to be dangling from our mooring lines.

Tony leapt into action to start pumping best he could trying to get the situation under control while I called our friend to see if he could help, he assured me he would be there in ten minutes.

Well, something inside me snapped at that point, I just grabbed my car keys and said to Tony,

"I'm out of here".

We had sold our house; the boat was our home such as it was, fitting out had been a trying time, often intrusive when you're trying to live around the proceedings. Adrian, bless him, always very conscious of this, would ask if it was a good time to carry out whatever needed doing, apologising for any inconvenience beforehand. OK, it was us that needed the work carried out, but he was always the perfect gentleman and so thorough.

I knew as I left the boat it would be alright, I just needed some space and who could blame me?

In the strange way of things, on my way out of the marina complex I saw something that even in my totally depressed state reached out to my normally optimistic nature. It was nothing earth shattering just one of those little delights you want to share. However, now was not the time.

Those familiar with Port Solent would no doubt know of Portchester Castle, that timeless fort that has stood at the northern reaches of Portsmouth Harbour since the period of the Romans. As I parked the car in the attractive leafy grounds that quiet summer evening and looked up as the sun set behind the aged battlements, I wondered what the hell I thought I was doing. Did we really think we could sail around the world in a small boat? That's what I'd been telling people, but deep down I couldn't make myself believe it. Something my brain had trouble processing. The distance to be travelled might as well have been on par to the number of grains of sand on a beach, or the stars in the universe, it was just an unbelievable reflection.

I'd told Tony I couldn't promise any further than the Atlantic crossing, it was bad enough getting my head round that. At least if I did, I could focus on the thought of visiting friends we had worked with in Tortola in the British Virgin Islands.

A lot of work, money and planning had gone into getting Cayuco ready for the off, no matter how far we got, we would have to take it one step at a time.

It was almost dark now and the castle grounds were deserted except for one or two people taking their dogs for an evening romp.

I was aware that I had walked away from Cayuco this evening because I could, in the months to come, when a problem arose, whether big or small, I would not have that luxury. It would be down to the two of us to sort it out and our solidarity would have to see us through. I started the car and drove slowly back home to my little ship and her Captain pondering my thoughts. Tony and Adrian were still busy in the stern cabin as I stuck my head over the side.

"Hey" I called;

they looked up dubiously, wondering what was to follow,

"Did you know", I continued, "The swans have still got all their seven cygnets; I saw them as I left the marina".

The release of baited breath from below was audible; Adrian rose to leave and promised to return our carpets in the morning, assuring us they would be fully steam cleaned. We thanked him for all his help and prompt action and bid him goodnight. Tony and I looked at each other.

The pair of swans I was referring to were on to a winner. They had the safest most secure place of all to raise their family away from the less caring members of the human race. It generally caused amusement when they left or arrived via the Port Solent lock system; sometimes having the whole lock to themselves.

"I suppose" I said, "I'd better put some hot water bottles in the berths, could be a bit damp in there tonight".

For some reason we both laughed and saw the funny side of that, the kettle went on for the bottles and then for a cup of coffee. We sat in the cockpit and talked about the near catastrophe of the last few hours, the full enormity of just what we were taking on and who in their right mind would be contemplating it?

Chapter 1

The Start

Tony

The big day dawned, Cayuco, together with 30 other boats was motor sailing down to the start line off Europa Point in Gibraltar, well, 29 boats in fact, one had already radioed in a problem with his steering gear, I wondered whether his butterflies were as active as mine.

We were a husband and wife team, as were nearly half of the other boats in the rally, all of us were off to sail round the world in our small yachts, what the hell were we thinking of? More to the point, I wondered, how many of us would be left at the end of the voyage. Would we with Cayuco make it all the way round? She was a wonderful sea boat, we had already established that, even so I was aware of her shortcomings and I would have to add our doubts to that as well.

We'd bought Cayuco in Greece in 2002 then sailed her through the Mediterranean and back to UK over a two year period. The next few years were spent fitting her out for an extended voyage, I was thinking about sailing round the world, my personal childhood dream while Audrey (my wife), was probably not on such ambitious lines.

Every one of us had joined the Blue Water Rally to "Sail our Dream" it's certainly easier to make the decision to go when you know lots of others are doing the same. This rally is a bi-annual event and follows the trade wind route around the world; it uses the Panama and Suez Canals while visiting some of the most exotic islands in the world.

Our choice of yacht, Cayuco, was a centre cockpit ketch and designed by Laurent Giles; she was built in UK in 1971 and was his "Salar 40" class of yacht. Although not quite the smallest boat in the fleet, she was the slowest and to complete the equation also the oldest. It was in essence all we could afford but we had not let that detract from the work, sweat and tears that had gone into her fitting out during the last five years. We had done the best job possible with the available funds but were still short of a few luxuries that would have made it easier, namely a generator and a water maker, not essentials but we would regret not having them later.

This period had not been without incident, one night while on the marina in Portsmouth we had nearly sunk the boat, getting up from the table and stepping into sea water already over the saloon floor was not recommended to instil confidence. The new automatic bilge draining system recently fitted had malfunctioned and back siphoned into the bilge, if we had gone ashore, Cayuco would have been lying on the seabed very quickly.

Leaving Port Solent Marina we experienced the worse channel crossing ever and then in the middle of our three day crossing of the Bay of Biscay, Cayuco had started taking water through the newly fitted propeller shaft seal. Solving that problem had only led to another, a drain pipe had slipped off a sea cock and was again pouring sea water into the bottom of the boat, simple to remedy after you have found the correct pipe; there are a lot of underwater inlets on most boats. We had pulled the boat apart, opened every locker, looked under the floorboards and checked all the sea cocks before finally finding the offending opening. Once again a considerable amount of sea water had entered into our home, this was becoming a habit. Here we were setting off on a round the world cruise in a small sailing boat and we could hardly keep the thing afloat getting to the start line.

Towards the end of our Biscay crossing a gale had sprung up, we finished that passage surfing into La Coruna harbour at over eight knots with seriously reefed sails and a north-west force eight behind us, at least it was daylight. When trying to leave port a few days later the anchor winch refused to work which caused further delay and meant a trip ashore to find some spare parts, all this was not a good omen. My mother always used to say,

"Bad start, good finish", oh Mum, if only you knew the truth.

Audrey

Sailing a small boat round the world had never been my dream but I had tentatively agreed to go as far as the Caribbean, we had worked at an island resort there some years earlier and it was my excuse for going back and catching up with old friends.

Just before we set off, both the wives of our two sons gave birth to grandsons, another reason for not being away too long. I told Tony, going sailing was for a two year maximum, being separated from them when they were young was acceptable but not any longer. Hence the Blue Water Rally, a bi-annual two year circumnavigation; however, as I already intimated, when we left, I had only agreed to go as far as the Caribbean.

There are many reasons for choosing to go on an adventure such as this with an organised rally, the camaraderie of many people with similar interests, organised stopovers with assistance, a daily radio schedule, access to a supply network in case of emergency, regular briefings with information and navigational warnings for the next passage and updates on present occurrences about where we were heading to name a few.

A few long distance yachtsmen seem to regard sailing with a rally as against the spirit of adventure and taking the easy way out. For us it was a logical and safe way to go, when you consider some of the problems in the world today it made sense, it fitted in with our time scale and also got us up in the morning and forced us to get on with it. All round the world we met people who had taken years to get where they were, this is OK if you can finance it. We also saw many abandoned dreams, there are some fine yachts lying decaying and rotting in forgotten corners of marinas and harbours all over the world, they are always a sorry sight.

Being a live aboard is in some ways an alien world, when you first go long distance sailing, the constant movement and the concept of always keeping one hand for the boat and one hand for you is odd but a necessary part of the learning curve. One of the more difficult tasks is learning to prepare meals without having to scrape them up off the floor, another responsibility is the night watches, they require a certain degree of alertness and dexterity. Sleeping in a sea berth with the continuous noise and trusting the person on watch to keep you safe is another leap of faith. It all adds up to a completely different frame of mind, sometimes ecstatic, sometimes scary, the one thing you can guarantee is; it's never the same.

Tony

We had been in Gibraltar for a month; it had gone very quickly, there was a lot to do on Cayuco apart from all the necessary administrative work for the Blue Water Rally organisers. Every boat is checked, a bit like a scrutiny, this ensures you are carrying the correct safety equipment and know how to use it. It is part of the work that helps to keep the rally so popular and as free from danger as possible, nobody will deny that there aren't still risks, but a very rigorous attempt is made to alleviate these where possible. Every entrant receives a detailed list of the suggested modifications well in advance, the recommended spares to carry and the paperwork necessary to satisfy government authorities around the world is also included in the information. The BWR have been organising these events for many years and are well versed in all the requirements needed.

An important part of the rally is the social programme, although everyone sails independently between stopovers, when ashore many functions and tours of the area are laid on. In Gibraltar there were sailing club, tourist and official government parties, tours to Rhonda over the Spanish border and other places of interest, a cable car excursion to the top of the "Rock" and a walk back down, with many other outings arranged independently.

Of particular interest to me was the special cave society expedition inside "The Rock", I went caving with a few others from the rally on an out of the ordinary expedition not usually part of the tourist agenda, It was fabulous; taking us right down into an underground cavern with a large pool and some serious alternative climbing, not recommended for the faint hearted as it does involve a degree of agility and can feel claustrophobic.

The final briefing had given us a head's up on possible weather conditions and the intricacies of getting out of the Gibraltar Strait against wind and current, you also have to dodge the predictable heavy commercial traffic. Current in the Strait is almost always easterly due to evaporation of the surface water in the Med. and the predicted wind was light westerly so both were expected to be against us for the first few hours. A good talk by the local sailing school instructor gave us an insight into avoiding the worst of the current and the start timing had been chosen to give us the best shot.

Saturday evening before the start was a sober affair, nobody wanted to overdo the partying bit, there was a distinct possibility the full enormity of what we were about to undertake was upon us all.

Everyone without exception was up early on Sunday morning; we had completed all the documentation the day before, one by one we slipped out and made our way down to the start line between Europa Point and the Navy Minesweeper anchored offshore. The cannon on the point fired its ten and five minute warnings, then the start gun and we were off.

The yachts ranged in size from 36 to 63 feet (10.8 to 19 metres) and included two catamarans; the start was timed for 10-00 hours on Sunday the 28th October 2007, we were just happy to be on our way at last. The wind as expected was light and we had a slight adverse current, most of us motor-sailed across the line, (well it is a cruising rally) and then continued out through the Gibraltar Straits.

Approaching Tariffa at the end of the strait around 13-30 hrs, the current was now in our favour, our log was reading 3.9 knots but the GPS confirmed we were actually doing 7.9 knots over the ground, this is most unusual here but we weren't going to question it.

As soon as we got past Tariffa the current eased off and the further west we sailed the better it was. We were heading out in the Atlantic looking for the northerly trade winds, these normally start about 50 to 60 miles offshore and as soon as possible we changed course to the south west. Keeping close to the Moroccan shore would not be good for us, long unlit offshore tuna fishing nets and an adverse current made that shorter route a dubious advantage.

Getting clear of the land as soon as possible worked well and the next day saw us finding the northerly trade winds, we headed south. Setting up the twin jibs with the wind vane self steering gear made the watches much easier to manage, apart from the occasional tweak to the vane we only had to keep a look out and fill in the log, Cayuco was now sailing by herself. Both of us got plenty of rest and we soon settled down to a regular routine, even our meals could be taken in the cockpit together while still keeping a look out. We run a simple watch system; both of us are up during the day while the night is divided into four approximately three hour sessions between 20-00 and 08-00 hours. This gives us both six hours sleep and either one of us can go down for an extra hour or two at any time during the day.

All went routinely until three days out when the conditions deteriorated towards the evening, a wild night ensued; we did our best to reef the twin jibs but still charged along way above our comfort zone. It was a very dark night, any moon we had was obscured by the clouds, I didn't like sailing this fast without being able to see anything but there was not a lot we could do about it. We reasoned that there would probably be many other nights like this on the way round so we may as well get used to it. The next day on the 10-00 hour radio schedule everyone had recorded the same conditions, it was confirmed that all the yachts had a really rough night. The wind continued to blow until mid afternoon on the fourth day, by then we had done 132 miles in 24 hours so we were happy with a 5½ knot average speed. One of the larger yachts reported 240 miles in the same period, phew, an average speed of 10 knots, there's just no substitute for waterline length! Under normal circumstances I would have shortened sail further to slow our headlong rush through the night, it was exhilarating to be moving through the water at close to our maximum hull speed and I just didn't want to slow down. Long distance ocean sailing is a different ball game and it is much more important to be cautious, I would have to watch my exuberance, a calculated risk may be acceptable sometimes but taking chances had to be a big no-no.

The reefing gear on the twin jibs worked well but with both of them on the same roller furler I considered the force required to reef the sails in a rising wind excessive. I would have to go back to the drawing board again and improve the system, it was an essential part of our rig and if we overloaded and damaged the gear, it would have serious consequences.

Figure 1: Cayuco moored stern to in Marina Bay, Gibraltar waiting for the off.

Figure 2: You cannot possibly go to Gibraltar without climbing the "Rock" and taking a picture of the Barbary Apes, they are not as friendly as they seem though.

Figure 3: Rhonda, up in the hills of Spain is reputed to have the oldest Bull Ring in the country.

Audrey

I saw Lanzarote through the haze in the early morning, Tony was still sleeping, the dolphins were swimming and diving around Cayuco and I was starting to realise that this was a normal phenomenon for them at dawn. I waited for Tony to wake up before putting on the kettle for a cup of tea and having a light breakfast. During the day we closed the shore and ran down the coast, the wind had gone light so we took a while to arrive and did not get into the new marina at Puerto Calero until 17-00 hrs. After the preliminaries we enjoyed a good night ashore with our fellow rally members, everyone was happy to be safely in. Nevertheless the No1 topic of conversation was the forthcoming Atlantic crossing. It is probably worth mentioning here that within hours of leaving Gibraltar no other yachts were seen until near Lanzarote.

The usual round of social parties and tours of the island courtesy of the tourist board took up much of our time. We had complimentary island excursions with visits to the local island sites of interest, a volcano and demonstration water spout from the hot interior, a call at the cactus gardens and a wonderful social night at an underground restaurant within the lava tubes of the natural volcanic caves, wonderful.

At some point during the time we were there, our friend with the steering problem we had left in Gibraltar turned up, he had gone back, got it repaired and sailed down by himself, it was good to see him, all the yachts were together again.

Figure 4: Cactus flowers in the Cactus Gardens in Lanzarote.

Tony

Our run down the African coast under twin jibs which were both slid up the same twin groove furler gear had shown up some difficulties associated with the rig, I was very concerned by the loading forces on the fittings and our single forestay system in rough conditions, my engineering brain was working overtime and I just could not see the components standing up to the forces exerted on them for a sustained period of time, a modification would have to be devised to give me more peace of mind.

While pondering this inconvenience a sailing yacht slipped into the next berth, that's funny I thought, looks like another Salar 40, odd, there's not many of them about. Sure enough, it was another one, but from Australia and heading back that way. It had a twin forestay arrangement and that was the basis of the idea in my head, all I had to do was fit a second forestay, that would neatly solve the problem of flying the second jib, plus it would give the fore part of the mast another means of support, Eureka, simple!

A local rigger gave me a hand to cut in the shroud support plate and roller at the top of the mast, while I got on with the exit plate at the bottom and fitted a new jammer for the second jib halyard. This arrangement worked very well and later on I was glad that we took the decision to fit a second stay. A "U" bolt was also fitted to the starboard side deck so the spare stay could be secured out of the way when not required. The lower end of the stay finished with a highfield lever so this arrangement facilitated moving the stay from the bows to its stowage point on the side deck. Again, much later on in the rally while crossing the Pacific Ocean, I was delighted to be able to use this new "U" bolt once more for a far more important reason.

We were scheduled to stay in Puerto Calero for 14 days, it was very pleasant. An organised shopping trip to restock our provisions for the Atlantic crossing was arranged and we visited local chandlers for last minute spares. I helped with engine and mechanical problems with others on the rally while generally everyone readied themselves for the long voyage.

The day before the off we were all called to a rally planning meeting; this is where information is discussed regarding the next leg. It deals with requirements for leaving, radio schedules, weather patterns known at the time and any special arrival information needed. Our destination was Antigua so the talk also included any special navigational dangers regarding the two most likely harbours we would be using.

For obvious reasons the organisers like to keep all the participants as close to the sailing schedule as possible. Although we all sail independently it is amazing how all the yachts spread out after leaving, a few hours is all it takes for you to be sailing along in your own bit of sea. This is why our SSB radios were so important, we had scheduled times each day to talk and update weather and position information. This was then passed on by the network controller of the day to rally headquarters who updated the internet site, very reassuring for people back home that followed our progress, of course, there are safety precautions built into this facility.

While on the subject of radios, there are many networks specially set up for long distance small boat sailors, you soon find out their broadcast times and frequencies. In general they are voluntary, free to all and can be a useful aid to safety or any other emergency, one of their most important functions is to pass on the current weather situation and future predictions, most skippers keep a chart near the radio of the more useful networks.

Audrey

The usual social gathering was organised for the night before leaving, everyone was behaving themselves and being sensible, nobody wanted a hangover the next day.

The start of the Atlantic passage was for Saturday the 17th November 2007, the time was set for around 10-00 am, in reality yachts left as soon as they were ready. As it is a cruising rally some of the smaller yachts had already left a couple of days earlier knowing they would be overtaken by the faster yachts later, that is what it's all about, everything is very flexible and with hindsight, we should probably have left with them.

Our decision was to wait; the weather men were forecasting no wind until Thursday, another 5 days. We wanted to sail as much as possible and didn't relish the idea of using most of our diesel motoring down to the area of trade winds approximately 800 miles away, we watched all the others leave and waved them off.

A couple of the yachts left and motored down to the Cape Verde Islands, after fuelling up down there they were able to sail the trade wind route to Antigua virtually all the way. This is another alternative but I was not convinced, we had been getting conflicting information about the availability of fuel supplies, it would have been a long sail to find fuel was scarce on arrival. In reality there were no problems at all and the yachts that used this ploy did not experience any difficulty.

Cayuco has two large fuel tanks, we also carried extra fuel in cans on the deck, this gave us enough fuel for nearly 1000 miles, with a passage of approximately 2800 miles we would still have to sail the majority of the way.

A few yachts also stayed in Puerto Calero with us, two were still waiting for spare parts and another three for the same reason as us. At least it gave us a couple of days to reflect and get a few more jobs completed. Eventually, exactly on time, the wind came in from the north-east and on Thurs. 22nd Nov we left for the longest passage of our lives so far undertaken. We tried to remain cheerful and keep the inner feelings to ourselves; neither of us was under any illusions. Cayuco was the oldest and slowest boat in the rally, very comfortable and extremely seaworthy but we had never sailed across an ocean before, this kind of loneliness was a new emotion.

For us, it was the point of no return; we were taking on the Atlantic Ocean with just the two of us on board. What it had in store we didn't know, but it was too late to back out now, whatever happened, we would have to deal with it ourselves.

Chapter 2

The Atlantic Ocean – Canaries to Antigua

Tony

We left Puerto Calero at 10-00 hours on Thursday 22nd November 2007 and waved goodbye to the two remaining rally boats that were still waiting for some spare parts to arrive.

To say we were apprehensive would have been a massive understatement, all the other rally yachts had left days before and the passage we were about to undertake ostensibly alone, was way beyond anything we had ever sailed; we tried not to think about it. Although it was exciting to be heading out into what was for us an unknown situation, for me it was the culmination of a lifetime of planning, acquiring skills, information and hard work, it was also the start of potentially the most dangerous journey we as a couple had ever attempted.

Motoring for the first 3 hours to give a good offing and get into some clean air, we took advantage of the wind acceleration between the islands as soon as possible and sailed south. The temptation was to head closer to Tenerife on the way through in case we decided to rest a while but we resisted, it was better to just get on with it and deal with whatever happened as we went. It would be beneficial for us to get to Antigua before the 16th December, that's when the BWR support team was due to fly back to UK. There was no desire on our part to rush or impose a time scale on the Atlantic crossing; safe arrival was all we ever required.

Before leaving we had filled up all our spare fuel tanks and lashed them on deck, we had also borrowed a fuel bladder from another rally member who did not need it. This held a further 140 litres of diesel and was stored and tied down on deck in front of the mast. It only goes to show what a great boat the Salar 40 is, all that weight above the waterline and in the bow section of the boat made no discernable difference to the speed, stability or the handling; she just got on with it.

Audrey - Crossing the Pond.

So now it was time for "the big one". Well, I'd said I could get my head round this one, hadn't I? Even if the Caribbean was as far as I got.

One of my incentives was to re-visit a small island off Tortola in the British Virgin Islands. Tony and I had enjoyed one of our more remarkable overseas contracts on Cooper Island, an ultimate getaway location just 6 miles from Road Town and across the Francis Drake Passage. The Cooper Island Beach Club Resort consisted of 12 hotel chalets and a popular restaurant used by yacht charterers; it has mooring buoys and a good anchorage. The island was largely uninhabited except for one local family living on the opposite side and the small team of about 14 people running the resort. We were privileged to become part of that busy team working in this idyllic spot for the period between 1999 and 2000; it was magical to see in the new millennium at the end of 1999 from this vantage point.

Tony was the maintenance manager looking after all the resorts facilities, he also took the guests and supplies backwards and forwards to the mainland. I looked after the hotel accommodation and also became a dab hand in the cocktail bar. We had become a close knit community while we lived and worked on the island, even cooking for each other and eating together as a family. It was no wonder I would consider sailing across an ocean in order to return to this place, I had really enjoyed working there and at this point in time, was not seriously considering going any further.

The support team had tried to encourage all the boats to leave Puerto Calero on the same day, for various reasons, this didn't happen. There were a few rebels, Cayuco being one of them, we preferred to wait for a more favourable weather forecast and wanted to sail as much as possible, Tony did not want to use the majority of our diesel just getting down to the trade winds, about 800 miles away in a south west direction. I can't blame the organisers for trying to get us all to go at the same time; I think they were worried that we may change our minds after everyone had left. It was certainly more difficult to leave later by ourselves, the worst part is thinking about it, when you've moved out and are on the way, it's not so bad. As they say, "the worst part is leaving", after that it's in the lap of the gods, we set off with the prospect of at least three weeks life on the ocean ahead of us.

After a few spots of rain it was a fine day with a calm sea as we motored through the shelter of the islands. When the Atlantic swell hit us I wrestled with my initial queasiness and was glad I'd seen fit to take a tablet. I normally suffer from seasickness during the first day or two, fortunately we enjoyed a beautiful star filled first night and averaged 4 knots with our twin jibs quietly pulling us along, the air was warm and the moon full, it was certainly a good send off.

At 10-00hrs the following day we caught our first rally roll call of the passage on SSB radio, we were able to pick up weather reports and log the positions of all the other yachts. For some positions, including our own, we had to use the relay system. The radio net controller of the day would send an e mail detailing all the yacht positions, any relevant weather conditions and a brief summary of significant remarks to base control in UK. All information would then be correlated and entered on the official website daily. This was a boon to loved ones at home and the facility was well used throughout the rally, it was also re-assuring for us to know that those left behind could easily obtain updates. The site was password protected, this hopefully made it more difficult for unauthorised people seeing information about our individual positions, after all, none of us wanted to come up against other aversive elements. Later on when passing through pirate territory, another set of more secure arrangements would be instigated.

Throughout the course of the rally the daily net became a most welcome lifeline. If a yacht was in trouble, going to be delayed for any reason or people just wanted to chat, the radio was always there. It was normal procedure to turn on the radio for two minutes every even numbered hour, this served as a listening watch in the event of any emergency, floating objects in the water, interesting sightings, all these could be reported with the Lat/Long position. The radio came into its own for advice and assistance, anyone with specialist skills could be called upon to answer relevant technical questions within their field of expertise, it was not uncommon to hear a discussion being debated regarding a medical, electrical or mechanical problem.

Our second night at sea was the complete opposite to the first, the moon was obscured, the weather was dreadfully squally and we endured a mixture of rain, wind, thunder and lightning all night long with plenty of sail changes. At one point we were going back to the Canary Islands at great speed for about half an hour before we could change the sail configuration over, eventually we managed to continue on an approximate course to the south west.

We had our first whale sighting on our third day, just a big dorsal fin but exciting all the same. On the fourth day I awoke at 06-00 hrs to a pod of dolphins playing around the boat. They were speckled in appearance with pink underbellies, later in the day we were visited by another huge pod, this time of the bottle-nosed variety, didn't really expect to see this many.

Tony

As Audrey said, all round the boat there were lots of dolphins jumping and whales spuming from their blowholes, I enjoyed watching them but there were some problems appearing on Cayuco. The starboard fuel tank had started leaking and the bilge pump kept running at regular intervals, every time we ran the engine, cooling water from the header tank leaked sea water into the bilge, it was not going to get better. As we had only been out a couple of days I was not overly impressed. On top of that I could not find the other water leak which was making the bilge pump work every few hours, I found a trickle of water coming from the anchor locker, this did not seem enough to be our problem. Anyway, nothing seemed serious enough to warrant going back to the Canaries or putting into the Cape Verde Islands. The wind had picked up a bit, we were sailing nicely and saving our diesel fuel, this was the whole idea of waiting for five days at the start, our noon to noon runs were 110 to 120 miles a day so all was right with the world, ...nearly.

I was surprised at the amount of squalls we were having, every few hours night and day it was shorten sail, change course, then back on course and set sails again, some of them were very vicious and quite alarming. We had decided to head for a position below the 20° north meridian and cross it between 25° and 30° west, then as soon as the trade winds started blowing we would alter course for Antigua. All this time the wind had been blowing from different directions and it was not always possible to use the downwind rig. It is very time consuming to constantly change from fore and aft to running rig, plus, it is also hard work as I always work alone on the foredeck. Audrey stayed in the cockpit, ensuring Cayuco stayed on course as we were on wind vane and she also kept an eye on the proceedings in case anything went wrong. I was always harnessed on but if I went over the side she was in charge of bringing the boat to a halt and extracting me from the wet stuff. We had rigged up a pulley system which used the end of the boom and a block and tackle to winch me out should the worst happen, fortunately it never did. We had two rules while sailing, the first was regarding falling overboard which was "DON'T", the second was, "If you do you're dead". It was how we looked at the reality, if you think the worst; you take more care, etc.

Audrey

On day five we were still playing with our sail rig, eventually we adopted a traditional "Goose Wing" rig, i.e. jib poled out one side with the main out the other and a preventer rigged to stop the inadvertent jibe. This system proved to be the most successful and on day 6 we were still going well in this fashion, our speckled pink-bellied dolphin buddies continued to lead the way, ducking, diving, jumping and generally amusing themselves at the bow!

Cayuco did not carry a lot of battery power, about 450 amp/hours, according to Tony we could have done with double that. When fitting out we had decided to fit a freezer, we didn't fancy living out of cans or on dried and reconstituted food for the long ocean passages, it was a good call and worked well. The freezer was quite small 37 litres, it was top loading, had been fitted with a keel cooler, a new efficient motor and then double insulated in its own compartment. It used very little electricity, less than 1 amp/hour and was more efficient than our ordinary refrigerator. Even with this advantage, it became clear by the seventh day that we were going to have re-charging problems. When under sail we had our solar panels but only if the sun shone, the wind generator was not very efficient downwind and the tow-gen only worked well when sailing fast whereby it then took about three quarters of a knot off our speed, at slow boat speed it was hardly worth the effort to rig it up. At this time we did not have a big enough petrol generator to charge the batteries, this meant we had to run the main engine twice a day, we timed this to coincide with the radio schedules at 10-00 and 18-00 hours so charged the batteries at the same time.

Our wind vane steering system saved an enormous amount of electrical power as we did not need to use the auto pilot, to save more amps, we opted to turn off all the instruments and continued with just the compass while using a dead reckoning system once a day. To be honest this was all that was necessary, we were hundreds of miles from land, there was nothing around at all, the whole voyage we only saw one ship and a couple of sailing boats.

Each day at noon Tony would estimate our position, note it on the paper chart, log the distance run and check it all with a hand held GPS. We did carry a sextant in case of emergency with all the necessary paperwork but even Tony admitted he would have to get the books out again to remember how it all worked. When the engine was charging the battery we would occasionally switch on the radar and chart-plotter, this was more to keep it active than serve any useful purpose. It was soul destroying watching the chart plotter screen seeing what little distance we had covered on the grand scale, even worse was to see how far we had to go. The really good thing was the radar; at night we turned it on for five minutes every hour, it was brilliant to see the squalls before they arrived and many times we were able to dodge them. In the end we didn't bother and just kept going as fast as we could, squalls and all. We learned that as the squall hit, we could run before it much faster so this in effect took a couple of knots off the apparent wind speed. Cayuco stood up to her canvas well so we just let her run, it got quite exhilarating, though in really hard squalls it was necessary to take over the wheel and steer by hand for a while, this broke up the watches and it was good fun as well.

Tony

On Thurs 29th November 2007 at 15-30 hours we crossed over the 20° north latitude line at 25°-45´ west, we were now supposedly into the westerly trade winds, unfortunately, no one had told the trade winds that they were supposed to be blowing, we slowly slogged even further south in search of them. I went on deck and put up the twin jibs again, surely the wind would come up soon, even as I was winching up the last bit of the second jib we were hit by a 30 knot squall, Cayuco took off like a scalded cat, I scrambled back to the cockpit and had to steer by hand as the wind vane had been over powered by the force of the wind. It was fantastic, Cayuco loved it and so did we, plus for once, it was in the right direction. We hung on to the sail for the next two hours and afterwards the wind did not really die, it went down to 20/22 knots and we just kept on going. At last we were away and these windy and squally conditions were set in for the next sixteen days of the crossing.

Our engine problems however were not over, by next day the heat exchanger was leaking sea water badly and it was obvious something would have to be done. Also, I'd run the engine during the night to charge the batteries, a high pressure oil pipe from the oil pump to the oil cooler had split and we lost all engine oil pressure. Not only that, the oil had sprayed all over the alternator which had now stopped working.

It looked like I would have some work to do when daylight came. To make it even more interesting, we still had the problem of the bilge pump running every few hours and had not yet found out where the water was coming from.

Ho hum, it never rains but why it pours.

Early morning at first light I assessed the situation, removing the alternator I dismantled it and cleaned up the parts as best I could. There did not appear to be anything physically wrong with it and all the continuity tests checked out ok. I was limited as to what I could do and hoped that it was only oil ingress which had stopped it working. Fortunately it was an old 24 volt A.C. heavy commercial vehicle type and was fitted with an external regulator, because of this, the regulator had escaped damage. While the alternator was off, it allowed me better access to the bottom of the engine where the split oil pipe was fitted, this was my next job.

The steel lined high pressure rubber pipe was damaged beyond repair and I did not carry a spare, another solution would have to be found. After a little thought, I reasoned that as long as we didn't run the engine for too long at a time, it may be possible to disconnect the oil cooler altogether. At the moment we were only running the engine for approximately one hour intervals to augment the battery charge, as long as this status quo remained, the rest of the cooling system would probably cope. There were two pipes, an inlet and an outlet, I removed the damaged pipe altogether, carefully unscrewed the end of the remaining good pipe from the oil cooler and refitted it to the engine side of the oil pump. The pressurised oil from the engine would now come from the oil pump, round the pipe and back into the engine oil pressure system, OK, it wouldn't be circulating around the oil cooler anymore but it was the best I could do. Refitting the parts I topped up the oil level and started the engine, there were no oil leaks, the alternator was working although not charging quite as efficiently as before and we would have to watch the temperature gauge carefully, it looked like it would get us out of trouble.

The bonus was, I had it all up and running by the time of the 10-00 hour radio schedule. The batteries by now were fairly well discharged but it did not take too long to get them serviceable again, we both breathed a sigh of relief.

Losing the ability to run the engine and subsequently charge the batteries would have been a body blow, I didn't want to think about the significance. If I had not cured the problem it would have meant no engine, an electrical shortage, probably no radio and consequently no communication, navigation would have had to revert to the old fashioned methods. This in itself would have caused unnecessary worry for everyone outside our little world apart from a big inconvenience to us.

We found out later that family members were following our progress avidly on the rally website, later, when three days late getting into Antigua we couldn't contact anyone by radio, our family became concerned and called rally support for information. The site only records your updated position if you can inform them by radio, when the radio co-ordinators have arrived in port the site can go unaltered. This is a normal problem as we found out during the rally, the SSB radio is meant as a long range means of communication at sea, in port it is affected by high ground, electrical disturbances, masts and radar from surrounding vessels plus any manner of other influences. That night an attempt was made to contact us and a weak signal confirmed we were alright, the family was informed but it does demonstrate the importance of having another means of contact such as a sat phone. There is a good network now and as the price continues to reduce they make a very reliable alternative. The amount of use is only determined by the depth of pocket, unfortunately, our personal depth of pocket decreed that our itinerary did not include one.

Audrey

The thing about ocean crossings is there's none of this nipping down to the local supermarket for what you are running low on. You adapt with what you have and become quite creative in the galley. Many of the ralliers became expert at baking their own bread, I tried but was not one of them and my efforts were pretty dismal. On day 8 we reached the place where the butter is supposed to melt which is around 20° north, we were then supposed to turn right for Antigua, as we still had little wind, we carried on south west, hoping to find the wind before too much longer.

People ask about our watch keeping and which system we adopted, in effect, the system adopted us. We fell into a pattern of sleeping for 2½ hours each on the first watch, followed by 3 hours each on the second. The watches started about 20-00hours,

Tony would do the first on watch and I would sleep, taking over my watch about 22-30 to 23-00, we would change again in the early hours of the morning around 01-30 and then again at dawn or about 04-30 to 05-00. It is amazing how you get used to the changing sleep patterns and there are no hard and fast rules about our system. On some nights we changed and had longer periods of sleep, this proved to be beneficial for both of us. During the day we mostly stayed awake but either of us could go down for a nap if they wanted to catch up. The bonus was our secure sea berth in the centre of the boat; it was comfortable, always warm and dry and unless Cayuco inverted, it was impossible to fall out of.

Up until now the wind had been coming and going, by the 10th day it looked like we had reached the trade winds, an indication of how strong the wind blew overnight was given by the number of flying fish trapped on Cayuco's decks, more flying fish on day 11 but by day 12 it was calm again. Well, I say calm; we were doing 120 miles a day easily and averaging 5 knots so maybe I was just getting used to it, whatever, it was good for Cayuco.

Another major consideration is having enough fresh water, many of the other boats had a water maker but on Cayuco we just had to make our quota of about 400 litres (75 gallons) last. We used our salt water pump for rinsing off dirty dishes, washing vegetables and anything else we could think of. We also took around 100 litres of drinking water securely stowed in the forepeak and all in individual two litre containers, only losing one plastic bottle during the whole circumnavigation. Taking a shower was not an economical use of fresh water so we only allowed ourselves one strip wash each per day. However, that did not stop us getting the occasional shower, on day 14 we were watching a squall coming up behind us, it looked like a big one but did not appear to have a lot of wind associated with it, just a lot of rain. We both grabbed our shampoo and stood naked on the stern deck, the rain shower was quite warm, very refreshing and we both got a good cleaning off well before all the rain had gone.

A lot of the rally boats were just two up same as us; obviously this causes a few problems with watches when it would have been an advantage to have a larger crew. We had decided beforehand that if we were going to do it, we would do it by ourselves. Generally speaking though, if you are to spend over three weeks at sea in a confined space, you will probably survive the experience better with the one person you know best of all. You can have a good old hissy fit, swear like a trouper and walk around stark naked. Anyway, why wear clothes when it's hot enough most of the time not to bother, there's no-one to see you, it saves using fresh water for washing them and cuts down on the laundry when you eventually arrive.

Well, if we were looking for trade winds we eventually found them with a vengeance.

Tony

Our progress had not been startling and our recent average had been 100 to 110 miles a day, the wind had been fickle and was not at all steady. This was about to change, a tropical wave was reported to be coming up behind and to the south of us, nothing spectacular, but the forecast was talking of a continuous 30 to 35 knots of wind.

It hit us on Wednesday the 5th December when we were about $17°$ north; although the centre was over two hundred miles further south of us we felt the effects. Early morning while it was still very dark, I was on my off watch sleeping peacefully, there was a tremendous sudden squall, Audrey grabbed the wheel as the wind vane had been overpowered and she called out for help. We were flying along at a pace far above ours and Cayuco's comfort zone when there was a terrific bang. Something had given out and not having time to get dressed properly, I appeared on deck most inappropriately attired. My wife was more than relieved to let me take over the wheel but even I found it very hard to keep on course. There was a serious chance we could broach, it was obvious Cayuco was carrying far too much sail in the conditions and although downwind something else might give. I quickly switched on the instruments to get an idea of what we were dealing with, the wind speed meter was off the scale, pressed hard against the stop, I didn't want to know anymore so turned the instruments off again.

It was a wild night, lightning cracked around us momentarily illuminating the wild seas, it all looked surreal. By this time Audrey had grabbed all the electrical instruments she could, the GPS and the spare, hand held radio, etc., she fought her way down below and placed them all in the oven. In theory the steel oven surround acts like a Faraday cage and protects the instruments, you don't normally get a chance to try this out and whether it works or not I'm unsure, the instruments were OK afterwards is all we can say. At one stage a lightning bolt hit the water both sides of Cayuco instantaneously, the noise was deafening coming as it did at the same time as the flash, I think our hearing was impaired for some seconds after. The compass card spun like a top in its bowl, it was all very confusing. I remember looking up to the masthead to check if I could see Elmo's fire, the halo that is supposed to appear during lightning storms around the top of a sailing boats mast but I saw nothing, Audrey told me afterwards that she saw the whole mast and rigging glowing like a Christmas tree during the storm, she is not prone to telling stories so I believe her, I'm just glad she said nothing about it to me until afterwards.

I switched on the spreader lights, the sight on the foredeck was a mess, one of the big heavy duty spinnaker poles had bent double and snapped in the middle, the remnants were waving madly in the wild wind with the jib still attached to the end of it, there was not much we could do at the moment except hang on and hope nothing else gave way. All this had happened in the space of a few seconds and it was clear we would have to reduce sail, doing that however, was not going to be easy. The squall was a long one and almost certainly associated with the tropical wave south of us. We hung on until daylight by which time we were back to a steady 30 to 35 knots, it seemed better after dawn, but we were still over-canvassed. I tied an extension warp onto the end of the roller furler line and attached it to the main reefing winch, gradually we managed to pull in the line on the roller furler drum and reduce sail enough to calm everything down. It stayed blowing like this for the next three days, the seas became very big and the breaking rollers were continually sweeping over the stern and rolling along the side decks, then disappearing off each side at the bow. When we reached Antigua the teak side decks had never looked so good, the abrasive qualities of clean sea water is known to be one of the finest cleaning mediums for this kind of decking.

Everything in the boat was soaking wet except our wonderful sea berth, water was sloshing around in the cockpit, we bailed out by hand in an attempt to stop as much of the Atlantic as possible from getting below, the bilge pump continued to run every 20 minutes or so. It was so rough I thought it dangerous to go on deck and try to clear up all the debris from the spinnaker pole, we left it and just lashed down what we could, I would have to deal with it when it was possible.

After three days the wind calmed down to a steady 20/25 knots, the seas were still big but they were not breaking any more, or at least, not as much. I ventured onto the deck to try to sort out the mess, my eye caught sight of a large stainless steel nut jammed under the side deck cleat. Picking it up I thought I recognised the nut as the one which was holding the forestay and therefore the mast to the deck fitting, why was it lying here. A cold chill ran through me and I rushed to the forestay fitting, the bolt holding the forestay was half way out of the plate, if the rest of the bolt dropped out the whole rig would collapse. Friction was the only thing that was holding it together; the bolt had jammed in the plate half in and half out and had got stuck. With the wind behind us the rig was working backwards and forwards, it was only a matter of time before the bolt dropped out with obvious results, emergency repairs were needed, and fast. The first thing was to secure the rig with anything to hand, I undid the two spare halliards rigged to the top of the mast, clipped them on to the stem fitting and winched them both down hard on the mast winch making them fast to a cleat. I then took hold of two large hammers from my toolkit and a couple of spanners, with one hammer supporting the stem fitting I struck the bolt head on the other side, nothing happened, back to the mast and a few more turns on the winch, some more heavy blows on the bolt head and hey presto the bolt shot through the other side, quickly I screwed on the nut and tightened it with the spanners. To make sure it didn't come undone again I used the hammers, one to press against the bolt head while striking the threaded side of the bolt with the other hammer.

This burred over the threads and secured the fitting, unfortunately when I had to remove it later on to replace it, I had done such a good job it was an absolute pig to unscrew. Anyway, we had been lucky, the rig was secured, what was left of the spinnaker pole was cleaned away and the foredeck put back to normal, whatever that was. We both breathed a sigh of relief and put the kettle on, that cup of tea was one of the best ever.

A point to consider, normally I checked the rig and deck fittings every day on my walk round, due to the heavy weather I had refrained from doing this, it is a salutary lesson, I was suitably chastened.

On Saturday the 8th Dec at 08-15, we crossed over the imaginary line that said we had 1000 miles to go, psychologically this was a good day, we were romping along, our average daily mileage was up to 140 and above, wind was strong and we were covering lots of distance. I had to go on the foredeck to change a jib sheet which had snapped, while there I heard a snort and looking up saw a huge whale directly ahead of us. With no time to get back to the wheel, I called out to Audrey but she didn't hear me, looking up again we were still charging straight for the oceanic juggernaut. I'll never know why but at the last moment the wind vane gave a little twitch to port, we slid past the whales head with inches to spare. The enormous creature snorted again and by now I was downwind of it, by heavens their breath stinks terrible, thank god it didn't get angry; it was bigger than Cayuco

Audrey

Already we were well into December, during my watch one night around this time I started thinking about what I would be doing if I was back home in the days leading up to Christmas and I hadn't got involved with this silly game of crossing an ocean.

Little by little a poem began to form in my mind. It was to be the first of several and became our Christmas card message for that year to all our friends and family.

This is how it went.

Atlantic Crossing Christmas Card 2007

We'd like to wish a Happy Christmas
From our humble little ship
As I compose this I'm on night watch
While Tony has a kip.

It's an unusual circumstance this year
To write your Christmas card
While sitting by the fireplace
It never seemed so hard.

At least there's a full moon tonight
And the waves are only gentle
When we're coursing through the pitch black night
I think we must be mental.

What are we doing here?
Bobbing on the sea!
I should be up the high street
Buying the Christmas tree.

The winds are getting fickle
And the sails begin to flap
So where are these (bleep bleep) trade winds?
What is all this ....mishap?

As in the Christmas custom
We are following a star,
But in our case, it will lead us
To Antigua.

There's a place called English Harbour
That is where we're bound
Old Nelson had his Dockyard there
It has a homely sound.

So come on then you trade winds
No time to dilly dally
We have to meet our new mates
Who are also on the rally.

We'll have to scrub the turkey
Not to mention brussel sprouts,
But there'll be plenty other grub
I'm sure without a doubt.

So as you share your Christmas fare
Please make a mental note
To the two silly sods who crossed the pond
In their little sailing boat.

Lots of love and God Bless,
Have a happy Christmas and New Year.
From Tony and Audrey - xxxx.

Tony

Strong winds continued into day sixteen, I noticed that the tow-gen was not working so pulled it in and found that something had attacked the vanes and eaten them. We joked that we were looking for a gummy shark with no teeth left. I had to fit the spare set of blades, these were smaller and not so efficient but at least we were getting a little charge from it. Day 19, 09-15 hrs, we had just eaten a good old one pan fry up, the sun was shining and the sea was steady. It was one of those golden moments – and then one of the new jib sheets snapped, I had only replaced it the day before so it must have been a faulty one we bought in Puerto Calero. I cut off the damaged end, fortunately enough warp remained to still use it for a jib sheet, but only just. Whatever, we were still making good time, averaging 140 miles every day.

We were not to be let off so lightly, the leak from the heat exchanger was now so bad I would have to do a temporary repair. Sea water was pouring into the bilge all the time the engine was running and even when it wasn't. I had rolls of the famous duck tape, you should never sail anywhere without it, and I also had some two pot resin and hardener. This was going to be an almighty bodge job, even by my standards. After the 10-00 hrs radio check when the batteries were charged up and the engine was nice and warm, I turned off the raw water sea cock and cleaned up the end of the heat exchanger as much as I could with a bit of petrol. I know, I know, dangerous, but this was one of those calculated risks, I had nothing else that would evaporate off and leave me a relatively clean surface to bond to. Mixing up a good measure of resin and hardener I painted it around the end of the heat exchanger and then wrapped duck tape around the end, pouring the rest of the resin into the gaps around the tape. We crossed our fingers and waited for the resin to go off. After a few hours we started the engine and the leak was almost zero, as long as it stayed this way, it would get us to Antigua.

This was starting to become a voyage of attrition, no sooner had we solved one problem, then the next one reared its ugly head. What more could go wrong we thought?

Audrey

More squalls overnight, by now both of us felt we'd had enough, it seemed Tony had been down in the engine compartment continually sorting out one problem after the next. We were now experiencing really bad cross waves, working or doing anything on board became a lot more difficult. We were still making good time though and it looked like we might make Antigua in 3 or 4 days.

Day 21, due to necessity I was coming up with some strange food combinations, burgers with beans for breakfast and a bit of not very successful homemade toasted bread. We were looking forward to getting to Nelsons Dockyard in Antigua and "Ye Olde English Bakery"; both of us had been there before and knew that they made the most fantastic Cornish pasties.

A flying fish had landed with such a thud the night before during my watch that I thought something had dropped off the mast; it started flippy-flapping on deck as they do and in the dark it sounded like a much bigger fish. It brings a whole new concept to things that go bump in the night, as if we didn't have enough jitters already after our string of catastrophes.

On day 22 the steering vane developed a gremlin as well, Tony reckoned it would be OK after some adjustments, at least we didn't have far to go. We still had our diesel fuel bladder tied down on deck with 140 litres of fuel bobbing about; Tony decided to attempt to empty it into the port fuel tank which now had enough room to get it all in.

In the squally conditions I managed to tip two cups of hot coffee over myself but was fortunate to be wearing clothes on this occasion.

Tony

I noticed Cayuco was veering about a lot and realised the wind steering vane was not doing its job properly. On investigation I discovered that it seemed to have no link between the wind vane part and the steering rudder, it is a hydraulic-servo type and is usually very reliable. My suspicion was that the sacrificial link between the two controlling parts had snapped so there was no actual control at all. The link is internal and it's best to remove the whole gear and strip it down to replace this part, absolutely impossible to do at sea and especially in these kinds of conditions. On investigation later, this proved to be correct, I knew I had a spare link in the locker so it was only a matter of time before I got round to it. Cayuco being the kind of boat she is just carried on downwind by itself, I tweaked the sails so that they balanced better which slowed us down a bit, but with her long keel she carried on regardless, just yawing from side to side a tad more than usual. I knew we would be using the engine soon as we were less than 48 hours from Antigua, so just let Cayuco sort herself out. Our course was approximately correct and as soon as the engine was running I would be able to put in a course correction and switch on the auto pilot.

The next day we kept watch for our first sight of land in 23 days, the visibility was very poor so we did not see anything until 16-20 hrs when we were still some 18 miles from English

Harbour. I wanted to get in before nightfall as English Harbour is not recommended for a night entry, this however was not possible and we arrived at 19-30 hrs just as darkness closed in. The alternatives were to (1) stay at sea overnight, (2) keep on going until we reached Jolly Harbour on the west side of the island, or (3) attempt an entry with the gathering darkness. After 23 days at sea there was not really a choice, we were keen to get in so decided to use the chart plotter and the echo sounder to enter the first part of the channel and then find somewhere to anchor for the night.

All very well in theory but it was a difficult channel, there are no lights, no channel markers and very little to go on, plus, as soon as you enter the inner channel it seems there are hundreds of anchored and moored unlit boats. The expected full moon was not yet up high enough to help us very much. We slowly worked our way up the channel, using the chart plotter and the echo sounder until we had found enough room and dropped anchor, I then did a very silly thing, I put the engine into reverse to assist the anchor to dig in, there was a loud "clunk" from the stern and the engine stopped. In my urgency to get in, I had forgotten the tow-generator over the stern, the warp from this was now firmly around the propeller and Cayuco was going nowhere fast. The anchor not properly laid then started to drag and I had to pull it up. We were now drifting helplessly up into English Harbour in the dark with no engine or any control over our progress, "Ho hum, another shitty day in Paradise". Luckily for us, a man who lived on his boat in the harbour came past in his dinghy and watched our strange progress. He started wondering what we were up to and came over to see if we were OK, after a short explanation of our predicament, he calmly towed us to the fuel jetty a short way away and we made fast for the night.

Audrey

Before we arrived in Antigua and about ten miles from land I turned on my mobile phone and found I had a signal, I sent a text to both of our sons who just happened to be having a game of pool together in their local pub. Both of their phones went off simultaneously giving them a double whammy. When they both read the message which simply said,

"Land ahoy" they both grabbed each other for a hug and leapt around the place like loonies, the rest of the people in the pub must have thought they had cracked up. One of our sons was having a birthday celebration, which was the reason for them both being in the pub in the first place, he texted back,

"Best birthday present I could have had". They were both clearly delighted we were in safe and sound.

There were to be many more landfalls but for us and our family, none of them had the same significance as this first one in Antigua having just crossed the Atlantic.

Tony

To get ourselves in safely I had grabbed the first pair of shorts to hand and slipped them on, I hadn't worn much for three weeks so it seemed irrelevant that there was very little backside left in them, ocean sailing is very hard on shorts when you do wear them. As we stepped ashore for the first time in over three weeks our legs turned to jelly and we staggered around on the pontoon like drunken sailors. While recovering our equilibrium we heard a chuckle beside us, not sure if it was caused by my backside hanging out of my shorts or our sudden lack of co-ordination we turned to see a young couple smiling at us who introduced themselves as Dave and Ricki. After returning the introduction we explained the cause of the wobbly legs.

"Isn't that a Salar 40?" asked Dave. We told him he was correct and that we had just arrived from The Canary Islands after sailing her across the Atlantic. Our new friends were absolutely amazed that we had done the trip in what seemed to them, such a small craft. They were skipper and hostess on a 120 foot super yacht in which they had recently completed the same journey with a full crew and were quite in awe of our achievement.

Dave told us he was very familiar with the Salars 40's as there were many of them in his native Australia. In actual fact although being designed in England, there were more Salars built in

Australia and New Zealand than built in UK, down under they are a very popular sailing boat.

"Anyway", continued Dave, "You guys deserve a beer", so, not even checked in and completely illegal we enjoyed a beer with Dave and Ricki while we entertained both of them and our new saviour with the tales of our disastrous voyage from the Canary Islands. They suggested, between bouts of belly aching laughter that we should write a book about it.

Even more luckily for us, the guy that helped us in was a diver and he promised to be back early next morning with his gear to help us sort out the rope round the prop before the fuel jetty was open for business.

All went well the following morning and by 9 o clock we were safely ensconced on a spare mooring next to our new friend's boat. While freeing the rope from round the prop he also discovered that the propeller and nut was loose on the shaft. We got a bonus of having our propeller tightened up at the same time; something we had not even realised was loose which could easily have been a much bigger problem later on.

It had taken us nearly 23 days and 10 hours to cross the Atlantic; we had run the engine for 80½ hours and used approximately 225 litres of diesel, nearly all of it for charging the batteries. The wind was mostly strong and in our favour, but we had pushed Cayuco hard for the last 17 days and it showed on the amount of repairs we had to do. The average speed for the passage of 2883 miles was 5.2 knots so we had just met our 5 knot average speed target.

We were very happy to be safely in harbour and as it was a Sunday and the Harbour Master was not working, we spent a very pleasant day lazing around on board, some of our rally chums came out to greet us and were amazed that we were happy to just stay on board and not bother about going ashore yet. It was clear that we had a lot of work to do before we could go any further.

There is free sailing for six weeks when the rally arrives in Antigua but it looked like we would be working on Cayuco for quite a while. If we continued with the rally we would still need to be in Panama for the canal transit by about the 20th January

2008, it was now a race against time to get shipshape and seaworthy again.

We also had our first wake-up call on our finances; it was not envisaged we would have this much expense so early in the rally. Our onward journey would very much depend on the cost of repairs and our success in carrying them out by ourselves, boatyard charges were out of the question.

Figure 5: Cayuco alongside in Antigua undergoing repairs after the eventful Atlantic crossing.

Chapter 3

Repair Bills, Antigua and the Caribbean

Tony

While having a day off at anchor in Freeman's Bay, Antigua, our rally organiser had taken the trouble to seek us out and had travelled over the island from Jolly harbour. He was due to catch the plane back to UK that evening so we had only just made our personnel deadline; it was good to speak to him even if it was only on the VHF radio, we wished him well and hoped we would see him again at Panama.

After our rest day on Sunday we checked into Antigua officially on Monday the 17th December and arranged to go alongside the Nelson's Dockyard Wall. It was essential I started on the repairs as soon as possible, the main problem to this is sourcing all the suppliers and firms with the specialist trades required, we had arrived too late to pick the brains of the rally team. Although we had been to Antigua in the past, we had little idea where to obtain anything. It was also the week before Christmas and in Antigua the festivities start early and finish late. Fortunately our friend came to our rescue again, he was a mind of information and as he had worked in a marine engineering company in Antigua for some time he knew all the right places to procure difficult to obtain bits for boats. A local drinking hole called the Galley Bar just 10 metres from where Cayuco was tied up proved to be a good meeting place.

The jobs that needed urgent attention included, the engine heat exchanger, main oil pressure pipe, alternator, spinnaker pole, self steering gear, some leaks from various deck fittings and quite a large list of smaller items like steaming lights, stern lights, tow-generator warp, etc, etc. The file was extensive but I prioritised the list and started with the most important ones first, this enabled me to move on as soon as possible, it would also be necessary to chop and change between the jobs as parts became available. Starting with the heat exchanger as I suspected this was going to be the longest and most difficult job, I was shocked to see the extent of the damage, there was a hole, caused by corrosion, big enough to get three fingers in right through the housing. A new unit obtainable in UK was well over a £1000 and worse still, would take three months before delivery, just one of the problems of sailing a 36 year old boat. With our friends help and a few days frustration, I found a local aluminium welder willing to attempt a repair, but we had to strip it out and clean it up first. After welding this had to be machined to the right length and "O" ring grooves cut for sealing purposes, it was a very complicated repair and as I suspected took a long time and quite a few of our dwindling dollars. While this was underway I obtained some Muric acid and cleaned up all the copper components and oil cooler membranes so that the re-building part would be easier. I also solved the oil pipe, alternator and spinnaker pole problems, again with a lot of help and advice. A new high pressure oil pipe was located, fitted with the correct hydraulic connections and screwed onto the oil pump. A new 24 volt alternator was available but it required an electrical wiring harness made up to fit it as it was an internal regulator type, not like our old one; at least I was able to do that job fairly economically. It also needed a new fixing bracket to the engine block so that the pulley would line up with the driving pulley on the engine, all these difficulties were overcome but the testing had to wait until we could refit the heat exchanger and run the engine, this didn't happen until the New Year.

    We located a second hand spinnaker pole but the ends were different, whatever, the price was right so I drilled out the rivets from the old pole and fitted them onto the new one, worked beautifully and still does. The repair to the wind vane steering gear was as expected, the link between the hydraulic vane arm and the larger steering rudder had broken. I knew I had a spare link but the whole gear had to be removed to fit this in the right place. It's probable that the unit is constructed in order to replace this important part without removing and dismantling the complete unit but it was certainly easier to replace it while working on it in the cockpit. I received help to remove the heavy unit from some locals I met in the Galley Bar, they succeeded in losing my new spanners by dropping them overboard and breaking the stern light as the wind vane swung when it released from the holding bolts, they also wanted me to reward them for the assistance they gave. Needless to say Audrey and I replaced it ourselves without losing or breaking anything. Another valuable lesson learned.

A surprise phone call one evening between Christmas and New Year saw us meeting a cruise liner in the port of St John's at 10-00am the next morning, my sailing friend of long standing Sid and his wife Sally had decided to take a Christmas cruise and arrived in Antigua while we were still there. We spent an interesting day together introducing them to the very cheap local minibus service and used the opportunity to pick up some spares on the way.

These gaily decorated minibuses, (some of them resembling rainbows), are apparently not only used for people, they carry large and small bundles of vegetables and goods to and from the home to the markets. Nothing very surprising there you say, at least, that's what we thought, until we were sitting next to live chickens, buckets of wriggling fish straight from the bay and other varieties of live farm produce, all of which kept trying to escape from their tethers and roam freely up and down the bus. We soon realised that the minibus service is much more than you imagine, it's a vital link between all parts of the island, relied upon by the locals for their livelihoods and to get them about. The buses are invariably overcrowded and nearly always driven at breakneck speed while managing to avoid everything else on the road; at least they did while we were aboard! Sometimes they don't even keep to their route; they are prone to darting off somewhere else on an errand of mercy delivering and collecting, or just as likely to shoot off home for a cup of tea. Last but not least, the drivers are always happy and cheerful with great big smiles all over their faces; nothing seems to be a problem and everything gets done, eventually, that's the way it is.

Most of the repair and servicing work was completed by 3rd January, at least all the important jobs had been completed, there were still some minor items to do but at least we were seaworthy again. Christmas Day was the only day we took off and where possible we joined in with the festivities in the evenings and over the New Year.

It was time to be on our way again and we decided to leave on Sunday 6th January, we wanted to drop in at the French/Dutch island of Saint Martin on the way to the BVI, there are some large yacht chandlers on the island and we wanted to pick up another wind charger. Saint Martin has the reputation as one of the best and cheapest islands in the Caribbean for picking up bits for boats off the shelf.

In most of the places we visited you are given 24 hours to leave after you have checked out of the country so to get an early start next day that is what we did. Most of the other rally yachts had long since moved on so we quietly pulled in our very muddy anchor and slipped out of our berth about 08-00 hrs on Sunday 6th January and headed north. When sailing north or south in the Caribbean you can take the inside the island route or head out into the Atlantic, as the weather was unpredictable and still squally we went up the inside route. After Saint Martin we had planned to have a few days in the British Virgin Islands and spend some time with our old friends on Cooper Island. As we sailed along the south coast of Antigua we looked across to the island of Montserrat where a few years ago a huge volcano had erupted and more or less decimated the island, there were a few people starting to move back but the devastation was pretty much complete. It will take a long time before the island is really habitable again and it made us realise how close we were to it. The distance to Saint Martin was just less than 100 miles, we estimated that we would arrive early on Monday morning so would be able to check in and go ashore for our shopping. It was a good sail with a south east 4 to 5 and we rolled along passing Barbuda on our starboard side with Saint Kitts and Nevis to port, albeit a good way off. By 10-00 hours the next morning we were anchored in Simpson's Bay but on the outside of the south bridge entrance. Blowing up the Avon inflatable and fitting the outboard we motored up to the office on the bridge, this being a French Department, the check in was easy and straightforward. As we were not intending to stay for longer than 24 hours we were able to check in and out at the same time, this would make it easier later. Soon we were using the outboard to dinghy under the road bridge and into Simpson Bay Lagoon looking for a convenient place to tie up. There are at least three large chandlers and some of them have their own pontoons, this was all too easy. Unfortunately the wind generator we were looking for was not available and worse; the delivery was not expected for two weeks. Oh well, it was worth a try, our time scale did not give us the luxury to hang about for that long so we reluctantly motored back to Cayuco and set off for another night sail up to the BVI. Again it was a very pleasant night and we sailed gently, all alone, on a silver sea that was reflecting the moon, it was idyllic.

It's another 85 miles to Tortola in the BVI where we had to check in so early next morning we could see our destination. When coming from Saint Martens there is a deep water channel between Cooper and Ginger Island, it is better to leave an isolated rock near Cooper Island to port and then give plenty of room as you go round Manchioneel Point as there is a shallow ridge just off the point. By 12-30 we were tucked into Village Cay Marina in Road Harbour, Tortola and walked along to the customs and emigration, sad to say that checking in is not so easy here, the process is long winded, it costs more and the impression given is clearly not a welcome one, I suppose its luck of the draw who you get to do the paperwork. In general we found that all the French Departments were easy going efficient and welcoming, it was noticeable that in any of the ex English colonies, the attitude was surly, long drawn out, included lots of waiting time, personnel were too busy for you and did not make you feel welcome. Maybe we're wrong, but talking to other yachtsmen with similar experience around the islands, they all agreed that in general the assumption is about right, it seems a shame but we can only comment on our experience.

Audrey

When we got Cayuco sorted out enough in Antigua we took off for the BVI. On arrival we checked in and sailed the 6 miles across the Francis Drake Passage anchoring off Manchioneel Bay on Cooper Island. It is called Manchioneel Bay because of the

Manchioneel trees that used to line the shore, the fruit of the trees is similar to a little green apple and very tempting, unfortunately it is extremely poisonous, can make you very ill and can even cause death in small children. All the trees were felled in the beach club area years ago but there is one tree further along the shore and according to Henry, the one permanent local resident, there are more around the back of the Island. We had never heard of the Manchioneel tree before and to be honest, we've never heard of it since.

We called the Cooper Island Beach Club on our VHF radio and our old friend Vernon who hailed from the island of Saint Lucia was very surprised to see us, he came out in the club dinghy to welcome us. A very happy few hours was spent reminiscing and it was great to be back on the island among friends. Towards sunset Vernon picked us up in the dinghy and took both of us ashore for a wonderful evening with Chris the manager, we had a typical Caribbean meal of Mahi, Mahi, (fish steaks) and a few drinks. It was surprising how little it had changed since our time there in 1999/2000. We chatted about our voyage and explained that we were having second thoughts about carrying on with the circumnavigation; financially it was impractical to continue.

Now we had to make the big decision, pack it in or carry on? The repairs had been expensive and we were rapidly becoming aware that this circumnavigation was going to be more costly than we had first estimated. If we went back it would have to be north through the Caribbean, out to Bermuda, across the Atlantic to the Azores and then another decision whether to go back into the Med or home to UK and possibly sell Cayuco. We would also have to wait around somewhere until March or April as we would not want to start north until the weather improved in the north Atlantic. As we were in an expensive part of the Caribbean for normal foodstuffs and general living costs, this had to be factored into the equation as well. Apart from all this I still wasn't convinced I wanted to cross anymore oceans. Eventually, if we went back, we would have to cross the Atlantic anyway; Tony reasoned with me that the Pacific would be a gentler place to be if we continued, hence its name. I foolishly took this information on board, but something was starting to happen to me. I felt I wanted to take on this challenge. We came to the conclusion that if we gave in now we would never forgive ourselves. From my point of view I was no longer doing this just for Tony, I was doing this for me and neither of us are quitters.

So the decision was made, we put the Atlantic behind us and bit the bullet.

Our sons were totally bemused, on Wednesday 9th Jan 2008 in the evening we texted them to say we were packing it in and coming back the North Atlantic route, on Thurs 10th the next morning we texted them to say we were on our way to the Panama Canal, our decision was as quick and unconventional as that. In the county of Yorkshire where Tony was brought up as a child, they have an old adage which says something like this:-

"There's none as queer as folk", oh how right they are!

Tony

So there we were, on Thursday the 10th January 2008, motoring out of Road Harbour and turning right instead of left. It was a very calm day, the wind, what there was of it, was only 5 to 6 knots from the east, we had fuelled up and stored up before leaving so were prepared to motor for a few hours. The forecast was calm for the first two days and then we should pick up a good wind from the south east. We spoke to a cruise liner, "The Carnival Destiny", who crossed a mile ahead of us a few hours after leaving Road Town, he told us he had picked us up on radar twelve miles away, always re-assuring to know your radar reflector is working as you embark on another long voyage.

We had been informed earlier by the rally organisers and again by the harbourmaster in Village Cay that the worst time to cross the Caribbean Sea is in January and February, as we only had a limited time left to get to Panama there was not a lot of choice. It is just over 900 miles to the Panama Canal from the BVI so we were looking at a voyage of between 8 and 10 days, this would put us there in good time for the Canal transit.

Within two days the wind had increased dramatically, it started as a good force 4 and went up from there. As the wind was just abaft the port beam, we had opted for the fore and aft rig; it was a good decision. By Friday evening just after dark the wind rose rapidly to 25 and then 30 knots. Our progress had not been good up to now, around 80 to 88 miles a day; we were still trying to sail as much as possible while using the engine when we wanted to charge the batteries. Our next 24 hour run was very different, 135 miles and we were averaging nearly 6 knots again even with a well reefed main, later we were doing the same speed with only the jib and eight rolls in it. Once again the seas were big and we started taking water over the port quarter, the seas are very different to the seas out in the Atlantic, they are much shorter and steeper so Cayuco had less time for her stern to lift. It made little difference to her progress, Cayuco just charged on shaking everything off and driving through the seas, her heavy construction being the greatest bonus, even sleeping in the sea berth was still possible. The centre cockpit layout of Cayuco is normally very dry and little if any sea water gets shipped into it, the cockpit is also self draining so any water that does find its way aboard is quickly back where it came from. Sometimes water can get through the engine hatch and into the bilge but this is very rare. The main reason why this happens is because the cockpit seats are the same height as the stern deck and would normally be open for ease of access from the deck into the cockpit. There are boards fitted to fill this gap when at sea but some water can squeeze through the sides in really rough conditions or as in this case short steep seas from the stern. I sealed the edges with some old rags I had in the locker and this worked in the short term. I have now fitted sealed boards which come up about 80 mm on the inside of the large boards, this has cured our wet cockpit problem, if the cockpit gets wet from sea water now, we would have to be virtually laid flat anyway.

As we were short of time because of the repairs we missed out going to the ABC Islands, these are Bonaire, Curacao and Aruba which lay a day's sail to our port side. Most of the other boats managed to get to at least one of these lovely islands as they had gone south from Antigua and then sailed offshore of Venezuela. Because of the recent problems in Venezuela and Colombia none of us visited these countries, which was a shame; we were all on a deadline to meet our Panama Canal transit dates and could not afford to become mixed up in political squabbles.

The straight line from BVI to Panama passes Colombia about 30 to 50 miles off, far enough to avoid man made problems but not far enough off to avoid the "square" waves caused by the banks. The wind is usually strong in the middle of the Caribbean around this time of year and the seas kick up very short steep waves. The water is also quite shallow for a long way offshore so to be safe it is best to keep outside of the 4000 metre depth line. At least this makes it difficult for the waves to "feel" the bottom which causes the waves to break behind you and makes conditions worse. We sailed between the 3000 to 4000 metres contours and it was a rough passage. The waves in this area are known as square waves because of their shape and the short distance between crests, they are notorious for breaking onboard. By now we were half way through this section and the wind had increased to 35/40 knots day and night, this was probably due to the natural wind acceleration zone along this part of the Colombia coast. It was a particularly wet and uncomfortable motion with sharp changes between the troughs and crests of the waves. With the wind still on the port quarter we charged on regardless and Cayuco seemed to be chuckling to herself at the bow, we were still achieving over 135 miles a day.

We had an interesting incident on the 4th night out, I was watching the lights of what turned out to be a large tanker coming over the horizon; he turned away at about three miles to pass us port to port. On our AIS he came up as A8LX8 so I never did get its name, as he passed us I called him up on the radio to thank him for altering course, he acknowledged and asked us where we were bound and what size were we, I told him we were twelve metres long and bound for Panama, across the Pacific and back to England via Australia. His reply was very amusing,

"Oh", he said, "You do this for **sport**" a pause, then "**yes**?" It was a foul night and I replied,

"Not really, I think we must be mad". He wished us well and hoped we succeeded; the ship very quickly disappeared and rolled slowly off into the darkness. It was always interesting to chat to other vessels and especially at night they would sometimes call you up to find out your intentions, well, if they saw you, perhaps it helped the boredom of their watch keeping. We certainly didn't suffer from boredom, at night or any other time, sometimes it was too eventful

Audrey

About half way through our voyage to Panama we were still enjoying good winds but the conditions were making life interesting. I could not deny the virtues of Weetabix as a boat friendly breakfast, it instantly soaks up milk like blotting paper and friction ensures it stays in the bowl. Muesli on the other hand gets washed out of the bowl straight away. Guess who was having the muesli and who the Weetabix.
"Here is yours," I told Tony, "I'm just chasing mine before it goes down the sink".
We had a visiting bird as a passenger on one night, obviously needed a breather because the conditions were a bit grim. It was some kind of gull with webbed feet, he did a little dance on the wheelhouse roof until he managed to wedge himself against the handrails; at least he got a bit of a rest.
Got the tow-gen back in commission behind the boat using a spare set of blades, in these conditions it works well and we didn't lose any speed, just take out another roll from the jib to compensate, hope nothing decides the spinning blades look like dinner this time!
The next night still sailing fast with only the jib, Tony had just gone below for a sleep when there was a bang from the front of the boat. I turned on the spreader lights to see what it was; the Highfield Lever on the baby stay had somehow released itself from the foredeck fixing and was swinging around wildly. I called Tony urgently but he had already heard the noise and was heading my way, he quickly dressed and harnessed up, we were sliding down the waves almost surfing and in darkness, I did not want him to have to go out on deck in this weather. There was no choice; the stay with its lever still attached was banging into the boat at every swing, first one side then the other, it was only a matter of time before it took a window out or some other damage.

Tony hanked on to the lifeline and crawled along the deck, it was impossible to stand up. I was horrified that the stay would swing back into him and hit him, the consequences of which I didn't want to think about. Tony kept low and watched the stay, he made a grab for it as it went by but missed it, he was now on the wrong side of the boat, he waited until it swung his way again, hoping it missed anything important in the meantime Taking another lunge at it he managed to grab it and holding it close to his body he controlled its gyrations, the motion of the boat was violent and I could see him struggling to hold onto it. I was worried in case he slipped as he had no alternative but to use both hands to keep it under control, he wedged himself into the foredeck stanchions in order to keep his hands free, he needed both of them to re-attach the base of the lever to the foredeck fitting but the weight of the wire and lever were threatening to tear it from his grip. He continued to slide about on the foredeck for what seemed a long time before eventually succeeding in re-fixing the stay. He had taken a piece of line with him and he quickly tied this around the stay for extra security, as long as it held overnight he would be able to secure it properly in daylight. This kind of emergency is fairly common when you are on long passages, Tony used to make visual checks on rigging and fittings and would always try to walk round the decks once a day but there are still things that catch you out.

On the Caribbean Passage I put pen to paper again so it must be time for another poem.

It's New Year and we're off again,
Some people never learn.
We're on our way to Panama,
Let's hope our luck will turn.

The Atlantic gave us heavy seas,
Lots of wind and squalls,
We certainly found our Trade winds,
They'd got us by the balls!

Not what the doctor ordered,
Lots of things got broke.
But Tony's Mr Fix-it,
He's such a clever bloke.

The Caribbean has lots of verve,
We discovered whilst our stay.
Lots of wonders to unearth,
And find along the way.

Tiny houses brightly painted,
Little islands, often Sainted.
Kitts and Bart to name just two,
Croix as well, - there's quite a few.

Pelicans and Frigate birds,
Like David Attenborough's "Life on Earth".
Tree frogs sing their nightly chorus,
Could it mean they feel amorous?

Well OK, it's a struggle to rhyme,
At least we've reached here well in time.
The Panama Canal we're bound,
It has to beat the long way round.

Tony

The days run noon to noon from Tues 15th Jan to Wed. 16th was 145 miles, this was close to some of our best days run so far, we were not trying to break records, the wind was gale force continually and nearly behind us so with lots of sea room we just let Cayuco get on with it.

On 18th January at 09-00 hrs we were only 45 miles from the entrance to the inner harbour at Panama, we were still sailing well but the wind strength was declining and by noon we started the engine. It was possible for us to easily get in by nightfall if we motored so there was no contest. As we approached the entrance it was quite alarming how busy the Panama is, we called up the harbourmaster and he gave us permission to enter the main breakwater after the next large vessel had gone by. You have to be very careful entering here as the whole area inside and outside the huge breakwater is a holding anchorage and large ships are moving at all times of day and night. There are three possible recognised mooring areas for small boats, the Panama Yacht Club, reasonable prices, good cheap restaurant but has limited space depending on time of year, "The Flats", a fairly deep water (20 metres) anchorage area about a mile from the club but safe, no charge made but can be uncomfortable and you need a good dinghy to get ashore, or the new Shelter Bay Marina complex on the opposite side of the harbour in the old American army camp. That is where we were heading and it was an excellent choice but as always there are disadvantages, it is a long way from town. Safely in we had our paperwork in the system by 18-00 hrs so now we could relax. We were also pleased because nothing had broken on this trip which was a first and we had arrived a day early. The engine had only run for 24 hours on the whole voyage from BVI, the wind was such that we did not need it and the tow-gen worked overtime, we were very pleased with ourselves and hoped that the luck would hold.

The voyage from the BVI had taken 8 days and 6 hours over a distance of nearly 1000 miles so we were happy with that considering we had sailed most of the way. Our average speed for the trip was just on 5 knots but that was down to the first three days of very light wind and low speed, this was to be one of our major problems, Cayuco likes a good wind and if it's below 10 knots we struggle to make a reasonable speed. We had a big spinnaker but without a snubber it was a handful to fly and even worse to get in. A good cruising chute would have helped but with our stretched finances we would have to manage as best we could.

We had missed out on some of the islands in the Caribbean due to the amount of work we needed to do on Cayuco after the Atlantic crossing and our decision to go to the British Virgin Islands. We had also missed the San Blas Islands just south of Panama; this was a shame as we would have liked to see them. There was nothing we could do about this, when we decided to carry on with the circumnavigation we were already late, it was essential we made the canal transit dates otherwise everything would have stopped at that point.

The marina runs a free bus service to the local supermarkets in the morning with a pick up in the afternoon; care has to be taken all over this area. It is OK in Shelter Bay Marina and the Yacht Club as they both have 24 hour security but any trip into town, no matter what you are going for needs some sort of security and local knowledge. You are advised not to leave either place without taking someone who knows the area, muggings and robbery with violence are commonplace. The taxi drivers know all the area well and will take you to the door of your chosen shop, then wait for you to make your purchases before returning you safely back. We cannot stress enough how dangerous this whole area is.

Shelter Bay is a haven in the wilderness, water and electric at every berth, clean showers and toilets, in fact the toilets and showers are American style separate cubicles with all facilities in the one room, including some with Jacuzzi's. There is also an excellent cheap restaurant and the marina team are very helpful, they will arrange anything for you at very reasonable cost.

It is worth mentioning here for interest, no movement of any vessel, big or small, is allowed in the very large inner anchorage without informing the harbour authorities. All vessels have to get permission before crossing the shipping lanes from one side to the other, if you ever get as far as this, you will know why. Having said all that there are some unofficial anchorages in the shallow water around the edges and away from the deep water but there is no security, good if you are just passing through. Leaving your boat at anchor unattended anywhere in the inner harbour is not advised, if you can't leave anyone aboard when you go ashore the best bet cost wise is the Panama Yacht Club, they welcome yachtsmen of all nations, are a mine of information and will help as much as they can.

Chapter 4

The Panama Canal

Tony

This is where the rally organisation really comes into its own, Audrey and I were about to meet them for the first time since the Canary Islands. The paperwork for the canal transit is fairly comprehensive, all the boats have to be individually measured and an agent has to be used. It is not possible to arrange a canal transit by yourself anymore. The cost in 2008 was $500 (American) for each boat plus agency fees, as long as you were less than 20 metres, after 20 metres you need your own pilot and the cost jumps to over $2000. All can be arranged through Shelter Bay Marina, The Panama Yacht Club (Club de Yates), or through an agent, you can also try www.pancanal.com for all other information including if you want to watch yachts transiting the locks.

Our stay at Shelter Bay was a very pleasant interlude, nothing broken, most things working and just routine checks to make. We had an ongoing problem with the engine which I had not been able to solve; it would run all day if necessary at cruising speed, about 1200 revs, if we put the revs up over about 1500 it started to run a bit on the hot side. Not serious and I thought just change the impellor on the raw water pump. I had spares and was able to purchase more in Balboa on the other side of the canal. I couldn't give the engine a good run afterwards but it all seemed OK so I ignored what seemed to be a small problem and got on with other work. This entailed going up the mast to check the rigging, fit a new steaming light bulb and trying to find out why the spreader lights were working intermittently.

Some yachts had already arrived and others started to turn up gradually after visiting the San Blas and the ABC Islands, tales of their trip from Antigua were told over a meal and drinks in the club bar. A few of the boats, like us, had experienced quite rough seas on the way across off the Columbian coast, if anything they had passed even closer than we did to the shore and said the seas were really bad.

We all had a shock one morning when we heard that an Italian yacht on the rally with our friends on board had suffered a knock down. They had been laid flat with subsequent damage to the rig and quite a lot of gear had disappeared over the side or had been ruined by seawater. They were two up same as us and his wife had been washed overboard during the event, she'd clung on to anything she could grab, her harness had stopped her going all the way but it must have been a horrifying experience.

Everything on board had been soaked as a lot of seawater had got below, some of their navigation equipment went missing or was not working, their engine would not start and the rig damage to the spreaders meant they could not put sail up either. They had issued a radio request for help and then got on with trying to sort out the mess. The yacht had righted itself as they are designed to do but was drifting, the couple had sorted what they could and secured the vessel and were now trying to get underway again. In the meantime, a large Italian commercial vessel which by chance had been sailing through the area had picked up their emergency radio message and altered course to assist. The vessel stopped upwind to see if they could help while acting as a windbreak. After some hours they managed to dry out the electrics enough to start the engine and continue on their way to Shelter Bay. He thanked the vessel for all its cooperation and setting course they both resigned themselves to the fact that they would now have to motor all the way in to Shelter Bay Marina.

We in the marina knew none of the details and after the first radio call could only wait for more news. We waited for the next few hours until we could hear them on our SSB radio to find out what was going on. Fortunately they had a satellite phone which escaped damage so were able to keep in touch with our rally organiser who updated us and arranged assistance for them when they arrived. It was going to be at least 36 hours before they arrived at Shelter Bay but we all knew they were OK if a little ruffled. This is one of the great things about being with a rally; there is always someone somewhere to give assistance and/or advice. Normally another yacht on the rally would be close enough to render support as has happened on many occasions in the past, this time however; they had delayed in one of the islands and were a little late setting off across the Caribbean Sea. This meant they were probably one of the last yachts crossing and other rally boats were too far away to give immediate assistance, many would have changed course and gone to their aid had it been necessary.

When eventually they arrived, life rings, bits of canvas and various odd lines were hanging from the broken lower spreaders and the rest of the rig, the evidence of a serious knockdown was everywhere, we all assisted in berthing and his wife received a lot of hugs from the other rally members. As they described what had happened we all realised how close they had come to a complete disaster, caught by a squall at night while sailing fast and blown flat on the water, she was washed overboard and hung on by her lifeline. The cockpit dodgers and spray hood frame where ripped off, stanchions and guardrails broken, the starboard lower spreader snapped with subsequent danger to the mast, cockpit floorboards washed out and lost, charts and books floating in the water below. Engine compartment partially flooded and due to failed electrics would not start, all other electrical components were suspect. The outboard had been immersed and would not start plus there had been damage to other systems which were still being discovered. It was clearly their superb seamanship and determination which saved them; they are both very experienced small boat sailors and it showed, we took them up to the bar for a well deserved drink as they explained how they overcame all the problems and continued on their voyage. They were both very concerned about the amount of damage and wondered if they would be able to repair everything before it was time to transit the canal, once again everyone rallied round and gave assistance where they could. As it turned out they repaired enough to motor through the canal and carried on working on the Pacific side until fit and ready for sea again. Serious damage to ones vessel is always a possibility when undertaking a venture like this, many boats suffered damage of one sort or another but all kept going regardless, the spirit of the ralliers to complete the circumnavigation was very strong.

We all had to complete the paperwork trail for the canal transit and this took some time. In all fairness to the organisers and the Panama Canal authorities it was made as painless as possible. The canal agents and rally personnel did most of the legwork and all we had to do was wait in the clubhouse for everything to be checked and verified before filling in and signing all the documents. This was made all the more difficult by the quantities of alcohol consumed, the bar had flexible opening times and what else was there to do while waiting? We all somehow managed to remember who we were and sign our name correctly, hopefully in the right place but probably not as comprehensible as it would normally have been.

Our organisers had arranged for the rally to have their own dedicated lock so that all rally boats could pass through the canal over a five day period, this is not the usual arrangement. Normally yachts have to wait until a commercial vessel small enough to get a raft of sailing yachts behind it is transiting the canal and then you follow on behind with lines ashore, hopefully far enough astern to allow for the surge as the water is let into the lock. Alternatively you can tie alongside a tug or pilot boat which is going through, neither is as good as having your own lock.

All yachts are required to have four lines at least 120ft long and they have to be of a diameter suitable to control the boat. On the day assessors choose to scrutinise your vessel, someone from the crew has to be available and have the lines onboard, they will confirm the lines are there, if desired, you can also hire the lines locally but these have limited availability. Other checks include engine, lights and any items of equipment needed to transit, when satisfied of the vessels suitability they will tick all the boxes. There are strict rules regarding towing in the canal, towing of any vessel in the canal is not allowed unless undertaken by the canal authorities and the cost of this service if needed is prohibitive. The other rule that's important to know, each vessel has to have four line handlers on board plus one person to control the boat and then a local pilot making six people in all, even if you are rafted up with two other boats. This is so each rope i.e. two from the bow and two from the stern has a dedicated handler to control and keep the boat in the centre of the lock if needed. They insist on this rule i.e. four people, four lines whichever method is used for the transit and it's not negotiable. The argument is, anything can change during the passage and everyone has to be ready for a situation where centre locking may be required. It was also a part of the arrangement that the Pilot would be looked after while on board regarding his drinks and meals during the day, this is normally only soft drinks, coffee or sandwiches, something with rice etc so not a problem.

Audrey

To have a complete lock just for the rally yachts was a real bonus, the plan as outlined in the briefing was to have five separate rafts each consisting of three similar size boats. This would mean fifteen boats could pass through the locks at Gatun all at the same time with the other fifteen yachts following two days later; we were still a thirty boat fleet so this proposal fitted in perfectly. The authorities had also told us that as we had dedicated locks the water could be let in slower so that we wouldn't be thrown around so much, this was a real benefit.

All the boats had arrived by 23rd January so it was hectic for a couple of days getting everything in place by the 27th; this was the date set by the canal authorities for the first group and was not flexible. Every boat had to have a pilot or transit advisor onboard, it is difficult for them to arrange so many people at the same time and some of us had trainees on board. If for any reason one of us didn't meet the schedule it was up to yourself to rearrange another transit at your own expense, this is a canal rule and none of us wanted this to happen. The canal timetable is fairly rigid and required some crew manoeuvrability, each boat needed four line handlers and someone to steer and control the engine. As at least half the fleet had only couples on board, some tricky footwork was going to be needed. Basically, the plan called for crew from one boat to help another boat through the canal and then all hot-foot it back to Shelter Bay to help the other boat through the next day. It all worked well, but very early starts and late finishes over a five day period was very tiring, everyone was ready for a good night's sleep by the time we finished although no-one argued about the wonderful experience.

The first group set off after lunch and final briefing on the afternoon of the 27th January, we teamed up with the other crew on their yacht. The plan was to motor over to an anchorage called "The Flats" on the other side of the bay; there we were to await the arrival of our individual pilot or transit advisor.

All went well and after notifying the harbourmaster of our intentions we set off, by 15-00 hours we were all anchored and waiting. The transit start, scheduled for 15-00 hours was delayed for various reasons throughout the afternoon until around 18-00hrs. This was important to all of us, it gets dark about 19-30 hrs and we were hoping to be able to complete most of the first part through the Gatun Locks before dark, this was not to be. The port vessels which bring the pilots are big, tough, and heavy old steel workboats, typical of those seen in every harbour in the world, their manoeuvrability in confined spaces is limited at the best of times. The reputation for not being too kindly to the topsides of yachts is legendary, lots of fenders were advised and a couple of the yachts even went as far as hanging their empty diesel cans over the side as well. To counteract this possibility we had all attempted to anchor well away from each other to give the harbour launches as much room as possible. This was hampered by the fact that lots of other small boats were waiting to go through as well, space in the shallower parts was limited. To identify us as the boats transiting today we were all flying the Blue Water Rally flags in the bow, these flags are quite large so can easily be seen.

Then another delay as we waited for the chief pilot to receive the go ahead from the lock controller and so it went on. The consequence was that fifteen yachts eventually set off in gathering darkness to motor the five miles to the entrance channel, this channel alone is over a mile long before reaching the lock. It was dark before we even entered the start of the channel, large ships also moved up the waterway positioning themselves to enter a lock. As we approached our designated lock, the port side one, we also had to raft alongside each other in groups of three before entering, not a quick manoeuvre in the dark. The first set of yachts failed to get all three rafted together before reaching the lock so turned back to raft up and join the end of the queue. This changed the order of entering and a bit of confusion followed while we all tried to back up, it gave the pilot and crew on a large freighter trying to enter the starboard lock a bit of fun. In the gloom, a restricted space, fifteen yachts trying to find its own group, none of whom had done this before, I'm sure I can leave the ensuing chaos to your imagination.

There was a lot of chattering in Panamanian on the radios before eventually the first raft entered the lock. The plan seems simple; with all three yachts tied together they move slowly into the centre of the lock, the marináis, (rope handlers on the dockside) throw a line with a monkey's fist on the end of it from both sides of the lock at the same time. The line controllers on the outside of the rafts fore and aft, catch the monkey fists, make it fast to the long lines already prepared and then feed the long warps out to the marináis who pull the lines up to the dockside. With all four lines from bow and stern of the raft in the hands of the marinara's, the centre boat which is in the charge of a senior pilot motors slowly forward, the engines of the two outside boats are left running but do nothing to assist forward motion unless the senior pilot orders them to do so. The engines on the outside boats are mostly used to keep the raft in the centre of the lock and in a straight line. The first raft moves right along to the end of the lock and the marináis secures the warp to the bollards, the whole raft is then centred in the lock by the line handlers on each boat under the guidance of the Senior Pilot.

While this is happening, all the other rafts are moving into position along the lock; they all have their own marináis who stay with the same raft all the way through the staircase of three locks. The whole operation is very smoothly carried out but was a bit fraught because of the dark and being the first time we had done it, it certainly seemed easier the second time through with the next group.

The Marináis can throw their lines with the monkey fist extremely accurately and indeed practise this action on a regular basis; the thought that struck me was that they all wear hard hats. These lines have a lead weight inside the monkey's fist at the throwing end, what we couldn't understand was why, when the monkey's fist was chucked in our proximity none of us had any hard hats and we were probably the people that needed them. Ho hum, such is life. What is advisable though is to cover any vulnerable items of equipment, hatches, windows and solar panels are particularly likely to be damaged if caught a blow from the monkey's fist.

The first set of three locks at Gatun take the yachts up 85 feet and into the Gatun Lake, it is essential that the line handlers take up the slack on the warps as the yachts rise. As we left the locks, the rafts were released and we all made our own way in the dark to an anchorage off the Gatun Lake Yacht Club. We had checked out of Colon on the Atlantic side of the canal and had to check in on arrival in Balboa on the Pacific side, another rule. This meant we were confined to our designated yacht and were not allowed ashore during the transit. All the aforementioned delays meant we did not anchor for the evening until nearly midnight; the pilots were taken off the boats and went home promising to be back at daylight tomorrow morning. A quick coffee, a natter about the day in general and we were all asleep to await our next day's adventure.

We were all up at the crack of dawn preparing for what we thought would be a long yet interesting day. Once the advisors were onboard and we were all fed and watered it was anchors up and off down the scenic route of the Banana Cut. The main channel through the canal is about 60 miles but the Banana Cut is quite a bit shorter and it avoids the big ships for a considerable time. It weaves its way through narrow and shallower channels between the islands, you are much closer to the wildlife and it is far more interesting. The monkeys could be spotted in the surrounding rain forest and further on our travels crocodiles could be seen basking on the shore. It was a great experience as we motored through the canal; we even got the sail up on one stretch as the wind came up behind us.

The first of the "down" locks is at Pedro Miguel, this lock takes you down 31 feet to the Miraflores Lake, we went through the same procedure with the marináis but this time we had to let the warps out as we dropped. The yachts then motor another couple of miles to the next two high sided locks at Miraflores which dropped us another 35 feet. The difference in rise and fall is because the Pacific is on average 19 feet higher than the Atlantic and has a much higher tidal range. Seems odd but true, apparently it has something to do with the rotation of the earth and because the canal is basically on an East to West orientation.

The general direction through the canal from the Atlantic to the Pacific is oddly enough south east, so you actually go back east a couple of miles on your passage through, again very odd but true.

This was another special moment for everyone as we were about to begin a new phase of our voyage. It was Pacific Ocean "Here we come", no going back now. As the canal gradually opened into the port of Balboa, champagne bottles were at the ready to drink a toast as we sailed under the "Bridge of the Americas". At this point tradition decrees that it is good luck to throw a dime overboard and make a wish as you pass underneath. A berth had been arranged for this yacht at the new Flamenco Marina so this is where we headed, it was 19-30 hours and just before dark as we tied up. We packed our bags, grabbed a quick drink, then all jumped in the minibus to head back to Shelter Bay Marina. Tomorrow, we were all going to do the same thing again with Cayuco, it would be our turn to transit the canal.

Figure 6: Motoring through the Banana Cut, a shorter way through the Panama Canal for small boats.

Figure 7: Approaching the "Bridge of the Americas linking North and South America.

Tony

The second trip went well, we were all better prepared now and Cayuco was on our preferred mooring at the Balboa Yacht Club by 17-00 hours on the 30th January 2008. Although a fascinating experience it was very tiring and we were glad to spend the next ten days fairly peacefully. The Balboa Yacht Club run a very efficient free water taxi service from the moorings to the end of the pier 24 hours a day; in reality we gave the boat boys a Panamanian dollar once a day or depending on how many times we used the service. The club also has a friendly bar/restaurant and there is a free internet service. Everything is very reasonably priced; it is a wonderful place to meet up with other ralliers and adventurers from around the world, we loved every minute of it.

The supermarkets are cheap and well stocked; we were encouraged to fill all nooks and crannies with as many stores as possible in preparation for the Pacific. This was extremely good advice as we were to find the Galapagos rather lacking in supplies and French Polynesia very expensive. I had ordered a new wheel pilot steering mechanism from England to be picked up here but it never arrived; I was not to see it until Tahiti when the Rally Director met up with us and brought it out in his luggage, another very good reason for being in an organised group.

After all the problems getting to Shelter Bay we had another overheating problem going through the canal, I checked all the usual things, filter, blockage and pump but all seemed to be working. When we got to Balboa I stripped it all down again but found nothing that was causing the problem, the engine was perfectly OK at normal revs but did not like it when over 1500 revs. As we normally run the engine at 1200 rpm our economical speed which gives us 5 to 5.5 knots, it was not a real problem but something we could have done without.

While on the mooring at Balboa, John and Jane our friends on the yacht Penelope 3 had a problem with their small petrol generator. It would not run at all, they hiked it round the local mechanics but no-one could sort out the problem, one morning while I was between jobs I said I would have a look at it for them, I made a point of not promising anything. Within an hour I had sorted the problem and got the generator working as good as gold. The electrics appeared to be OK; this was partially confirmed by a 20,000 volt jolt of electricity shooting up my arm. I had removed the spark plug to check its gap and cleanliness, while trying to check if the engine was rotating properly I pulled the starting cord while inadvertently holding onto the end of the spark plug lead. The resulting electric shock running up my arm and in rapid succession made me jump backwards while exclaiming,

"Dear me, that was a silly thing to do", ----------- or words to that effect anyway. The problem turned out to be a fuel blockage in the carburettor, a small jet hidden in the bowels of the unit was completely blocked, a quick clean and blow through and the generator was working perfectly. As we were on a mooring and had to keep running our main engine to charge up the batteries on cloudy days, I tested it out by connecting it to our shore 240 volt system and putting on our mains charger. What a treat, a simple and quiet method of charging the batteries while away from shore power and cheaper than running the main engine. It was clear we would have to obtain a small generator ourselves as soon as possible. As it was portable it could also be moved around the boat to the most desirable position, bow or stern, depending on the direction of the wind and whatever circumstance we were in. We did have a small 12 volt petrol generator which we could use for the computer and printer but it was not man enough for charging our 24 volt system using the mains charger. It could only be used for the batteries if we disconnected them and charged them individually, obviously not a good idea and very time consuming.

All too soon it was time to move on, we would have enjoyed staying a bit longer but our next stop over was the Galapagos Islands, visiting these had been my personal dream since I was twelve years old and I was keen to be on the way.

Chapter 5

Panama to Galapagos Islands

Tony

Our stay at the Balboa Yacht Club was the most pleasant stopover yet, we had little work to do on the boat, replenishing our stores was straightforward, in fact shopping in general for anything was simple and inexpensive. We replaced some of our shorts, shirts, sandals, shoes and other non essential items, had our haircut and just chilled out. The rally social party was nearby and the evening was a great success, our rally organiser had done us proud. Local dancers performed in spectacular costumes, a buffet meal with just about anything you could have on a plate was prepared, the all inclusive wine flowed freely and everyone had a thoroughly good time. The next morning was very quiet, no-one was around too early; it was a mark of just how good the party was.

In due course we were all stored and fuelled up and it was time to be on our way again, we did not really expect the reception we had received in the Panama location, although you had to be careful when outside of the security areas in Shelter Bay or Club de Yates the Balboa experience was first class. I can only recommend the Balboa Yacht Club with the highest regard, it was one of the highlights of our round the world voyage.

Audrey

To prolong the chill out experience we checked out of Panama on 9th February 2008 and sailed over to the Las Perlas Islands. These beautiful and almost deserted islands are about 35 miles from the Balboa Yacht Club and are in the Panama City Bay. Commercial traffic is very evident so a close watch has to be kept while crossing to the islands, some vessels are moving in or out of the canal and others up anchor and start moving with little or no warning. All traffic is monitored by the Port Authorities so it is possible to listen in on VHF channel 12 and 16 but sometimes it's difficult to identify which vessel they are talking to.

We were sorry to leave the friendly club but dropped the mooring and were on our way by 08-45 hours. The wind was light but we managed to motor until we were out of the commercial vessel anchorage and the main shipping lanes. We anchored in about 10 metres off a picturesque naturist beach on the island of Contradora. The deserted beach looked very inviting and was only a short dinghy ride away, as it was nearly sundowners' time we decided to enjoy the early evening and watch the sun set in the perfect stillness of our own little world.

Early next morning we blew up the Avon dinghy while it was still cool and fitted the outboard engine. There was a small building hidden behind some trees, the previous night we had seen lights over there so went over in the dinghy to investigate. There was a small hotel and a bar called the Romantica Restaurant this had been run by the same family for many years, it catered for the few people who knew it was there and some local clientele with second homes on the island. The owners explained to us that the large area alongside the hotel had recently been acquired by developers, he was unhappy and when he showed us the drawings of the proposals we could see why. The hotel and resort that was planned was garish, out of context with the surroundings and would almost certainly finish off his home and business completely. We had a beer and a chat with him, another couple from the rally who were doing the same island tour joined us and we whiled away a couple of hours. As planned the night before, it was time to check out the naturist beach which was just half a mile along the shore. We motored along to the beach and pulled the dinghy out of the water to join a few like minded souls and the odd elusive iguana, after a very pleasant few hours we returned to Cayuco for sundowners and our evening meal.

Figure 8: Sunset on Contradora in the San Perlas Islands

Tony

The next day we sailed roughly south west and went between the islands of Chapera and Pearl on our port side and the town of Pedro Gonzales on our starboard. The wind was very gentle and we sailed slowly, the current however was running our way at 4 knots so our speed over the ground was over six. The tidal streams in the bays can run very quickly and currents speed up through the islands, fortunately it runs in a south west and then north east direction for about 6 hours each. The tides can be used to make a fast passage from island to island but it is essential to get the timing right. The current can also be used when setting off for the next destination which was the Galapagos Islands. Arranging to leave as the south west current starts gives a big boost to your speed for up to 6 hours and by then you are so far away that the current has slowed down, so then you don't get much against you.

We also passed Isla del Ray (Del Ray Island) to Port, this has a beautiful anchorage on its south side called Kingfisher Bay; it also has a river flowing into the bay which can be explored by dinghy for quite a way up, adds a bit more interest to the day. We were heading for an anchorage on the south side of San Jose Island where a German couple Gerdie and Dieter had taken up residence many years before. Even the bay was named after them, seeking solitude they had certainly found it here. This is a good jumping off place for the passage to the Galapagos Islands, the tide was perfect for an early morning start and the next day saw us weighing anchor at first light.

The passage to the Galapagos Islands is notorious for light or nonexistent winds; they sit right on the equator and there are horror stories of people taking three weeks or more to sail the 1000 miles. We had filled up everything we could with diesel and had even bought more cans to tie onto the side decks. It was expected that we would have to do a great deal of motoring; the long term forecast confirmed the lack of wind for the next few days. There seemed little point in waiting any longer as there was no indication of anything changing for weeks. If we were lucky it was possible we might get some wind further south but it was toss a coin time, we just had to suck it and see. As the Equator passes through the Northern Galapagos we would cross the 0° meridian between north and south hemispheres just before reaching our destination in Academy Bay on Santa Cruz Island.

The recommended route is to head south, this is supposed to give a better chance of wind and favourable currents. In the event we experienced neither, the wind was extremely light for nearly all of the passage and the current, except for the first day, was against us all the time. The first day we made 110 miles but after that it was a battle all the way. What wind there was came from right ahead, mostly 8 to 10 knots, rarely did we have a wind where we could sail a direct course, even then, it was only for a couple of hours. When we had any wind at all, I carried main, mizzen, genoa and the mizzen staysail if the wind was right, over 1000 square feet of canvas and still we were struggling to make 75 miles a day. On the 14th we had a tropical squall, vicious winds and rain for three hours while the wind slowly boxed the compass, we steered by hand to maximise speed and course, reefing and altering the sails continually to keep moving anywhere near the general direction we required.

It was my birthday on the 25th Feb. So I was keen to get in by then, nine days and 660 miles to go, normally it would not have been a problem but on this leg anything could happen.

Twice a day at 10-00 and 18-00 hrs we maintained our SSB radio schedule. The schedule at 10-00hrs was again used to update the positions of all the fleet to the net controller vessel of each day. It was clear we were not the only ones having difficulty making way; most of the boats were struggling to make any appreciable progress, the only ones covering a decent daily mileage were the ones who had large reserves of diesel and could afford to motor all the way. Probably half the fleet could do this, although none of them wanted to. As time went on the concerns from the others became apparent, quite a few were expressing doubts whether or not they carried enough diesel to motor all the way and all were experiencing the same conditions as us.

The wind and current were not our only problems, one night we were sailing slowly, still tacking on a course of 170°, nowhere near the course we wanted but trying to make more southerly. It was 03-40hrs on the 15th and it was very dark, I saw a row of white floats ahead and there was a faint white flashing light off to the starboard bow. It was a tuna net and it was laid right across our track. I tacked and we sailed along the net from marker buoy to marker buoy, these nets can be up to 12 miles long and there is no indication of which way to turn to get to the shortest end, so make a choice and stick with it. We were only sailing at around 3 knots so about two hours later we reached the end of the net which was marked by a much brighter fixed white light, as we were tacking it made little difference which tack we were on so I just kept sailing in the same direction. An alternative to this tactic is to hold your breath and sail over the top of the net, of course if you do catch it around any underwater obstruction, i.e. fin keel, propeller, skeg or rudder you are normally in more trouble than wasting a bit of time. Later on we accidently sailed right over the top of an unlit one and only saw it when the row of marker buoys was disappearing in our wake. I then realised that it was possible to do this with most nets, the marker buoys are normally about 30 metres apart, the tuna nets hang on warps from the buoy about 5 metres below the surface, with care and taking it slowly, you can sail up to the net and watching over the side you can slowly drift over between the buoys and see the net some distance below. The water at sea well away from land is usually clear enough to do this. You take your chance or sail round it, a word of warning though, not all nets are low enough in the water and it depends on what the fishermen are trying to catch. The other interesting point to make is fishermen will nearly always lay the net lengthways down tide or down current, I'm not sure of the reasoning for this but it is probably something to do with gathering the net in afterwards, keeping the net in a straight line or maybe the way the fish feed, one day, maybe I'll find out.

At least we could relay the position of these nets to all the other yachts on the rally. At the start of our 10-00 and 18-00 hr radio schedules there was a two minute silence period for emergency calls. During this time you could report the position of the net or any other danger you had spotted, or alternatively, request a time slot at the end of the schedule to give out the information, this facility worked very well.

Our daily progress was disappointing, on the 14th we covered 75 miles, 15th and 16th, 90 and 92 miles but with the engine and the 17th – 55 miles, 18th – 85miles, the 19th was special 65 miles tacking so actual straight line distance made good was only 23 miles. The piece de resistance was on the 20th when after tacking backwards and forwards in light winds and against the current for 24 hours we covered 11 miles back towards Panama. It was clear we would have to use the engine if we were to have any chance of getting there within our time slot.

This was the most frustrating passage we had ever made, we were constantly trying to mentally work out the logistics and sail on the most advantageous tack. One of the rewards of trying to sail in calm weather is that you are constantly trying to improve your sailing performance; everything on the boat is checked and double checked. I moved the genoa blocks on the runners, adjusted the tension of the halliards and the sheets and generally tried to make Cayuco as efficient as possible. It was interesting to discover how many small improvements I made, as most of the rally so far had been downwind it hadn't encouraged me to look too closely at sail settings, a few days upwind sailing in calm winds soon brings out the competitive side.

Audrey

We began the ongoing journey on the 12th Feb and were rewarded with the sight of more whale activity. A couple of gulls stole a ride, one of which remained overnight. We were to experience a mixture of thunderstorms, squalls and periods of calm which forced us to motor. Our southerly progress was reasonable, but conditions were preventing the westerly direction we also required. Also we began to experience an opposing current that seemed set to take us back to Ecuador instead of the Galapagos.

As if this was not bad enough, by the ninth day we experienced 25 knot headwinds pushing us north once more and undoing all our good work. Just when we were considering forgetting Galapagos and heading for Ecuador we started to do better. We thought we were beginning to discover the reason why these Islands were so remote and relatively unknown for so long; it was certainly causing us a few problems at trying to reach them.

We had acquired another passenger, this time a bit larger and more impressive than a common gull. We identified it as a blue footed booby which is mostly associated with the Galapagos Islands; we certainly saw a good few of his chums when we eventually arrived. Our blue footed booby, (who also had a blue beak), seemed quite happy perched on our pulpit and settled down for the night while Cayuco chugged on into a spectacular sunset.

Figure 9: A Blue Footed Booby who stayed with us for a few days on the way to Galapagos.

Tony

After having gone backwards trying to tack against the current in very light airs we decided to motor at our most economical speed. It was Wednesday the 20th February and we still had 330 miles to go in a straight line. Our friendly booby bird had decided to stay, probably because we were still travelling in the direction he wanted to go. It was amazing how friendly he was, I walked around the deck, almost right up to him, he just sat there, I emptied the diesel cans which were tied on deck into the main tanks and he never moved, just watched me. Audrey went up on deck and took some photographs; he still just sat there unperturbed. Emptying the fuel bladder was next and we expected him to take off after all the disturbance this would entail, but no, he was quite happy and just continued to preen himself. Occasionally he would fly off and circling Cayuco would dive continually into the water then come up eating something, after a little while and clearly having his fill he would fly back and settle in his favourite spot. We were happy to have him aboard and left him to his own devices although we never did find out if he was a male or female. The one thing we did find out after he had gone was the disgusting mess he had left behind on the foredeck; they must consume massive quantities of fish if the amount of his visiting card was anything to go by.

The speed of Cayuco was being seriously hampered; the bottom of the boat had not been cleaned and painted since in the UK eighteen months earlier, the antifouling was losing its effectiveness and we were slowing down. Cayuco also had large goose barnacles growing on the underwater sections and weed trailing from the waterline. The goose barnacles were also growing on the sides of the boat, they are strange things and they only cling on to the hull while the vessel is moving, the theory is, as soon as you stop, they are all supposed to fall off and go looking for another moving object. This is a fallacy, small boats are nearly always moving in one direction or another and as long as there is water movement they cling on. Small boats roll considerably at sea even in calm conditions, goose barnacles grow on the topsides, look dirty and ugly and they also cause an alarming amount of drag so slow you down considerably. As far as possible I tried to clean the worst of them off with the deck brush but I could only scratch the surface, the drag was not only slowing us down it was causing us to use more fuel as well. The bilge pump blocked again and I had to strip it down and unblock it, I think the rough passages we had experienced so far had loosened much of the sediment in the bilge and being an old boat I would just have to keep clearing it until it resolved itself. The goose barnacles were also trying to grow in the inlet of the raw water intake. My sea water filter has a window in the top and you can see through it when it is clear, every time I checked there was more and more growth and eventually I had to stop the engine, turn off the sea cock and clean out the filter

Most of the other rally boats had now arrived; another one a little way behind us was also running low on fuel. I estimated that we probably had enough fuel to make it but it was just too close a call, my estimates were being undermined by the dirty bottom of the boat.

We continued very slowly with the engine revs just above tick over which was giving us about 4 knots, the sea was glassy calm, not even a sign of a ripple. By Saturday the 23rd at noon we had 100 miles to go to Galapagos and were nearing the Equator. We watched the GPS very closely, at twelve minutes past two in the afternoon with our position at 88° 44.853´W we crossed over the equator and into the southern hemisphere. As a mark of respect to King Neptune we performed the usual ceremony of offering him a tipple of rum and thanked him for our safe passage so far.

My fuel calculations were still predicting a close call, we had around 24 to 30 hours fuel left depending on our speed and the consumption was slightly less than 3 litres per hour. The current was still against us and as we approached the islands it increased, I reckoned at this speed it would take us about another 26 to 28 hours to get there.

Figure 10: On 23rd of February 2008 we crossed the equator, confirmed by 0.0000 on the GPS.

Audrey

On the morning of 24th February we eventually had the Galapagos Islands in view. Our concerns about low fuel reserves had been passed on by radio to the other rally yachts that had arrived in Academy Bay. They had an impromptu meeting and one of the yachts very kindly volunteered to bring out some spare diesel fuel in jerry cans. We chatted for a bit on the radio and agreed a rendezvous point so that we could take on the extra fuel. At this time, only a few miles separated us from the other yacht behind so both of us arranged to meet up and proceed to the rendezvous point together.

I knew this was one of the most important locations of all for Tony as he had always talked about visiting these islands in his own boat, at last he was going to make it, and in time for his 64th birthday the next day, what more could he have asked for?

Tony

As I have already written in this book, the Galapagos Islands had held a special fascination for me since I was twelve years old, my dream of visiting them in my own sailing yacht was about to come true and just before my birthday.

Throughout my life I had held onto the belief that this dream was achievable, even when it looked hopeless and unreachable a little spark stayed alive urging me on. As we all get older and ostensibly more sensible, I believe there's a possibility we think too much about the reasons why we should not do something. As far as we know, there is only one chance at our life, such that it is, it really is not a rehearsal, live it, love it, take it by the scruff of its neck and wring the life blood out of it for all you can. There is no second chance and there are no prizes when in old age you turn round and say to yourself,

"If only", however you look at it ... you are a long time dead.

Now, here I was, only a few miles away from that childhood dream, to say the least, I became quite emotional.

Audrey

As we approached the waypoint where we were meeting the other yacht to take on board our emergency fuel supplies we could make out that the skipper was fishing. He was on the stern and we were just in time to witness him make a big strike with his fishing rod, we saw a fairly big wahoo which was firmly hooked and making wild gyrations, jumping out of the water and diving trying to throw the hook. To everyone's amusement and the skipper's disgust, the wahoo dived once more but when the line came up only a small portion of wahoo was left dangling on the end of it; the rest of it had gone. A couple of sea lions lurking behind his yacht were licking their lips after enjoying a free meal, they had stolen the wahoo off the end of the fishing line and right in front of him, he was not impressed.

Our fuel transfer worked very well, the sea was almost flat calm, they had brought some extra help and as we slowly motored alongside each other, the fuel in cans was passed across to Tony; they then repeated the same process with the other yacht. By 15-00 hrs. both yachts were carrying enough fuel to safely make port.

Fortunately for our fishing skipper, the sea was teeming with fish, so after the fuel had been passed over he set his line again and quickly had another wahoo even bigger than the one before, this one he landed successfully before the sea lions could catch up and steal it.

Tony

After taking the fuel onboard we could safely increase speed, we still had some miles to go and wanted to be in by nightfall. It was in quickly gathering darkness that we eventually dropped our anchor at 19-30 hours. Due to limited swinging room in the harbour our stern anchor was taken by a waiting boatman who neatly placed it in line with all the other vessels. Our rally organiser, who was also helping the boatman, came on board with our paperwork; we were quickly processed and then whisked ashore with our other late arrival.

The Islands being a huge nature reserve are not the cheapest to visit; there is little currency generation apart from tourism and this is being closely controlled by the Ecuador Government. In 2008 we were charged $100 National Park fee, (this gives free access to the Charles Darwin Centre), $135 Harbourmaster fee, this includes anchoring, lights, buoys, pollution charge and an environmental charge, $48 fumigation fee to rid us of any bugs we may be carrying and then you pay for rubbish to be collected as you are not allowed to dispose of your own ashore. By the time you've refuelled at $2-30 an American gallon and taken on fresh water at $70 for 150 gallons it all adds up, the justification of course is that it's a very special place and the Ecuador Administration is trying to maintain its exclusivity. We still would not have missed the experience for anything; it was worth it just to be able to say we have been there.

The Galapagos Islands were not to disappoint, although we would not have as much time as some of the others, it was to be a memorable and amazing few days.

Audrey

Our time in the Galapagos Group definitely lived up to expectations, we felt immensely privileged to be there and it was well worth the arduous conditions encountered on passage. The Ecuadorian Government is very concerned about the amount of visitors and tourism is strictly controlled. The first full day saw us and all our rally compatriots invited aboard the rally yacht which brought out the diesel for a fish and chip lunch. The large wahoo caught the day previous was gracing the table and it was also Happy Birthday Tony, what a great way to celebrate a special day, fresh fish and chips on board a sailing yacht in the Galapagos Islands, amazing.

Neither of us had ever seen such an abundance of wildlife as exists everywhere in the islands. Brown sea iguanas would swim around the boats at anchor, feeding off the seaweed, goose barnacles and algae on our hulls; they would peer into snorkel masks, as curious of the swimming humans as we were of them. There were sea lions and sharks in the harbour and whales just offshore.

All the way up the rock faces blue-footed boobies and their red-footed cousins would nest precariously, raising their chicks. Large orange crabs scurried at the water's edge and sea lions would make themselves at home on any convenient poop deck. Pelicans would patiently stand in wait at the fish market slab; heads all rising as one like expectant family pets. The fishermen cleaning the fish on the marble slabs would then throw all the fishy bits not required to the waiting mob of varied wildlife clambering around them. All life of any kind is protected in the islands, as a result all the animals and birds have nothing to be afraid of and are fearless where humans are concerned, they seem to realise that they will not be harmed in any way.

We paid a visit to the Darwin Centre where we met "Lonesome George" the last of his line of giant tortoises, along with his entourage of cousins. The tortoises were being bred in captivity to boost their population; it was fun to witness the very tiny babies to the huge fully grown adults in their different living quarters all within a few metres of each other. There was also an incubation shed where the eggs were kept at a closely controlled temperature while the young tortoises were hatched out. Yellow land iguanas of various sizes were all around the centre, some in captivity and some just roaming free in the scrub, and they all had a ready supply of food.

Unfortunately, even the mosquitoes seemed to be on the protected species list, they were huge and seemed very good at flying. Normally as long as you are anchored 50 metres or more off a beach, you rarely get bitten by a mosquito, they are not renowned for their ability to fly long distances, not so in the Galapagos. We arrived at our anchorage around sundown and were a good 400 metres out from any shore, I, clad in just a bikini was eaten alive in minutes. Quickly adjusting to the way of the islands, we soon learnt to cover up early, use a repellent on exposed skin and light up the local mosquito coils as the sun went down.

Our rally organiser was staying in a small hotel called "The Red Mangrove" it certainly lived up to its name. It was discovered through winding narrow paths leading through mature mangroves, cleverly lit up at night for extra atmosphere. Here in the very comfortable lounge rally members were invited to use the internet facilities, the service was well used and much appreciated. We managed a good simultaneous link with both our sons only then discovering it was in fact Mothering Sunday, this of course made the connection all the more special.

We were also recommended to walk up to the "Kiosks" about half a mile from the harbour for a memorable meal ashore. Here there is a road full of island restaurants, we went to one called William's and had a local delicacy known as "slipper lobster" this is a large crayfish they call "langoustines". The meal comes with all the trimmings for $10 about £7 and it is delicious, we went back and tried it again a couple of times later on. Other famous drinking dens and eateries in the high street were "The Rock" very popular with all yachties but could get a bit boisterous, a bit further on if you wanted more peace and quiet was the "Garanta Restaurant" which was excellent. I'm sure there are many more places to make merry but these were the ones that seemed to be "in vogue" at the time we were there.

A trip in one of the local tourist boats was also arranged for all of us across to another island called Santa Fe. This was a nature reserve so visiting was controlled and no landing permitted except by the warders. The island abounded with wildlife in and out of the water, swimming among the creatures and the fish was an experience not to be missed, I don't know where you would ever see so much sea life in one place again. Shortly afterwards when the shark appeared to be taking an unhealthy interest in all of us, swimming was not so popular. It was not only the fish that were abundant, the variety and amount of shellfish, sea creatures and birds was amazing, the whole island was vibrant with life, it just goes to show what happens when nature is allowed to take its course.

Figure 11: A giant tortoise in the Darwin Centre on Santa Cruz.

Figure 12: Pelicans and Sea Lion waiting for handouts at the fish market in the Galapagos Islands

Tony

There is a very cheap and efficient water taxi service laid on in the harbour to get yachties backwards and forwards to their vessels when required. It operates 24 hours a day and avoids the problems associated with using rubber dinghies against rough stone and flint walls. The other reasons were that there was simply no room to tie all the dinghies up, the quay was very small and even the taxis had to wait and queue up to drop people off. For the harbourmaster it was also more environmentally friendly to have controlled movement plus he did not want small fast ribs flying around all over the anchorage.

As is the case of all landfalls, replenishing water and fuel was of priority importance, many yachts had water makers but Cayuco did not have this luxury. Both these commodities needed to be ordered in advance, giving details of quantities required. It was advisable to be as accurate as possible with your calculations, you pay before delivery and are charged for what you order regardless of whether or not you can accommodate it. This calculation is true for water and fuel, then these important supplies are brought to your vessel by boat boys using a mobile bowser. This is an open boat which would normally be used for the boat taxi service but is temporarily fitted with large drums to contain either fuel or water. Try to check that the drum contains what you have ordered, the system is prone to mistakes and at the end of the day it is down to you to check all is OK. Another word of warning, the drums are not always used exclusively for one thing or another, check whatever you have ordered has not been contaminated or used for another substance, don't forget, you've already paid for it, when it's in your tank, it's your problem.

The other really serious problem is fuel contamination, diesel bug has been found by yachtsmen after filling their tanks here. The problem is, you don't find out until well on your way to your next destination. Liberal use of biocides when refilling your tanks with diesel fuel is recommended in most places around the world. I overdosed mine as I suspected the fuel was dirty.

It is also advisable to use lots of fenders if you value your topsides; the boat boys are very cheerful and happy go lucky, but are not professional seamen and are only young local lads trying to make a bit of cash on the side. As with all remote islands full time employment is a luxury not enjoyed by all, there is almost always a supply of labour for any job you have that you are not too keen to do yourself. For example they are happy to dive underneath and clean the bottom of the boat as far as they can; when I saw the amount of sharks swimming freely in the harbour I thought it was an excellent idea! There is also a fairly good chandler within walking distance, (3 kilometres) or it is a cheap taxi ride, I was able to top up my biocide stock for diesel fuel from here and it is usually hard to replace. He also carries a large stock of fixtures and fittings to be able to repair or modify most of the important parts as required.

Audrey

On the main island of Santa Cruz where the rally yachts were based, as expected there were many bars and restaurants. There is also a small supermarket and a fresh food market for meat, fish and vegetables. These facilities are very handy to replenish fresh stocks for the long passage to the Marquesas, if you have a small freezer as we did it is even better.

When we were expecting our supply of diesel fuel to be delivered, it was agreed that Tony would await its arrival on Cayuco, while I went ashore to pick up what stores I could lay my hands on. As I mentioned previously we had all done a good job of stocking up with as many tins and imperishable stores as possible before leaving Balboa, I'm afraid a good deal of this was in the form of tins of "Spam" in various guises. Anyway it was useful and we had obtained what we could, groceries and shopping on Santa Cruz was a bit hit and miss. A useful commodity discovered was tins of Anchor butter which would keep for long periods in the bilge. I had a fairly successful expedition and managed to purchase wholemeal bread and a couple of lettuces as well as fresh fruit and other items to vary our diet for the first 7 to 10 days on our way to the Marquesas.

As the water taxi dropped me back onboard Cayuco I was surprised to see a rather pert youthful bottom protruding from the engine room,

"My word" I mused, "This sailing round the world lark is taking years off Tony!"____ Well yes and no, pert bum belonged to one of the boat boys. The good news was our diesel had arrived, the bad being that the delivery guys needed to tap into our battery power to pump it into the tanks. Talk about a Heath Robinson organisation, they also had no way of communicating the stop command to the guy on the battery except lung power. As there were strict laws about diesel spillage they could not risk filling the tanks right to the top so the one down below kept trying to shout for information while the one with the tank was shouting to stop or go depending on the level, it was all extremely amusing.

Tony was highly suspicious of the quality of the diesel fuel we were getting; others on the rally had ended up with blocked filters and fuel lines plus gallons of water in the fuel tanks instead of diesel. It turned out his caution was justified; the fuel was a disgusting black colour and it looked like we had got the bottom of the barrel.

"This diesel is shit!" exclaimed Tony to the boat boy,

"Yes, Yes, it eez sheet", agreed Pert Bum. After all, it was only his job to deliver it, he wasn't into quality control. You had to giggle at the irony of it and as far as we were concerned, beggars can't be choosers, as we said before; we had to pay for it before they would deliver it. At least the fuel was some of the cheapest we encountered all the way round the world.

Tony

For information, I always used a Baha funnel fitted with a filter when I refuel anywhere, as the fuel looked so evil I also used a pair of Audrey's tights over the top, good for stopping water and large particles of sediment. It was a good call, not only did I have to clean the Baha filter many times during the refill process but I also had to clean Audrey's tights over and over again, the fuel was filthy. Having prevented most of the water and dirt from entering the fuel tanks I then used liberal quantities of fuel biocide to combat and kill off the bugs which would have got through. These bugs are so small that all my attempts at filtration to stop them would be useless, it is essential to prevent them propagating and growing in the fuel tanks hence the biocide. Even with all these precautions I still ended up having to change our fuel filters over and over again well before their service schedules, they just block up and stop the engine repeatedly. Many other rally boats had the same problems with some close encounters months later, their engines just stopped abruptly. Further on in the Pacific we heard of many other similar stories regarding the quality of the fuel. It is a hazard which is becoming more prolific as this diesel fuel bug problem occurs in more and more places.

Our time in the Galapagos was coming to an end; normally yachts are given a 14 day visa although our rally organisers had negotiated a 21 day pass for us if we wished. Some faster vessels had taken advantage of this concession, arriving early and leaving late. In Cayuco we could only make our limited time there as fruitful as possible, we were shortly to embark on the longest voyage between islands of the whole circumnavigation. The Marquesas are some 3200 miles from Santa Cruz and as Cayuco was one of the slowest boats of the rally we could not afford to dally in the Galapagos Islands..

Audrey

On the way to the Galapagos and during our stay another poem started to develop, I reproduce it here but it is just as relevant for our onward passage through the first half of the Pacific Ocean.

Off To the Galapagos and Beyond

We made our way through Panama,
And are now in the Pacific,
We stopped off in Galapagos,
The wild-life was terrific.

You can understand old Darwin,
Why he wrote his "species" book,
More creatures than you would believe,
Just everywhere you look.

Iguanas eat the seaweed,
It's something that they relish,
You'll often see them swimming by,
Though the currents can be hellish.

There's a bird they call a boobie
He has these bright blue feet,
He'll show them off in courtship,
It's really rather sweet.

Sea-lions came to meet us,
They thought we may have fish,
They'll hang around your fishing line,
And rob you if they wish.

We visited Charles Darwin's centre,
It was full of nice surprises,
Here was the famous Tortoise,
In all its different sizes.

They breed them here to keep them safe,
Then release them to the wild,
It was a privilege to see them,
We were totally beguiled.

And now we'll soon be on our way,
Further wonders to explore,
But there's a large expanse of water,
I'm afraid we can't ignore.

The Marquesas and Tahiti,
Are next on the agenda,

It will be worth it when we see them,
In their South Pacific splendour.

Well, that was it; the rally schedule meant we had to be on our way, it's not possible to extend your stay in the Galapagos anyway, unless it's an emergency, at least Tony had visited the most important islands on his agenda. It would be bravado to say I was not worried about the next bit, it made no difference, whatever; we were leaving tomorrow.

Figure 13: A beautiful rainbow before a passing squall between Galapagos and the Marquesas.

Chapter 6

Galapagos to Marquesas

Tony

We completed the paperwork to leave the Galapagos Islands and paid our respects to the remaining rally yachts who had decided to stay for a few more days. It was a sad and gloomy crew of Cayuco who left Academy Bay, we had only been there nine days and it was just not enough. Still, I had visited one of the most important places on my list, enjoyed the remoteness and wildlife while walking the same trails as my heroes of yesteryear.

Sailing out of Academy Bay shortly before noon we went well offshore to miss the reefs along the south of the island. It was very calm with a gentle breeze so as usual we motored to clear the land. As we were still very close to the equator no wind was expected until we were well south of the islands. Also, we had a bit of residual current against us instead of going with us which it should have been, another reason to make southwards.

We were off on the passage of a lifetime; the Pacific is nearly 8500 miles across and we had already sailed the first one thousand, the next land after the Galapagos is the Marquesas nearly 4 weeks of continual sailing away. There are no refuges, no islands to visit or take shelter behind, once started it's best to continue, returning means sailing against prevailing winds and current, for a sailing yacht it is all constantly moving night and day towards your destination.

After the Marquesas there is the Tuamotus, the Polynesian Islands, Papeete and Bora, Bora, Cook, Tongan and Fiji Islands, these as yet were only in our minds. Again we wondered how Cayuco would cope, more to the point, how would we cope, our experiences so far on this adventure had been sobering and weighed heavy on our minds, it was on the cards that along the way other calamities, breakdowns and gear failures were going to happen. Whatever, this remote part of the world was the start of the most interesting and fascinating part of our voyage, we would just have to overcome the inevitable problems, it was our decision to sail a now 37 year old boat round the world and we would have to live with it.

At least leaving just before midday gave us a simple noon to noon position fix and an easy 24 hour days run figure, the first day we covered 110 miles but most of this was on engine, we managed to sail for a few hours in the afternoon and then it was back to the iron topsail again. By next day we had got well clear of the outer islands, a breeze of about 10 knots came up from the south east and this was enough for us to start sailing, the jib, main, mizzen and mizzen staysail all went up trying to catch every bit of wind we could. With the distance to go we had to use our sails for the greater part of it, even with all our tanks, cans and fuel bladder full, it was impossible for us to motor all the way, not that we would want to anyway.

Again we used the 10-00 and 18-00 hour SSB radio schedule to charge the batteries by starting and running the engine at the same time. The morning schedule usually took between 35 and 50 minutes and we would copy each other's positions, this gave us a useful reference as to where we were in relation to the others. When we set off there was another 8 to 10 yachts behind us, all faster of course, the radio also gave us all the opportunity to pass on anything urgent or important.

The amount of battery power needed was more than I had originally estimated; we had been without shore charging facilities since leaving Shelter Bay on the other side of the Panama Canal. It was now the 7th March and we had been charging our batteries by periodically running the engine for 38 days. Our solar panels and wind/water generators gave us some charge but only in certain circumstances, we also had a long way to go before we could get shore power again, we guessed another 6 weeks. Another type of electric power generation was really important to us and this was becoming a necessity, at this time our small petrol generator could only be used for the computer and printer, we relied on our engine alternator more and more, this was risky and expensive on fuel.

Audrey

We began our voyage to the Marquesas on the 5th March; this was to be the longest sea passage we would encounter. My first observation was that the fresh stores I had purchased from Santa Cruz were not lasting well. For the Atlantic crossing we had bought up loads of the "Bimbo" brand of bread from Porto Calero in Lanzarote. I'm not sure how much preservative had been added in the baking, but the result was that it lasted far longer than any other sliced bread. One rally member reported that she found a loaf lurking in the back of a cupboard on reaching Antigua eighteen days later and it was still edible.

Unfortunately this was not going to be the case for this voyage; I was throwing out mouldy bread after the second day along with a good chunk of the fresh pineapple I had purchased, a bit disheartening to say the least. I managed to fit what was left of the bread in the top of the freezer and into a cool bag and hoped this action would save enough bread for the trip, my bread making operations so far had left a bit to be desired.

At least we were keeping the marine life fed with our discarded items. A large wahoo had got to know the way of the game and tracked us for days feeding off any scraps jettisoned overboard. We were asked why we didn't put a line over and try and land him, but truth be told he would have taken up our entire freezer capacity which would have meant ditching what was already there. It was a large fish. The wahoo was obviously not impressed when Tony, finishing off a can of Cola, pierced it with his marlin spike and dropped it overboard to sink. There was a loud crunch as teeth met aluminium and we never saw Mr Wahoo again. Although we do enjoy eating fish it does get boring eating it every day, the alternative is to take the parts of the fish you want and throw away the rest, we both think this is an appalling thing to do. If a creature gives up its life, the least you can do is eat as much of it as possible and appreciate it properly.

On our Atlantic crossing we had managed to obtain some long life vacuum packed meats which ostensibly keep well in the normal refrigerator. The same opportunity had existed in Panama for this type of victuals but we had rejected the idea, eating the various meats had not caused any ill health but the smell when opening the packets had put me off.

On the morning of the 7th March, the engine had been off since 22-30 the previous night. We had enjoyed a beautiful starry night watching the meteor trails across the sky and had then continued to average 4 to 5 knots sailing throughout the day. It wasn't to last however, on the 8th the weather turned miserable and poured with rain, at least we could shelter from most of it. Our fully fitted cockpit cover was made in sections which zipped up and around the whole cockpit; this gave us complete flexibility of coverage from the elements when needed, everything from a bimini over the top, to a range of side and rear panels covering every eventuality. Never mind, even with the disgusting weather we were experiencing, we were still sailing well and with the current now in our favour were doing 6 knots over the ground.

The bilge pump started its tomfoolery so Tony was once again down in the bilge trying to sort it out. This time it turned out to be a valve stuck in the open position and the sea water was running backwards and forwards in the pipe, triggering the sensor to operate the pump again and again. This was becoming tedious; it was happening too often, each time it took us some minutes to work out what the problem was and sparked us into emergency procedures in case this time it turned out to be more serious. If it happened on a channel crossing or an afternoon jolly to Cowes and back it would hardly be worth a mention, but we were hundreds of miles from no-where, we could not run for safety or pull in anywhere, we just had to keep solving the problem and carry on. Whenever it happened, it was always gratifying to realise that in fact, we were not sinking.

For the next three days we made good progress, fine weather, good winds and the current still helping us at about 1 knot. We implemented the steering vane and tow generator, there was a bit of a dip in the wind about the 13th March but then back to our average again. It was looking like we would make the Marquesas before April fool's day.

Tony

We continued on, in my log on the 8th March it reads, 2648 miles to go, bloody awful weather, Bilge pump keeps going, wind light, drifting, got to get better than this.

On the 10th I altered course to miss a sea mount ahead of us. These sea mounts can rise from the sea bed four miles below to just a hundred feet or so under you. It's best to try and avoid them if you can, the current even at only 1 knot can flow up the sides of the mount and cause a very confused sea on the surface. It's a weird phenomenon, and we have seen some really bad seas caused by this which throw the boat around a lot just like overfalls and worse, this also puts an excessive amount of strain on the rig and masts. It's all very odd on a flat sea with no wind to speak of. You also get a peculiar surface when two opposing currents meet, one minute you're sailing along nicely and then you notice a strange bubbling noise, the waves sit up in small peaks and cause a sort of rattling along the sides of the yacht, after a few minutes you just slip into a smoother sea as if nothing happened. Saw this a lot in the Pacific Ocean where the position of the easterly and westerly currents move north and south on a daily basis, it's best to find your current, sail well into it and stay there, saves a lot of miles and subsequently time as well. Another phenomenon is the cut off point, in calm weather it's possible to actually see where the east and west going currents meet, both bodies of water, moving in opposite directions, appear to slip past each other on a sheer plain only millimetres wide, it's most unusual.

When ocean sailing, it matters little whether you arrive in 21 or 22 days, the really annoying thing is to get to your destination just after nightfall and have to hang around offshore until morning. This has happened to us in the past, but now, when we are a few days away we start to work out our required mileage and try to gauge it so that we arrive in daylight, most of the time it is possible to get it right. Of course, if you are arriving in a port which can be entered safely at night it doesn't matter, but there are not many of them for a sailing yacht in the Pacific, most of them seem to have an off lying and dangerous coral reef.

We heard on the 10-00 hour radio schedule that another one of our rally boats only two days out of the Galapagos had lost their auto pilot. This meant they had to manually steer the boat, maybe OK for an afternoon jolly but not for a three or four week stint across the Pacific Ocean. They were too far behind for us to help but another rally yacht near them offered to try and help. He was able to carry out a temporary repair to the auto pilot mechanism which enabled them to continue to the Marquesas with a working unit. This kind of spirit prevailed throughout the whole rally and almost everyone in their turn was able to offer some kind of help and assistance at some point or other. As I was the diesel engineer of the fleet, you don't need too much of an education to work out what I was called on to doctor.

Lots of wind on the 11th, 151 miles in 24 hours, a very near gale and we just let her run, she was really enjoying it, A frontal system moving across our position had given us 30 to 40 knots of wind from the south east nearly the whole day, really felt like we were getting somewhere. The weather then eased a bit and for the next few days we bowled along with 20 to 25 knots of nice steady similar winds, we and Cayuco loved it.

Wasn't to last of course, around 4 o clock in the afternoon of Friday 14th March, I thought I'd go below for a little catch up on some sleep, no sooner had I put my head on the pillow when the boat gave a lurch and we were hit by a rogue wave from the port side. This had been happening all day, a disturbance thousands of miles away in the Southern Ocean was sending up big cross waves. Occasionally two waves from different directions would converge right at the same time as Cayuco rolled by, one of the waves coming up from astern and one from abeam. The result was a steep fall over to starboard; water would cascade right over the port gunwale and pour into the cockpit. This was not very friendly and apart from the water getting into the bilge it was damned uncomfortable and everything within range got soaked. You also had to keep aware of this event because if it caught you out, it could damage the boat and us, the motion during the roll was quite violent

On this occasion, just as I laid down there was a bang from above, Audrey shouted out that something had broken on the mast; I was up and out in an instant and saw the port lower forward shroud swinging freely around all over the place, it was no longer attached to the deck where it was supposed to be. The current wind was from the south east so this was serious; the damage was on the windward side. On examination I discovered that the chain plate itself had snapped at deck level. I threw a large box of bits from the boson's locker at Audrey with instructions to find another "one of those" and clambered on deck with lots of bits of warp to lash it down temporarily. It didn't take Audrey long to realise that there was not another "one of those" anywhere in our supply cupboard. The only thing resembling the broken one was on the other side of the boat, holding up the starboard side of the mast. She made this observation to herself while shoving the contents of the box around with her fingers. Not being too sure of my reaction to her suggestion that I take the starboard chain plate off as well and fit it on the port side, she kept quiet, after all, it did seem to be a bit extreme even if the thinking was sound.

As she put it later, it was a typical Star Trek situation, she said, "This is the only logical conclusion Captain".

After tying everything down to the other chain plates for safety and lowering all the sails to take the pressure off, I returned to the cockpit for a briefing as to our next step, at least we had saved the mast. This breakage was unexpected; all rigging had been tested and checked or renewed before leaving. No-one even contemplated breakage of the chain plates; they were enormous, six half inch thick stainless steel plates, they looked strong enough to hang the boat from them. On examination of the broken ends it was obvious what had happened, the continual stresses had caused metal fatigue, a small flaw, obviously very tiny at first had just grown with the constant movement and spread right across the bar. The constant south and south easterly winds which we had experienced almost all the time since leaving the Canary Islands had been putting strain on the port shrouds and fittings for thousands of miles.

This wind from the same direction was about to come to our aid, I reasoned that as we are always sailing on port tack, the chain plate on the starboard side was not doing its fair share of the work, this fact may come to our rescue, i.e., why don't I put the starboard side chain plate on the port side. I ran the idea passed Audrey and she admitted she had already thought of it but didn't want to voice it as it seemed so excessive. Audrey immediately went below to clear out the lockers behind the sink and worktops, while I rummaged around for some big spanners and a socket set. I also took the precaution of once again using the spare spinnaker halliards to lash down from the top of the mast to each side of the boat. At least the mast was not going to go anywhere just yet, even if we weren't getting anywhere very quickly either.

I prepared to remove the starboard forward chain plate, took out the split pins and released the bottle-screw taking the load off the rigging; I then removed the split pin and clevis pin from the chain-plate and re-attached the bottom of the shroud to a smaller ring bolt used to house the baby-stay when it was not being used. At least this would give the starboard shroud some kind of support, even if it wasn't as strong as it should be. Before trying to fit the other plate I had to ensure all broken pieces from the port side were out and the holes were clear. My only hope now was that the holes in the starboard plate were drilled in the same places as in the port plate. We were in luck, although the holes were not an exact fit, they were close enough to be able to work the starboard chain-plate into the port side. It was getting late and before I had completed all the tasks it had become quite dark, normally that happened around 18-30 hours at our present position. I managed to get the main fixtures in and tightened up, then completed the rig adjustments with a torch, pinning and securing the bottle-screws and clevis pins before being satisfied. With a lot of trepidation I hoisted sail again and we started moving, I vowed to re-check all the fittings again tomorrow morning in daylight to make sure everything had been pinned and secured correctly.

Our next task was to try and replace the chain-plates, it was clear that if one had broken then all of them must be suspect. We were on the radio next morning trying to work out how we could get a new set of plates. It was looking like we would have to have a set made up, although where this was going to happen we had no idea at the moment. We knew facilities in the Marquesas were very limited so didn't think we could get any made there.

As we sailed westward along our track it got dark earlier and earlier in the evening and stayed light longer in the mornings. We had to alter our clocks by 2½ hours between the Galapagos and the Marquesas due to the time difference between them. For some reason the Marquesas are - 9.5 hours UTC, this is unusual, as it's normally rounded up to the nearest hour, in these islands it only goes to - 10 hours UTC when you reach Tahiti. On the 17th March all the yachts on the rally synchronised their watches and we all changed our clocks after the morning radio schedule, this meant that in theory on our next radio call we should all be listening at the same time. We had already gone back by one hour shortly after leaving the Galapagos Islands so we were now all on Marquesas time. This time difference as you sail west or east can be confusing, it doesn't really matter what time you use as ship time, as long as you change the clocks when you arrive, problems can occur when you go ashore and find out you are a couple of hours adrift.

Our own problems were not over yet, day 13, Tuesday 18th March, got up to a nice day, good breeze, a following calm to moderate sea, not a care in the world. I did my usual morning visual inspection, glancing around the deck, checking fittings and security, looked up the rigging, all correct until, bugger! The top section of the jib furling tube had separated from the rest of the spar, I was sure it was OK the night before. It had obviously parted company sometime during the night but all speculation was useless, something would have to be done, and quickly. The gap between the top sections had left the genoa without any support; it had not taken long to wear through the bolt rope and tear the sail right across almost to the leach. I quickly rolled the damage part around the rest of the pole and was surprised to see the sail continue to set although not with a good shape and with a greatly reduced area. As the wind was mostly behind us, it was just possible we may get away with it. For now we had another problem, we knew there was no sail maker in the Marquesas and the genoa was going to need professional facilities, sail repairs we are equipped to do, sowing in new bolt ropes was a completely new ball game. We carry a spare but smaller jib so I rigged this up on the baby-stay to compensate for the lack of sail area and we continued on with little loss of speed.

Later that morning, on the 10-00 hour radio schedule and after we had completed the roll call, I reported our dilemma to the other rally yachts as a routine update of our situation. It transpired that a rally yacht a few miles behind us had a spare flying jib that they did not use. As it was a faster boat than Cayuco they offered to pass the sail over to us while sailing past. This seemed like a good idea so preparations were made to transfer the sail at sea, as we were still over 1500 miles from our destination it would be an extra safeguard to have another spare jib.

It took two days for them to overhaul us as we were both still sailing nicely; we talked to each other regularly by radio to update our relative position, it was important that we met up with them, if they slipped by in the night, it would not be possible for us to catch them up.

When you are at sea and your eye level is only a few feet above the water, the visual horizon is only two to three miles away, it is very easy in the vastness of the ocean for another yacht to sail past without seeing them. When they came into VHF radio range we discussed the proposed transfer method and agreed our modus operandi. We would both drop our sails and start the engines, then Audrey on Cayuco and the skipper's wife on the other yacht would manoeuvre the yachts at the same speed and on parallel courses as close together as safety allowed. I and the other skipper would then carry out the tricky task of transferring the sail. Although it was not a rough sea, the waves were too big for us to make a close alongside pass; this could easily result in damage to both boats. The proposal was for him to tie the bag to a rope from his masthead sheave, probably a spare spinnaker halyard; he would then throw another rope, already tied to the sail bag, to me. I would catch the rope, he would haul the bag up into the air, I would then pull the bag across the gap as he paid out a bit more rope. The whole operation relied on a fast pass-over and had to be a slick smooth procedure, we did not want the sail bag dropping into the water.

It all went beautifully, that is until I had to release the rope so that he could pull it back aboard his yacht, it took just a fraction too long to undo it and the whole thing nearly ended up over the side as I struggled to hold onto it. In general, the whole process went well and we had a spare jib aboard, sending thanks across to the other yacht we both re-set our sails and resumed sailing mode. A little later on, sitting in our cockpit with a cup of tea, we watched as they gradually pulled ahead and sailed off into the evening sunset.

It was now day 15 of the voyage, Thursday March 20th, we still had over 1200 miles to go, the conditions were moderate, only 10 to 15 knots of wind, mostly we managed to cover over 100 miles a day and we still had a nice bit of current with us. It became frustrating, some days we had wind, some days none at all, we tried to catch every little zephyr we could as we still had to be careful how much we ran the engine. At least everything seemed to be holding together, we did not want any more traumas with gear breakages. There was very little to see; only a couple of fishing boats, one of them steamed up to us from the North West and on a converging course. Although he was not flying any fishing identity and technically we had right of way I was forced to take avoiding action and passed close under his stern. There was not a sign of anybody on deck or below and he roared by completely oblivious to his close call. Repeated radio calls had no effect and as we could see straight through the wheelhouse when he went by, there was no one in there either, you pays your money and take your chances.

On day 17 we crossed another milestone, only 1000 miles to go and on course for a finish before April fool's day although it was going to be a close call. I kept busy, emptying the fuel bladder and our cans of diesel into the tank. We heard another rally yacht on the VHF radio, they were overtaking us so were not far away but we never got a visual sighting. He was concerned about his low fuel reserves as due to the unusually light weather they had been motoring more than expected. Of more immediate concern to him were his stocks of refreshment, he was nearly out of beer and that was much more important.

With 600 miles left to go, day 20 saw another front developing and we got the usual squally conditions with the associated wind, rain, thunder and lightning etc. It was just what the doctor ordered and we started to make 120 to 135 miles a day again

We had been at sea for nearly three weeks and it was amazing how fast the goose barnacles can grow and attach themselves to your topsides, they were disgusting. I was hoping the speed and conditions would deter them or cause them to fall off, but no, they just clung on and got bigger. After a few days of this weather a big three metre sea was running and once again we started taking breaking waves over the stern, running along the side decks as before. Fortunately, our new glued in panels stopped the sea water from sliding under the weather boards and the cockpit remained mostly dry and comfortable, we didn't care anymore, we were making fantastic time and couldn't wait to arrive in the Marquesas.

On day 25 the engine fuel filters blocked while we were charging the batteries so the engine stopped, probably due to the contaminated fuel we had received in the Galapagos Islands. I had to change the filters, clean out the system and bleed the engine while charging along under sail at 6 to 8 knots surfing down the waves; at least we were making good distances.

Unfortunately the alternator did not seem to be charging properly and the batteries were nearly flat. Everything electrical was already turned off; we don't use anything electrical unless we have to on long voyages. I turned the battery switch to the "all" position and wound over the engine with the injector pipes undone; this bleeds fuel up to the injectors quicker and helped to save what little electrical power we had left. It was clear I was not going to get many chances to get the engine started. I was lucky, the pipes bled up straight away, I tightened them up, tried the starter again and the engine burst into life. We left it running for a while to give the batteries the best charge we could, it was not charging well but at least it was putting in about 15 to 20 amps. Clearly we would have to be very careful with the batteries plus, we would have to look at the new alternator that we fitted in Antigua, something was wrong with it and we may not be able to do very much about it for a little while.

At noon on day 25 we had only another 130 miles to go, the wind was very light, it would take about 30 hours sailing at our current speed, the important thing was to arrive with fully charged batteries so we decided to use the engine while it was calm. We'd managed to sail most of the way and conserved fuel when we could so we had plenty of diesel left, as we approached the first island of the Marquesas the wind again increased so up went the sails.

The first island was Va Huka and Audrey spotted this at 07-30 hours, we had about 50 miles to go to Nuku Hiva and as it was March 31st, it looked like we would be in before April fool's day. The island of Nuku Hiva was seen through the haze at 12-25 hours, we were ecstatic; but it was going to be dark by the time we arrived. All the other rally boats had beaten us in and were talking on the radio to welcome us. We were going to arrive just in time for the famous "Island Piggy Roast" especially arranged for the Blue Water Rally fleet and we were looking forward to it. As we arrived just after dark our friends from the other rally yachts came out to meet us and guide us to a suitable anchorage in Taiohae Bay. The bay and harbour were very busy with commercial vessels, fishing boats and other yachts so their assistance was appreciated. Cayuco had sailed over 3200 miles in 26 days and 8 hours, at an average speed of 5.2 knots, we had weed, goose barnacles and all sorts of marine life growing on our hull reaching half way up the topsides.

Without waiting for any formal clearance we were whisked away in the dinghy to the festivities, it was great to be in safely and for a while we forgot about the damage to the mast, spars, sails and alternator.

We would have to sort out and repair that later, for now, tired as we were, the adrenalin flowed, it was party time.

Figure14: View from the hills behind Taiohae Bay, Marquesas.

Figure 15: Anchored in Taiohae Bay in the Marquesas, it was a privilege to be one of the few people who sail to this island.

Chapter 7

Polynesia

Audrey

It seemed wrong to be leaving Cayuco at anchor while we darted across the harbour to join in the fun; she had brought us all that way across the ocean safely and it felt like we had discarded her within minutes of arrival. The feeling did not last long; we dragged the dinghy up the beach, tied it to a log and walked into the garden where the Piggy Roast was well underway. As we walked in, all the rally participants gave us a standing ovation, they clapped, blew their hooters, screamed and shouted, it was deafening, of course they had all heard of our rig and sail problems and were happy we had overcome them. As usual we were the last to arrive, a position with which we had got used to, nonetheless; it was humbling as we were led to a table. They had even saved some of the piggy piggy for us, we filled our plates with island produce and with a glass of wine for me and a cold beer for Tony, we toasted with all our friends.

An Island dancing group had been laid on which were spectacular, colourful costumes, loud singing and mock battles were fought in front of our eyes. The evening ended with us all having a sing song, Tony was performing with his usual exuberance, the skipper from a French yacht asked him to give him an example of a typical English pub song. He thought about it for a second and the only one he could come up with at short notice which he knew all the words to, was the French song "Alouette Jaunty Alouette" so that's what they got. Within seconds everyone joined in and we brought the house down with the rendition, it resounded all round the bay and bounced of the hills for many a long minute, two very tired and weary people made their way back to Cayuco after midnight.

As it had been dark when anchoring the night before we had noticed little of our surroundings. The next morning somewhat bleary-eyed I stumbled from our stern cabin berth and into the cockpit to greet the day.

I was instantly overcome by the beauty before me; Cayuco was anchored in a bay that can only be described as majestic. Soaring green mountains encircled a natural harbour which seemed to gently embrace the flotilla of weary yachts that had made it to these shores. Every single one would have its own tale to tell of the struggles they endured to reach this magical place. I felt proud and emotional to be part of this very exclusive club, the last passage had been the longest we would sail and signified another major milestone.

We were requested to be on the jetty at 08-30 am in order to complete the entry formalities, sadly, we didn't make the deadline, but we did manage to drag ourselves ashore by about 10-00 am, in the Marquesas, it really didn't make any difference.

Tony

As well as the necessary paperwork we also took the chain-plate fittings, or rather, we took what was left of them, we needed to find a machine shop or at the very least a welder, I didn't fancy going any further until I had strengthened the fittings holding up the mast.

Another problem was water, in these islands, if you don't have a water maker, every time you go ashore you also have to take the five gallon jerry cans, this can save time later on when you want to fill your tanks. We had done very well with our water consumption, we only have capacity for about 75 gallons and after 26½ days we still had enough water for another week at sea, this meant the two of us had used less than two gallons a day for washing and cooking. Our arrangement for keeping drinking water was working well; we had about 70 separate 2 litre bottles well protected in the bow cabin and we used these as required, only one had broken so far. We reckoned that with our normal drinking water requirements we had supplies for about 35 days, and then emergency rations for about another 15 to 20 days. These water bottles could be replaced easily and cheaply anywhere we went and sometimes we could purchase separate 20 litre containers and fill up our empty bottles by siphoning, an even cheaper option. In fact having a couple of siphons on board was a good idea; they make transferring liquids very easy, we used them for water, petrol and diesel but we were very careful to keep the siphons in separate compartments.

After we had completed our check in formalities which are very easy in the Marquesas, we were directed to a man on the quay that knew a welder and could repair our chain-plate, there was no machine shop facilities available so welding was the only option. With the welding underway we returned to Cayuco, taking with us our refilled water containers for the tanks and some limited stores that we were able to find. In these islands you have to get what you can and when you can, potatoes and onions for example were not available until Thursday when the boat came in, and then only for a day or two until they were all sold. The locals still use the barter system; nearly all have a fairly large garden and most that are fit enough will spend hours tending their produce. They will swop what they have grown with each other depending on the time of year and what's available, walking around the island you can find notices posted selling all sorts of tropical fruit and vegetables.

The Marquesas are beautiful islands but very limited facilities exist for the yachting fraternity which is odd considering how many yachts must pass through here every year. There was no alternator service either, so I removed ours from the engine, stripped it down, cleaned and checked all the windings for continuity, and replaced it, adjusting the V belt at the same time. It appeared to be working a bit better but I was not happy with it, I had fitted it new in Antigua and had a nagging feeling it was about to give up on us. We were not the only ones suffering from electrical problems; it was without doubt the most common fault throughout the whole fleet. Even the ones with their own small generator sets were experiencing faults which ranged from ordinary servicing problems to whole electronic circuit board failure.

Audrey

While waiting for the welding to be completed, our rally representative for the Marquesas organised a "round the island" trip in four wheel drive vehicles, because of the numbers of people who wanted to go, it had to be done in two groups. The trip took up most of the day and although our finances weren't healthy it was impossible to resist. What an incredible day, the views, the scenery, the feeling of complete isolation was awesome, the whole trip was fantastic and we really enjoyed it, this is what it was all about. Everyone enjoyed a fabulous lunch in a beautiful bay on the north side of the island, the trip back to Taiohae Bay went by another track and past some high waterfalls, I already knew it was going to be sad when the time came to leave these idyllic islands.

Tony

We still had a problem with the roller furler spar up the forestay; I had removed the genoa which was badly torn all the way across and the bolt rope had snapped. How to repair the split pole at the top of the mast was another matter, I didn't want to have to lower the spar to repair it. This is where Brad, an independent Canadian yachtsman, sailing with his family from the yacht "Cairngorm" came into his own. The family, Brad, father and Jackie, mother, Tyler 12, Jasmine 10, and Bowen 8 had left Canada on an adventurous cruise round the Pacific, having nearly completed their list of places to visit they were heading back home for work and school. Their yacht was a 1978 MC39 built by Marcos Yachts in British Columbia, Canada, just like Cayuco it was an old heavy displacement yacht very comfortable and seaworthy.

The repair to the furling gear was a two man job and I knew it would be impossible for me to carry it out alone. I made up some new screws from my boson's locker, cutting and shaping until they resembled the originals. Brad, whose climbing skills came into their own, hung from the spinnaker halyard like the professional he is, while I did the tailing bit. He managed to refit the sections of the pole, superglue and screw them together, at the same time as clinging on to the furling gear with his legs 45 foot above sea level. We left it a couple of days to set and re-checked that it was OK, as it looked good we put the No2 genoa up on the furler and coiled it around the spar. I had already made sure before leaving UK that both of these sails would fit to the furler, the 2nd genoa was smaller in area but it would get us to Tahiti where I hoped to get the main genoa repaired.

The welded chain-plate was returned and I fitted it to the starboard side, I wasn't happy with the weld so thought it was better on the side that was doing less work, we still expected to get a majority of south easterly winds.

We had to fuel up and as we wanted about 450 litres of diesel I didn't fancy taking the cans ashore one by one. We would have had to make at least 5 separate trips ashore, each time with 5 x 20 litre cans and then somehow get them to the garage and back again, we were a quarter of a mile out in the bay, it was just not feasible with our small dinghy.

In Nuku Hiva, apart from cans, the only way to fuel up while afloat is quite tortuous; we enlisted some help from 2 young lads in another yacht and with their dinghy went over to the wharf. We dropped anchor well off the wall and reversed up to the quay, this is where the dinghy came in useful. The ladder up the wall is a long way away and round the corner of the jetty, you use a very long line and pull it back afterwards. The operation is further complicated because the prevailing wind is blowing you away from the quay and your warps try to go under the boat, to make it more interesting the quay is designed for commercial shipping and is 15 to 20 feet high (5 to 6 metres). With the dinghy, two young and agile lads and some nimble footwork we ended up safely anchored with our two stern lines secured to the bollards. You then send another line ashore to attach to the fuel hose, this is over 100 metres long and comes from the garage on the main road, the trick is to pull the fuel hose out to the boat, without dropping the nozzle in the water. When you are 80 to 100 feet off the wharf, this in itself is quite an accomplishment. Other points of consideration, as it's a commercial quay, it's in deep water, anchorage ground is poor and can be foul, a heavy swell comes in from the open Pacific Ocean and then bounces of the quay wall. The boat rolls considerably, takes on a yawing motion and moves in and out from the quay with the wave action. Nothing about this operation is easy, after filling the tanks we still had to fill up our fuel bladder on deck and all the fuel cans. The whole procedure can take a few hours; only one boat at a time can take on fuel and if other boats are waiting it adds to the pressure. Not many yachts can be refuelled in a day and it's just a case of waiting your turn, also, if fuel stocks are low on the island, you have to wait until the next fuel boat arrives. If a mercantile vessel arrives, there's only one commercial quay so all refilling is suspended, it's not an operation for the faint hearted and can be very fraught.

While we were fuelling up we had another distraction to contend with, just a few feet out to sea, a large manta ray about 8 to 10 feet across was attacked by a shark, the shark bit a large piece of wing off the ray and as you'd expect there was considerable turmoil in the water. We were told this was rare, but there it was, happening right in front of us. This frenzy continued after we had fuelled up, left the jetty and re-anchored in the bay. It looked like it started with just one shark but as time went on a lot more joined in; strangely enough no-one wanted to go swimming to check it out. Since witnessing this event we have discovered that sharks sometimes attack manta rays but rarely kill them, usually they just take a bite out of the wing, this then heals up as the ray produces a blood clotting agent and it just swims off. This was probably an isolated incident and all sorts of different catalysts could have caused it to happen.

Audrey

Nuku Hiva is a unique island, one of the most remote in the world, very quiet, few people, peaceful bays, amazing scenery and most of the island when you get out of town is deserted. In reality all of the Marquesas are much the same, the people are wonderful, relaxed, easy going and helpful. There are some colourful characters who we will never forget, one of them, working in the only bar and restaurant open along the seafront while we were there, deserves special mention. His pizzas, produced from local produce and anything else he can get hold of were delicious, he ran the place almost single handed, was always cheerful, even when 30 ralliers descended on him at short notice. I can recommend his "Tuna Special" pizza, the tuna arrives fresh most days on the wharf, anyone can walk along and buy what they want, if you ask the fishermen if it's fresh, you'll be told it was still wriggling less than an hour ago. We spent many a pleasant evening in the bar, sometimes able to watch the BBC news on the TV while sharing our stories and a beer with friends. It is easy to see why they are a happy people; there is never any rush, never any need to do today what you can put off till tomorrow, life is gentle, children are respectful, as one of the locals said to us, nobody here wants to be a millionaire,.... we already are and it's nothing to do with money.

For us the Marquesas were a welcome rest after nearly four weeks at sea, our days at anchor had allowed us to complete the repairs that we could do and victual the Cayuco as much as possible for the next leg, regretfully, it was time to move on.

Tony

We left after only nine days, it was sad to leave such a beautiful place, the bottom of Cayuco was still very dirty, we had tried to clean off what we could, but we were still slow. With our economical 1200 revs on the engine it was just about managing four knots through the water, even worse, the propeller was foul with barnacles and this was exasperating the situation. We had managed to make arrangements for a lift out in Fiji but that was over two thousand five hundred miles away and it would be another three months before we arrived.

There were a few yachts wanting sail repairs in Tahiti apart from us, one yacht wanted to replace a blown out cruising chute and another was looking for major repairs to his mainsail and in boom reefing system due to an unexpected jibe off the island of

Va Huka on the way in. Apart from the yachts with us, there was another large rally arriving in Tahiti at the same time as we were due and a race regatta week shortly after that. We knew there was only one sail maker currently working a sail-loft in Tahiti and we wondered about our chances of getting the genoa repaired.

At 11-00 hours on the 10th April we said goodbye to Brad and family on Cairngorm and slowly motored out of Nuku Hiva laying in a course for the Tuamotus. The island of Uo Pou was on our port side a few miles after leaving Nuku Hiva, some of the rally had been visiting here and we heard them talking on the radio as we sailed by. Apparently they had been ashore and were having some difficulty returning to their yachts. Whether this was due to the steepness of the cliffs and difficulty of negotiating the walkways to board their dinghies or some other more inebriating quality we never found out.

It was five or six days sailing to the Tuamotus so we settled into our daily routine and were soon watching the Marquesas slip slowly below the horizon.

I suppose the first significant event on the voyage happened at 16-00 hours on the day we left, I broke one of my back teeth, not good I thought, 1st day out on a week's passage and I have a broken tooth, oh well, at least my dentist had told me not to bother about breaking a tooth, apparently, as long as you get to a dentist eventually, it doesn't matter too much. Audrey had a tooth repair kit in her medical kit, but I didn't think it was bad enough to have to glue the bit of tooth back into it.

The next morning just after nine o clock we had a surprise visitor, a large whale, as big as Cayuco, surfaced on the starboard side only 30 foot away and gave a blow, it had a massive fin and we watched as it just sank slowly below the surface and disappeared again. At least it was on the lee side so we didn't get fish breath wafting all around us like before, if you ever have the undesirable opportunity to experience whale breath first hand, you will understand what I mean. Later on that morning what looked like a large pod of whales but could have been dolphins were spotted, each one was about three metres long, they had flat fronted heads, were yellowish brown in colour and had a large curved dorsal fin; we watched as we sailed past, they seemed to be swimming in circles, maybe they were feeding.

On day 3 we were drifting along at about 4 knots, not necessarily in quite the right direction, we were still experiencing squalls day and night; they usually came up quite quickly and disappeared just as fast. They lasted from 20 minutes to a couple of hours and entailed a rapid reef of the sails, then a bit of hand steering as the vane was overpowered, a wait of a few minutes to ensure it had passed, then sails out again and carry on.

Along our path lay the island chain of the Tuamotus, known on the chart as the dangerous islands, these are all coral atolls and none of them are more than 15 feet or 5 metres above sea level, usually, the first and highest thing you spot when approaching are the palm trees fringing the lagoons. For us and the rest of the rally, the main problem was going to be picking up the islands and being able to correctly assess their position. They are so low lying that you don't see them until only a few miles off and even then their position on the chart is not accurate. Many of the Tuamotus have not been properly surveyed and quite probably some of the reefs are not yet discovered. Many a yacht has come to grief navigating around and through these Islands, Thor Heyerdahl ran up on a Tuamotu Atoll at the end of his voyage when sailing the reed raft "Ra" across the Pacific and this is where Francis Chichester's ex yacht "Gypsy Moth IV" came to grief in 2006, there is a good reason for referring to the atolls as "The Dangerous Islands".

Another problem for the small boat sailor is the distance travelled to get there; you have to sail 600 miles across the ocean from the Marquesas and try to identify an island you're not going to see until less than 3 or 4 miles off. Navigation has to be accurate, the currents through the Tuamotus vary in direction and speed on a day to day basis, weather conditions prevalent at the time can dictate what you find and it can change quickly.

As the islands are not on a main shipping route, no one has any incentive to carry out a detailed survey, the result is a mix-match of data from a number of sources dating back to the 1700 and 1800's which is used to chart the area. There are updates where specific items have been reported, but the best course of action is to treat everything with a certain amount of caution and leave very wide margins of error while negotiating these atolls. The charts include warnings like, "last surveyed by the expedition of Captain Cook in 1768" etc, so when sailing around here, only believe what you can see, touch, feel or smell.

When we left the Marquesas our intention was to stop at a couple of the Tuamotu group, we had picked out Ahe and Rangiroa as possible places as they were right on our route to Papeete on the island of Tahiti.

Unfortunately this was not to be, our alternator was not charging properly, there was not enough regular wind to use the wind generator and the solar panels weren't getting enough sun. We were making fair progress but our electric problem was serious, we turned off the freezer and all our electronic navigation aids and for safety steered Cayuco by hand as much as possible, in these hazardous waters the "dangerous islands" demanded a lot of respect from us.

We also had to run without lights at night although we could turn them on in a second if necessary and we did keep a powerful torch handy in case of emergencies. Our batteries were very low and it was uncertain as to whether we would make Tahiti before losing all electrics completely. On the 14th April while still trying to charge the batteries as much as possible, the engine overheated and had to be switched off. The problem was traced to the raw water pump which had stopped pumping cooling water around the engine, a fairly simple problem to solve and I fitted a new impellor. This cured the overheating problem but the starter motor was obviously unhappy as I re-started the engine. It was clear that the batteries were not being properly charged and there was a fair chance that if the engine stopped again, I would not be able to get it going next time.

By now we were very close to the Tuamotus and it was obvious we would not be able to visit these lovely islands, with our electrical problems we just couldn't afford to take the chance. Getting stuck here was not an option; it would mean a long wait to get any repairs or to order any parts that we required as well as the expense. For us, this was a continuous problem, our faithful Salar 40 is a superb sea boat, but as our mechanicals were old, most of the peripherals are either out of date or had been exchanged for alternative units, the fact that the system was 24 volt made it even more difficult to obtain spares.

The approach to Ahe was made in the dark and we felt our way round the coast between 01-00 and 04-30 hours, we had been warned about their charted position being incorrect, maybe by up to 1.5 miles. In actual fact my suspicion is that the islands charted position is even more inaccurate than that, according to our GPS positions on the chart we rounded the northern point between 4.5 to 5 miles off. The entrance lights looked very close and still watching the voltmeter I switched on the radar and chart plotter for a few minutes, according to the rings on the radar we were only 2 miles off the reef. This is a constant problem around these atolls, inaccurate charted positions; variable and unexpected currents, very low lying islands and the long distances to get there create problems. GPS is a boon and although like all navigation aids it needs to be used with caution, it does give a good indication of where to start increasing your vigilance. It was upsetting to be able to see the entrance lights of the lagoon on Ahe looking so tempting, it would have been wonderful to enter the inner harbour at first light and anchor for a couple of days. The other yachts which managed to visit these islands were given a fantastic welcome and really enjoyed the experience.

We rounded the north and west sides of Ahe and laid a course between Rangiroa and Arutua, there is a 20 mile open passage between the two islands but the safe passage is only about five miles wide. It is impossible to pass through all the islands at this point in daylight, if you are forced to go straight through like we were; you have to negotiate either the first bit or the last bit in darkness. There are many safe passages through the Tuamotus but nearly all take up to and more than 24 hours, its better if you can stop and enjoy at least one of them.

Rangiroa is one of the few places in the world producing black pearls. Some of our rally friends anchored in the lagoon and were taken on a visit to the pearl beds and then around the workshop where the pearls were prepared for market, it is possible to purchase these rare pearls at very favourable cost while visiting. If you are ever lucky enough to visit these Atolls in your own yacht, remember the current through the entrances to the lagoons can run very fast, we're talking 5 to 9 knots here. It's partly due to the sea breaking over the coral reefs at one end and the excess sea water trying to leave through the few natural passages at the other end. Sea level changes due to weather activity and surges maybe hundreds of miles away can also cause these effects. Obviously, small sailing vessels rarely have enough engine power to overcome this amount of current, the trick is to wait offshore till high water and slip in just before the top of the tide, alternatively, if there is enough depth, you can enter at low water. Sometimes this has the advantage of being able to see more of the reef and avoid them, it also means, that if you do touch, you have a better than average chance of getting off. Usually there are anchorages just off the reef where you can wait for the correct moment and if you're lucky, the islanders will see you and help you through the passages at the right time. Most of our friends reported that they had assistance wherever they went in the Tuamotus. It's also been known for the current to slacken off well before or after high and low water, so local advice is always a bonus and if available is recommended.

Our alternator problems continued but it appeared that the batteries were holding a part charge, the wind came up and we had a memorable sail between the islands for most of the day. The solar panels and water generator played their part and by nightfall we were heading out and away from the Tuamotu group with only 140 miles to go.

During the night the wind died and we re-started the engine, the wind continued light and I had an excellent night's sleep, by

04-00 Audrey picked up the lights of Tahiti, we changed watches and it was her turn for a snooze.

By daylight we could clearly see the outline of Tahiti, as there was still no wind whatsoever we continued to motor and arrived outside the reef around 15-00 hrs, calling up the harbour authorities we were advised to wait until the next ferry had entered before proceeding into the harbour. The entrance is very narrow so extra care is needed, the port authorities are careful to ensure everyone keeps out of the way and obeys the rules; the entrance is also on the direct flight path to the very close international airport and can lead to extra excitement.

Buoyage inside is confusing as the flow in and out of the harbour is different to the buoyage along the inside passage of the reef, just take care and common sense will prevail as you get used to it. Another word of warning, if you turn to starboard after entering and take the passage from the harbour to Marina Taina east of the airport, you have to pass the western end of the flight path for planes landing at the airport, the runway is built on the inner reef, passage is not allowed until contact has been made with the airport authorities. Large planes land literally alongside the boat channel; you can only proceed east and west after receiving clearance. The height (air draught) of a yachts mast can easily cause a problem for the pilot when entering or leaving the airport. Another entrance through the reef further south leads to the marina, this is much better when you have got used to it as the channel is a bit vague and is dangerous in heavy onshore breaking seas. Channel markers have to be observed closely, sometimes holding off and following a local boat in can be a better option; a local pilot book is invaluable.

After avoiding all these hazards, the inner harbour which is to port of the main entrance is a very pleasant and peaceful place, mooring is stern or bows to the jetties and water and electricity is available.

This was the first mains electricity we had managed to hook up to since leaving Shelter Bay on the other side of the Panama

Canal. Our batteries seriously needed a good charge; this was not helped by the supply being interrupted when more boats arrived and wanted to run their air conditioners, ice makers and other electricity hungry equipment. The electric supply on harbour walls in most of the islands, even if you can get it, is only low amperage and a bit of common sense is required when using it. The port authorities had allowed 10 amps per berth as a rule of thumb which only really ran a battery charger and maybe a small kettle for boiling water, sometimes not even this, we got quite adept at running up the quay to re-set the trip on the main box.

Tahiti is a shock to the system, the yacht harbour is right alongside the main road and after many months of tranquil bays, few people and lots of peace and quiet, we were surprised by the noise, pollution, volume of traffic, and how overcrowded and commercialised it is.

After checking in which is an easy operation carried out in the office just along from the quay, I located the local sail maker and together with John from Penelope 3 we got our sails into him for repair. As expected he was a busy man, we explained our time frame and he said he would do his best to get them finished for us.

The next job was to have the alternator checked, so I took it off the engine and next day saw me dragging it around the industrial park on our wheeled trolley. After being directed from one place to another I eventually found a Bosch dealer who had the equipment and could check it over for me, he told me to come back tomorrow for the report on its condition. Next day, back in his workshop as requested, I was shown an open tray with lots of very sad and extremely burnt bits of alternator. Apparently the stator windings had burn out and had then virtually destroyed every other piece of equipment in the unit. Repair was a possibility but would cost more than the price of a new alternator and this, only if he could locate one on the island. Again, our 24 volt system, being a non standard layout, looked like causing us more problems. All I could do was leave it with the experts and see what he could come up with. In the meantime I had to chase around for a couple of new batteries as the alternator had cooked the old ones, at least I had only ruined one bank of batteries. I had suspected early on that there was a fault with the alternator and had tried not to use the other bank. He kindly pointed me in the right direction and once again I trundled off with my trusty trolley.

We had also decided to invest in a small portable generator, Cayuco's electronics are not that sophisticated but to have an alternative reliable charging facility for our 24 volt system was becoming crucial.

Our computer had a messenger facility; this was really helpful in places where we could get a wireless link from a marina, hotel or cafe. It was a real bonus being able to speak to family while sitting onboard on the occasions when a connection could be established. Our secondary system for running the computer was a 24 to 240 volt inverter fitted on the bulkhead; the power supply came from the batteries. If I could get hold of a larger petrol generator, we could use this for charging the batteries which in turn would make the computer more reliable, it may not be the most electrically efficient method, but it works.

Sadly our Wi-Fi experience in Tahiti was marred by technical difficulties, the private local system needed a new and expensive aerial and booster, for us this was not financially viable. In the end, a nearby bar let us use our computer with their internet link and we succeeded in chatting to family for an hour here and there, of course, being a bar, we had to partake of the occasional glass of beer or wine to keep them affable, shame! It was particularly enjoyable for Audrey to be able to keep in contact with the family, we could talk quite cheaply using the computer but the phone call costs prohibited anything but a brief chat.

After many hours searching we found a new portable generator which had a lot more power and would charge our 24 volt batteries, we also managed to sell our smaller unit to another rally friend who wanted to be able to boost his 12 volt system. The expression "portable" in regards to our new generator was questionable, technically it was portable, but only if you were a gorilla with muscles of steel. We decided to permanently mount it on the rack we had built over the stern cabin, the arrangement worked well and it gave us the emergency electricity we needed. The drawback, being a commercial unit, was the noise it created and occasional exhaust fumes when the wind was in the wrong direction, we also had to be careful where the exhaust went and make sure the stern hatch was closed when it was running. As we already used petrol for the outboard that was not too much of a problem, but the quantity we had to carry rose considerably, we stored it on deck and as out of the way as possible.

Audrey

In between sails, generators and batteries we joined in with the rest of the fleet for some well needed rest and relaxation. The Tahiti tourist board had laid on a "round the island" trip with visits to Cook's monument, the bay where Captain Bligh's Bounty had anchored for some months before the mutiny, then to the famous artist Paul Gauguin's and the Tahiti museums. We all had a fantastic local lunch in a bay on the east side of the island which split up the day nicely and everyone enjoyed themselves immensely. There was also a colourful reception with Tahitian dancing girls giving us all leis around our necks, this is customary in Tahiti and we all had an opportunity for some vibrant photography.

Eating out in Papeete or anywhere in Polynesia is fairly expensive, however, just along the shore from the pontoons in the harbour is a large park, in the evening this is taken over by the aptly named "Cockroach Hotel". This is a gathering of a multitude of mobile cafeteria type vans, they descend on the park every night from 6 to 9 pm serving fast food in all varieties imaginable, don't let the name put you off; it has nothing to do with the quality. It is an open air arrangement and all very politically incorrect I'm sure; it would probably never be allowed in Europe with our EU health and safety laws. However, by

Polynesian standards, the food is cheap, very tasty and covers a wide variety of different cuisines, there's plenty of it and it's certainly a culinary experience not to be missed.

Figure 16: Cayuco, dressed overall in Papeete, Tahiti.

Tony

Our alternator contact had chased out another 24 volt unit for us, once again it had a different bracket fitting so it was back to the drawing board with hacksaw, files, drill and lots of modifications to make it fit. In the end I had it lined up with the engine pulley, wired into the system and once again we had a working alternator, it only gave a maximum of 30 amps charge but it was the best we could get. It would have been nice to fit one of the proper marine units with a 100 amp charging capacity, but the expense and the loading on our single V belt pulley plus the technical difficulties prevented us. This ongoing electrical problem was one we should have sorted before leaving UK, hindsight is an amazing faculty.

Again I had to change the fuel filters, like many others on the rally we were still suffering from the dirty fuel purchased in the Galapagos Islands. Before leaving UK I had purchased and stored a dozen of each of our different fuel and engine oil filters, the fuel filters were now being consumed faster than predicted, I would have to obtain some more soon but decided to wait, my thinking was that they would be cheaper further down the line and supply would be easier.

While we waited for all the various bits and pieces to be ready we managed to clean and polish Cayuco's hull. After thousands of miles of hard ocean work she really did look the worse for wear. We blew up the dinghy and used it alongside to scrub, clean and polished, it took a long time and wasn't easy but it was worth it. Due to the heat during the middle of the day, we got up early and did a section at a time before it got too hot. A few days working morning and evening and soon she looked her old self again, we also scrubbed the waterline and cleaned as far under as we could get. The barnacles on the hull and propeller were slowing us down and we were looking forward to our lift out in Fiji.

Audrey

Another surprise was the mail from our family; it was soon to be my birthday and have to admit I was missing them, the mail helped; I had some birthday cards plus a long letter and some DVD's from our son. The DVD's turned out to be of our grandsons playing in the snow and then some of the 2008 Snooker World Championship, we both enjoyed watching them all and it brought everyone a bit closer.

Most of the other rally boats left for Cook's Bay in Moorea, the island was only an afternoon's sail away; we were all due to have a briefing about the next leg of our voyage at the Balhi Hi Hotel in Cook's Bay. As Cayuco was not ready to sail we went across to Moorea on the early morning ferry with some others who were stuck, we were met by John and Jane from Penelope 3 who had rented a car for the day and before the meeting we had a tour of the island, I think it's fair to say we all enjoyed the excursion immensely, Moorea is a delightful island.

Tony

After the meeting it was back to the grind again, on board Cayuco I started searching for the cause of our engine overheating problem. Again I checked all the water passages, heat exchangers and impellors, I couldn't find anything to blame, I started to think about blocked exhausts and hose outlet problems but could not isolate anything as to the cause, it was becoming very frustrating.

We eventually had Cayuco up and running again, apart from the overheating problem. Some lads from another yacht had swum underneath in their scuba diving gear and cleaned off most of the barnacles from the hull and the propeller for us, that was a real bonus and deserved a few free beers in the local hostelry.

Before continuing we needed to top up our fuel tanks, the only place fuel was easily available was at Marina Taina the other side of the airport. We decided to take the inshore passage, this runs between the outer reef and the airport runway, from the pontoons this was the easiest way. Leaving our berth, we crossed the channel and waited at the entrance between the reefs while we called up the airport tower to await instructions. After a few minutes we were given permission to cross the flight path and preceded on our way. It was out of the ordinary negotiating the passage inside the coral reef, similar to other channels we have sailed but more exotic, little did we realise, how much more of this type of sailing there was going to be. We arrived at the marina but as it was their lunch break we had to wait before being able to fuel up; a series of events determined what happened next.

In my mind I was trying to sort out somewhere to take Audrey for her birthday, I had thought about the hotel on Moorea but it was now getting late, I met some rally friends who had come back from the briefing and spotted a pretty restaurant in the marina almost at the same time. The restaurant was called "Casa Bianco" and an idea began to materialize. After a little chat we decided to give Audrey a surprise birthday party in the evening with as many friends as we could muster, it isn't often these events happen on trips such as this, you have to grab the moment and go with it. We fuelled up to be ready to move on and as it was now too late to head off, I made an excuse to stay in the marina overnight and told Audrey we would sail over to the island of Moorea tomorrow.

There were more rally yachts in the marina than I first thought; the result was that a band of 16 happy ralliers met on the lawn of the restaurant that evening for sundowners and gave Audrey a surprise birthday celebration evening. It was a very jolly party and I think it's safe to say everyone enjoyed themselves; it was so good, that we spent another few days in the marina getting over the night before, socialising, and enjoying the company, such is life.

Audrey

On the 9th May 2008, a few days after my birthday celebrations, we set off for Moorea and were looking forward to spending a few days in this calm and tranquil setting. Leaving the marina and negotiating the east passage we had a really good exhilarating sail across to Moorea, dolphins played around the boat riding the bow wave, circling us and jumping high out of the water on both sides, what more could anyone ask for, this was real South Pacific cruising. Late afternoon after negotiating a passage through another reef we arrived in Cook's Bay anchoring off the Balhi Hi Hotel. This bay is extremely photogenic, when we were there it was extremely quiet and peaceful, it felt like you never really wanted to go anywhere else, a lot of the anchorages throughout Polynesia felt the same.

The next morning we blew up the dinghy and went exploring, starting with scrambled eggs and bacon for breakfast in the hotel we then walked round the bay. As it warmed up we found plenty of places tucked out of the way for a quiet beer, the whole scene was breathtaking, we walked and sat and then walked and sat some more, we contemplated the accomplishment to get here and looked in awe at our surroundings.

While we were in Cook's Bay, Brad and family on the yacht Cairngorm who we'd met in Nuku Hiva arrived. This was unexpected as when we left the Marquesas they were off to Honolulu. From what Brad told us, they had decided to sail down to Tahiti and Moorea after we left because they wanted to, and, because it was there. As Brad said, they didn't know if they would ever get another chance to sail these islands again, best do it now, for our part, it was great to see them again.

Our idyllic life was not to last, normally Tony doesn't take the cover off the anchor locker to flake the chain down, it's inside the fore cabin and awkward to get to, being a deep locker it doesn't usually cause any problems. This time, as we weighed anchor to leave Cook's Bay and for some unbeknown reason, he decided to flake the chain after all; how lucky can you get.

Figure 17: Bali Hi Hotel in Cook's Bay, Moorea.

Figure 18: We were all invited to a tourist dance where we were all presented with "Leis" a flower garland around our neck.

Tony

We were in 22 metres of water and had 75 metres of chain out, maybe subconsciously this was the reason I had decided to flake the chain down in the locker. It was a good call, as Audrey, on deck, used the electric anchor winch to pull up the chain, there was a bang above my head and flames shot out of the winch, not only that, the flames continued to burn. I shouted to Audrey, "stop", but the noise of the winch and my distance from her meant she could not hear, I pushed open the fore hatch and shouted again, at the same time grabbing a nearby fire extinguisher. The winch stopped turning, I managed to tell Audrey what had happened and put out the flames all in one go. It's a good thing I obeyed the rules and made sure we had new and working extinguishers in each cabin.

The winch however had short circuited and with the high amperage loading at the time it had melted all the connections. This was going to be a problem, it's very hard to get up anchor chain by hand on Cayuco, the manual handle is almost impossible to use due to the fitting position, I had tried to remedy this in the past and had been beaten by the age of the winch, the only real solution was to fit a new and more modern system. We pondered what to do and were thinking of using the sheet winch and a pulley system when our friend John from Penelope 3 called us on the radio to check if we were OK. After explaining what had happened, John, an electrician by trade said he would come over and have look at it. We spent an hour examining possibilities of removing and repairing the winch but to no avail, John's prognosis was not good, he knew the problem and how to cure it, but without a proper workshop it would be difficult to affect a long term solution. However, John did know of a very good electrician who operated from a small unit in the marina back in Papeete, he had comprehensive workshop facilities and the silver solder techniques we would need. With much heaving and grunting, John and I managed to raise the anchor and with no possibility of repairing the winch, we decided to take Cayuco back to Marina Taina and seek advice from the electrician. It was unthinkable to continue without an effective anchor winch, we were in the middle of the Pacific, most of our stopovers for the next three months would be at anchor and in some deep water, we had to find and affect a repair.

Back in Marina Taina I consulted Richard the electrician, he as expected was a very busy man, he advised that if I could remove the motor from the winch mechanism he could probably repair it. This I knew was not going to be an easy operation without unbolting and removing the whole unit, it was fitted underneath the foredeck and I would have to work upside down, with my head inside the anchor locker and in almost pitch darkness. I needed time to think about how I was going to tackle this ticklish project. In the end, working in the locker as described above i.e. upside-down etc, I managed to drop the offending bottom half of the motor away from the top half. The reward to this was that the bottom half included all the offending bits that had caused the trouble. The bulk of the winch mechanism was still bolted to the foredeck so this method saved valuable time and my sanity. Our electrician had little trouble replacing the burnt out parts of the motor and within a day I was presented with a modified but workable bottom half of the motor at very affordable cost. Of course, on removal, working upside-down in the locker, gravity had been on my side and the heavy motor had dropped down uncontrollably almost doing me a serious mischief in the process.

Putting the heavy unit back up again was going to be a very different matter. Basically, I had to support the motor, spring the armature brushes onto the commutator, slide the whole unit up into place, align the motor body onto its pegs, while at the same time fit and screw the long locating bolts into the top half of the unit. I also had to be careful not to damage the new silver soldered joints and ensure that no electrical connections were trapped between the casing and the base plate as the whole unit was screwed together. A simple operation if only I could turn Cayuco upside down, balance her on her mast and get gravity to help me again, what I really needed was a very clever octopus. I then realised, working upside down in the black hole of the anchor locker, it was not possible to do all this with one pair of hands. As it was impossible to get anyone else in there with me, I was in a predicament.

After a deal of thought, I managed to accommodate all the necessary requirements with a series of blocks of wood, little sneaky hooks of wire holding out the brushes to be released later and a whole lot of luck. Audrey in the meantime had taken herself of shopping in order to save herself from the stream of colourful language emanating from the dark depths of the said anchor locker. Whatever, after a few hours lying on my back, in a succession of intricate and agonizing positions, I succeeded in getting the motor back together and working, we tested it as best we could and declared it fit to carry on.

During our trip to Moorea and back I had been suspicious of our other battery bank, they did not seem to be holding charge so I dug out the hydrometer and I tested them. Low and behold, they showed evidence of short circuiting too; we could not take the risk of continuing with batteries below par, it was impossible to know when we would be able to replace them. There was nothing for it but to purchase two more deep discharge heavy duty batteries, I searched around and got the best price I could, at least I got a lift back to the marina in the works van with the batteries.

By the 15th May we were on our way again, this time we were heading for Raiatea about 120 miles away and only a stone's throw from the famous island of Bora Bora. We made good time and managed to sail most of the way arriving off the Irihu Passage through the reef about 11-00 hrs the next day, good timing as it is easier to see and feel your way through reef passages with the sun above and behind you. Our chosen anchorage for the night was Faaroa Bay just inside the passage; this is a very large bay with good holding all the way up to the shallows. The bay is very peaceful, calm and quiet; we spent an extremely pleasant evening with our own company all alone and watched the sun go down. It is amazing how you can still find a completely deserted anchorage in these islands, there's just not the numbers of yachts or people about.

The next morning we took a leisurely sail up inside the reef, once again trying to distinguish between channel markers and withies stuck on isolated coral rocks, most of which are just below the surface. You have to appreciate there is not much small boat traffic around these islands; buoy-age and marks are usually kept serviceable by local helpers and fishermen who know where they're going anyway. Leaving early in the morning with the sun behind you shows up the reefs and shallows really well, you soon get used to reading the colour of the water and learn how to avoid all the hard bits, a pair of eyes in the bow or better still up higher in the rigging is a real boon. You can con yourself all the way through shallow reefs and coral outcrops to the most incredible anchorages. As the water is calm and clear with excellent visibility and your speed is generally low, even if you touch, you can just reverse a bit and try again somewhere else. With little tide or current to worry about and almost perfect weather, it is not surprising how many yachtsmen get waylaid by the beauty of these islands and spend years being mesmerised before able to escape and carry on with their voyage.

We were heading for the north east corner to the small town of Uturoa on Raiatea which surprisingly for the Society Islands actually has a free town quay; you can stay for a few days without being charged. It is a charming little place with most facilities for the visiting yachtsman, even down to refilling your gas bottles at very reasonable rates, there is also fresh water but sadly no electric outlets. There is a Chinese Restaurant near the Quay, open for snacks, a cold beer, or a full blown meal in the evening at very good value. These facilities were well subscribed by the ever increasing number of rally yachts arriving as the word got around by virtue of the evening rally radio net, very soon there was no more room on the quay and yachts were double and triple banked but a good time was still had by all.

On Wednesday the 21st May we moved down to Atooria Marina to fuel and water up, this is unusual in that it is another roadside garage with a fuel dock behind it, here at least we could pull up alongside, our next destination was back to taking cans ashore.

Before leaving Raiatea we went coral dodging again up through the reef to the island of Tahaa, we had heard about a place called the coral gardens where you can go ashore and walk for miles through the coral in water no deeper than your knees. Our anchorage was just off the gardens in about 8 metres and we took the dinghy ashore, the underwater gardens are truly incredible, the sea life can be seen in all its glory while colourful reef fish just swim around your legs. It has to be a photographers dream and it's all free to yachties, all you have to do, is get there. It was so beautiful we stayed at anchor another day and rested, we marvelled at the unbelievable sunsets and to top it all, the moon was full. We sat in the cockpit all evening, ate our meal and drank a beer, marvelling at the brightness of the moon which turned the night into a surreal kind of daylight.

Would you believe it, Audrey once again put pen to paper and wrote the next poem. Guess what now? Written in the Coral Gardens with a little bit of license as to the exact position of the Longitudinal Meridian.

Audrey

Half Way Round

We are here!

No ocean liner brought us

Or jet plane flying high.

No package tour

(Here today, gone tomorrow)

Just us two, by and by.

One eight zero degrees
Half a circle
Round the world already.

How can we explain?
How difficult
When our nerves are none too steady.

The moon is full
The air is warm,
The anchor holding fast.

We deserve this,
when you contemplate,
The problems of the past.

You'll say, "You lucky bastards"
But it was not luck,
which brought us here.

God's intervention,

His sense of humour

And a lot of blood, sweat and tears.

This poem was written one evening in a beautiful calm bay, which was sheltered by a surrounding coral reef. This had to be very carefully navigated to find the entrance safely. The water in the anchorage was so crystal clear we could see the anchor on the sea bed 25/30 feet below. I wrote it, not to make the reader jealous, but to describe the most incredible feeling that **this** is what it is all about. After battling with the elements and feeling like you are trying to sleep in a tumble dryer, these moments stay with you forever and they make you feel that you have truly earned them".

Figure 19: The Coral Gardens on the reef near Tahaa, a truly magical place.

Tony

Audrey wrote those comments after the poem, I know what she meant, I remember that anchorage as clear as when we were there.

All too soon it was time to move on; we had a date to meet the rest of the rally yachts in Bora Bora the next day which was to herald the end of our Polynesian adventure. On the morning of Saturday 24th May we up anchored and started to thread our way back through the coral reef and out through the passage just south of Tahaa. It was less than 20 miles to Bora Bora over a calm sea and once again we negotiated the now obligatory coral reef passage at the entrance to the island; we picked up a mooring buoy just off the famous film star retreat of Bloody Mary's Restaurant at 12-45. Bora Bora is still famous as the island where the film "South Pacific" was made, and Bloody Mary's the drinking hole where the actors relaxed after filming. The place is full of pictures and photos of the actors and other famous people who have stayed at the place since, even now you never know who you will be sharing the facilities with. There is only one main town called Vaitape where it is possible to moor to the town quay for a few hours while storing up or there is also the Yacht Club. As you would expect there are many secluded and fascinating anchorages around Bora Bora but great care must be exercised negotiating the coral reefs, water is generally shallow and navigation can be tricky. It's not possible to circumnavigate the island by sailing yacht inside the reef due to very shallow coral banks on the south side; however, it is possible to do the approximate 30 km round trip by hiring a bicycle or to take the local bus.

The rally yachts that had arrived organised a night in Bloody Mary's and we all enjoyed a meal, dancing and a few drinks, it was extravagant for us to participate but we argued that we would never be this way again so what the heck. We dragged ourselves unsteadily back to the dinghy tied to Bloody Mary's private jetty around 01-30 in the morning, the moon was still almost full and we motored back to Cayuco in the half light. It was a clear and windless night, climbing aboard we sat in the cockpit for a few minutes, it was time to leave these enchanted islands and the friendly people we had met. We were all stored and fuelled up; it was going to be hard to say goodbye to this tranquil and serene little outpost at the western end of the Society Islands.

Little did we know what was in store for us in the next few months, perhaps if we had, we may not have left at all.

Chapter 8

Bora Bora to Rarotonga and Tonga

Tony

The weather was calm with a light southerly breeze as we left Bora Bora; it was Monday 26th May and by the time we got away it was 14-00 hrs. All the rally yachts were slowly leaving the anchorage, after the night before no-one was too eager to get underway before they had recovered. Another problem was the weather forecast, the report told of a front associated with a low pressure system heading our way, also the South Pacific Convergence Zone, (SPCZ), which usually stays north of our position was yet again forecast to come further south than was usual. We did not really have any choice, time in Polynesia was up, we had checked out and everyone wanted to make the deadline for the next rally stopover in Tonga.

By now, we had got used to setting off and dealing with whatever the weather gods threw at us, let's face it, when your hundreds of miles from no-where, it matters little what weather conditions you find, you just have to put up and get on with it. It was more than 500 miles to Rarotonga and well over a thousand miles to Tonga itself, we had not yet decided which island to go for but we had stored and fuelled up for either, our next destination all depended on wind direction and what happened weather wise. Other Cook Islands include Aitutaki, Atiu and Niue but weather and shallow channels may prevent entry, some have mooring buoys outside for visiting yachtsmen in reasonable conditions.

The first 24 hours was flat calm, no discernable wind from any direction, we used the main sheeted in hard as a steadying sail and our own speed through the water gave enough to fill the mainsail and stop us rolling too much. It was 16-45 hrs the following day before a light 5 to 10 knot breeze came in from the south and all available canvass was hoisted, even the mizzen staysail. The light breeze continued but at least the engine was off. Just before midnight on the 28th wind came in from the north at 10 to 15 knots, by 08-15 hrs the next morning it was NW 25 to 30 knots and we were sailing on a broad reach nicely off the wind. Well reefed down by this time, the decision of which island to go for had been made for us. Tonga lay almost directly to windward so at 65 degrees off the wind Cayuco was flying along and heading for Rarotonga

It was a very wet sail, sea water was cascading right over us and as it was raining hard we were getting a real dowsing, the seas were running at 2½ to 3½ metres (9 to 15 feet) and rising. The crests of the waves were already breaking and Cayuco's speed was throwing sea water well up into the rigging. The waves were their normal Pacific mixture of wind related and a heavy swell from the south, it made for an uneasy motion and we were having to hang on to anything we could when moving about the boat. This swell from the south presumably from the roaring forties, had been evident all the way from the Galapagos Islands and made life aboard somewhat uncomfortable, I pondered that the seas were being made worse by one set of waves opposing the other. It was invigorating and exciting to be charging along at this rate but I was very aware of the damage we had already sustained to the rigging, plus we were on the tack where the welded chain plate from the Marquesas was taking all the strain.

It was also getting wet inside the boat, the pressure of water finding every little leak and after a few hours I shortened sail further, we lost a bit of speed but it was a far more comfortable motion. We had the water generator towing behind us and had good charging for the batteries; with the wind generator as well we did not need to run our engine or our new petrol generator very much. Unfortunately, with the solid cloud base, the solar panels did not produce any electricity at all.

The depression to the south west of us had deepened considerably, it had moved east and had also tracked a bit north; this put us in line for a beating. At the same time the wind had gone from NW to SW and showed every sign of going round further, this had produced an even worse confused and uncomfortable sea and once more we were off course. All we could do was hold on tight and wait until the wind had gone round further before changing course again for Rarotonga. While waiting to tack we were hit by a tremendous gust from the SW, Cayuco lay over on her ear, the port deck disappeared under water and I grabbed the wheel to assist the grossly overpowered helm. Audrey leapt for the mainsheet and released it but we were still laid over, all attempts to make headway had been abandoned, it became a damage limitation exercise. There had been no warning of this gust, the weather had been overcast and threatening for hours, we heard later that another rally yacht 10 miles away had recorded 65 knots on his anemometer; our meter gave up completely and never worked again for the duration of the rally. As Cayuco is a very long keeled sailing yacht, it does not round up very quickly when hit by strong gusts of wind, it is such a well balanced yacht that it is easy to take over the wheel and let her keep ploughing ahead. The gust lasted for over fifteen minutes and even though we managed to release the pressure in the jib she just kept on forging ahead, burying her nose, throwing water everywhere with the side decks under water.

By the time we had reefed further and got some kind of control back into her, the wind had started to die down but even then it was still blowing at 45 knots. Cayuco continued to punch into the waves while the wind screamed in the rigging, both of us hung on and let her sort it out. I take my hat off to Laurent Giles when he designed the Salar 40 class of sailing yacht. I have sailed many yachts during my life as a delivery skipper and for charter companies in many parts of the world, but I have never experienced such good sea keeping qualities on any forty foot (12 metre) sailing boat as the Salar 40. They may not be the fastest 40 footer out of the blocks, but by God they look after you when the chips are down, we were to have an even better affirmation of this later in the voyage, as yet, that experience was still to come.

The weather continued to be awful, the good thing was that as the low pressure system south of us tracked east, the wind backed to the south and then to the southeast. This enabled us to keep sailing towards Rarotonga although our rations consisted of muesli bars and anything from a tin. The wind direction had been erratic during the storm so the distance to our destination had suffered; we only managed 78 miles in the right direction even though our speed had been 6 to 8 knots over the ground.

Figure 20: How not to come through the reef in Raratonga

Sometimes we were going in the wrong direction completely but there was little we could have done about it. The last 24 hours had been very unpleasant but by the 30th it had calmed down and we resumed our course. Mauke, the first of the Cook Islands was spotted at 08-15 on our fifth day out; we sailed past with only 150 miles to go to Raratonga. Another instrument we had lost was the speed and distance log, although I had removed and cleaned the paddle several times it still refused to register, this was annoying but as it was not an essential piece of equipment I removed the paddle and fitted the blank, at least this would stop the paddle wheel from fouling up.

Day 6 on the 31st and a hazy Raratonga appeared on the bow at 07-00 hrs, this was another place where shore power was not available so we started the engine and motor sailed in to give the batteries a good charge before we arrived. At least with our acquisition of a petrol generator from Papeete we would be able to re-charge the batteries on a daily basis without using the main engine. We arrived in Avarua Harbour about midday and managed to moor stern to the small quay, Audrey's notes said, great little place, had a good night at "Trader Jacks", bar, good food and "live" music.

One of the problems which continually occur in these small harbours is mooring and anchoring space. All our rally fleet had taken their own route to our next stopover at Tonga, some like us visited Rarotonga, and others went to Aitutaki, Atiu and Niue, room is limited at all these islands so the 18-00 hour radio net was buzzing with who was going where and how long they proposed to stay. Another consideration is depth of water, nearly all of the islands have shallow passages through the surrounding reefs and some you have to anchor or pick up a mooring buoy outside the reef. The weather plays its part as well, if you arrive and it is blowing hard, some of the harbours are impossible and dangerous to enter, imagine sailing for 5 or 6 days, arriving and then having to wait around or sail onto the next island which may be 2 or more days away. It is frustrating, after sailing half way round the world, then not being able to visit the island you want to, worse still, knowing that you will probably never get the opportunity again.

We spent a few lazy days in Rarotonga, filled up with diesel from a tanker on the quay, replaced stores, had a tour by bus round the island, had lovely toasted sandwiches in the bus depot cafe, found an internet cafe and had a good chat with family back in UK. We were really enjoying our time here but as usual it was over much too soon, the decision to leave for Tonga 814 miles away was arranged for Thursday 5th June. It was approximately eight days passage time to Tonga which fitted in with our rally support team's arrival schedule. Almost directly on our route was the Island of Nuie, if we made good time it was feasible that we could spend a couple of days on here as well, so with that thought in mind, we left.

Well, the thought was there, we had arrived in Rarotonga fairly early, dropped our anchor and reversed onto the quay, other yachts arriving later had done the same, as we left and pulled up our anchor, two other anchors came up with it and caused a bit of confusion on the quayside. Fortunately for us both yachts had also decided to leave, just not exactly at that time, I have been in this situation many times in the Mediterranean when other people have accidently dropped their anchors over ours so I was not worried about clearing the other anchors. Audrey took over the wheel and controls while I grabbed the boat hook, a length of rope and hot footed it to the bow. The trick is to make a loop in the end of the rope, pass it under the chain of one of the fouled anchors and use the boathook to pull the loop back on board then make the rope fast on a cleat. You then drop your anchor again and with a bit of luck it will swing away from the other anchor, you then simply pull up your anchor and drop the rope off the cleat holding the other one, the owner can then pull in and re-set his anchor. Unfortunately with two anchors caught, I had to carry out the operation twice and this took some time, We had some help from one of the other rally yachts who saw our predicament and came out in his dinghy to assist, when he saw we had two anchors caught up, he said,

"I've seen this before with one anchor but two is just being plain greedy".

A good laugh was had by all, in the meantime the other two boats had decided to bring their leaving time forward so it was made easier to drop the other two anchors, I then backed off while the other two sorted out their own anchors.

The weather on the day and subsequent forecast was not appealing, 20 to 25 knots of wind with occasional gusts to 30 knots, it is amazing how we had got used to setting out on a long ocean voyage with double reefed main and jib and thought nothing of it. It was a wild night and we were charging along at an average of between 5 to 8 knots depending on how we caught the waves, I swear Cayuco was trying to surf, before nightfall we reefed the sails a bit more for safety but it made little difference to our speed. The morning dawned with an angry sky, very red and aggressive looking, the seas were large and breaking waves were rolling along both our side decks, water was finding its way everywhere. It continued like this all day and into the next night, the South Pacific Convergence Zone was very active again.

Why this year has it decided to move so far south we asked ourselves, the answer may have been that it was an El Nino year, although it was not a particularly active one, it was bad enough to cause us a few headaches, we carried on and let Cayuco do what she does best.

Around 05-00 hrs the following morning there was another loud bang from the front of the boat, a quick flash of the spreader lights confirmed our worse fears, the port forward chain plate had broken again. This was starting to get tiresome. I quickly took all sails in and went forward to secure the flaying shroud, this action left us under bare poles, surprisingly it didn't slow us that much, we were still moving at 2½ to 4 knots over the ground. Fortunately I had managed to obtain some similar fitting chain plates from Tahiti for emergencies such as this, they were not exactly the same size but I had checked them and they would work as a temporary measure. Working in the dark with the spreader lights on, I managed to change the chain plate and refit the shroud, adjusting the rig as best I could in the circumstances. It was daylight before I finished but I was getting used to this operation and soon we were once again ploughing into the waves. Confidence comes with experience and it was a satisfied skipper who had an unruffled breakfast that morning, Cayuco under wind vane steering and greatly reduced canvas was once again sailing herself on course for Tonga and all was right with the world.

Audrey

The recent weather had meant neither of us had got much sleep in the last two days, the forecast did not give us much optimism, a front caused by the SPCZ had formed ahead of us, we were heading straight for it, and it, was heading for us. Another low pressure system travelling east and south of New Zealand was destined to pass below us in a couple of days so the outlook was not favourable. Everything on board was suffering from the damp and humid conditions and with the solid water coming aboard the only relatively dry place was our one and only sea berth, when we could use it. The fore cabin once again looked like a tip, not only had all the lockers emptied themselves again, but we had been using it as a rapid response tool chest. Oh hum, such is the ocean wanderer's life.

Around 11-00hrs we were surrounded by whales, ahead, astern and both sides, they looked like a pod of orcas and/or others. Later in the day we came much closer to another group of much larger whales, they came very close so we had a good view of them, seemed like a family, the adults were as long or longer than Cayuco and they stayed with us for some time. We could see and hear them snorting as they blew air and water from their blowholes. One of them came so close we could clearly see his or her whole length in the water and we both started to worry, we could have stepped off Cayuco onto the whales back, Tony hoped it didn't flick its tail and damage the rudder. It may have been a mother protecting her calf, we've read the stories and all you can hope for is not to inadvertently get between her and the baby whale.

Another really crap night, we only had the well reefed jib up now and with a strong quarterly wind it was enough to give us 5 to 6 knots over the ground, water swilled about in the cockpit, it was impossible to stop it, sea water broke over the stern regularly. All our cockpit cushions were soaking so we relegated them to the stern cabin and out of our way. The bilge pump kept pumping excess water out so we started monitoring it and wrote each cycle in the log book, it was our way of finding out whether the sequence of pumps was speeding up. During the night the mizzen sheet horse snapped and the mizzen boom started swinging wildly from side to side, Tony had to go out onto the stern deck to secure it, this was becoming another eventful trip.

It looked like it was going to clear up as daylight slowly started to brighten the day, it was a false dawn, more squalls again all day, this is more like English Channel or Bay of Biscay weather not the Pacific, very disappointing.

Tony

At last the wind died down and by nightfall we were sailing along with a reasonable wind almost behind us, the sea however would take some hours to calm down and remained very uncomfortable. When we started the engine for the 18-00 hr radio schedule an unpleasant smell started to pervade the boat, it was attributed to the asbestos matting around the exhaust pipe which had got very wet during the storm, it seemed water had indeed got everywhere. The wind continued light but the evening radio chat with our friends Hugh and Shan on Stargazer did not bode well, they had told us about the low now approaching from the south east and to get ready for another blow. We had been blown north and off our great circle track by the previous conditions, this did not worry me as it put us further away from the next lot. Eventually the seas calmed down and we had a fairly good night, we both caught up with our sleep pattern. The next day the sun came out and everything started drying out, we even managed to spread out the cushions and have a modicum of comfort again. We knew of course that this respite was going to be short lived so decided to just enjoy it, we were still over 400 miles from Tonga, we had only been on passage for four days; it seemed longer.

The Island of Nuie lay on our direct course, it was two days away and it may have been possible to get into shelter at the main town of Alofi on the west coast. There is a small harbour here, again through the reef but even if we couldn't get into the harbour, the bay is protected from easterly gales and makes a reasonable anchorage. The wind stayed light so we continued to motor in an attempt to keep up with our daily average mileage, at least our unpleasant smell had disappeared.

On the 9th June around 20-00 hours the wind started to come back, by 22-00 it was 40 knots and once again we were well reefed down, at least it was still blowing from our port quarter so there were no Olympic gymnastics required but getting a good sleep became difficult. Next morning June10th, and day six of our voyage it took forever for dawn to break, there was total cloud cover and it was like a dark winter's morning in England, the only exception was that it felt a bit warmer. We wondered what it was going to do next.

As you approach Tonga you have to deal with a strange time phenomenon, you have to cross the International Date Line. This has you crossing from one day into the next, in our case it meant going from the 10th June into the 12th June over a period of a few hours. Also because of the distance travelled from Bora Bora we lost another hour of time due to our movement. The actual dateline is just east of Tonga, but to keep all rally boats on the same radio schedules we had all agreed earlier to change on a set day regardless of our position. For us, this meant it was 10th June until 18-00hrs, then the 11th June from 18-00 hours until midnight when it became the 12th June. Because of the lost hour it also went from 12 hours behind GMT to 11 hours ahead of GMT, all very confusing but it seemed to work.

A note in my log reads "Date Line 18-00hrs Tuesday 10th becomes 17-00hrs Wednesday 11th, therefore Thursday 12th starts at midnight seven hours later, good game isn't it?

Our course took us north of Nuie and by early morning on the 12th we were about 6 miles off and had decided to carry on to Tonga. The wind was already 30 to 35 knots and rising, we argued that to close the island would have been dangerous, two other boats from the rally and an independent yacht which had caught us up during the night all did the same. The independent yacht had appeared behind us less than a quarter mile away and had taken us by surprise. I called him up on VHF and we had a chat, the yacht was a catamaran, running under bare poles and still doing 6 to 7 knots. The owner was worried he would reach Tonga too early and in the dark so was concerned and wanted to slow down, the best advice I could give him was to tack downwind and cover a greater distance. I personally do not like towing warps to slow down on any boat, on a catamaran it can be positively dangerous and the relatively low buoyancy of some catamaran hulls at the stern and the extra drag can pull you under backwards. I stress at this point that this is my own personal view; everyone has to make their own minds up. My catamaran experience says, keep it light, keep it moving and hope you have plenty of sea room.

The last two days from Nuie into Tonga it blew a force 8 to 9 gale, once again we battened down and hung on, at least with our relatively slow speed, we would not see Utula'aina Point at the northern end of the Vava'u Group of Islands in Tonga before sunrise on Friday 13th June.

Audrey commented that Friday 13th was a date to conjure with, very apt considering this passage and a good day to arrive in Tonga. The weather was awful, visibility was down to 100 metres and less at times, this was a worry, a lot of rally boats were all converging on the same waypoint just to the north of Tonga and all at around the same time. During our regular radio schedules we all decided to monitor our positions closely and use our radar and VHF when close together. During the night it was particularly disturbing, the rain, spray and height of the waves restricted visibility to a very small area around you, it would have been easy to miss another small yacht until you were on top of each other. We knew at least one rally yacht in our vicinity whose engine had failed and he would not be able to work on it until safely in Tonga, he had sailed nearly all the way from Raratonga without the engine and was very low on battery power, he may not even be able to use lights at night.

On the last wild night into Tonga, at 00-30 hrs, just after I laid my head on the pillow, there was a heavy roll to starboard quickly followed by another loud bang from just above my head, almost instinctively I knew what it was and leapt out of my berth. Switching on the spreader lights confirmed my suspicions, the port forward shroud had parted at the bottle screw and once again I had to fabricate an emergency repair. Fortunately I had secreted some different sizes of bulldog clips in my boson's store for just such an emergency. After furling the rest of the jib I quickly donned my safety harness, grabbed the bulldog clips, some stout line and a spanner to fit the bulldog grip nuts. As it was too rough to walk along the deck, I crawled along on all fours again, this was becoming a habit, I clung on as best I could getting a good soaking every time Cayuco rolled her port deck underwater. Within a few minutes, I'd grabbed the swinging shroud, bolted on the clips, secured the stay to the chain plate with the line and using a Spanish windlass system and the natural sway of the mast as the boat rolled from side to side, I sweated it all up tight. Back in the cockpit, unfurl the jib and we were off again; what a wonderful life, again I thanked our lucky stars that no further damage had been done but it was obvious we were in serious need of some major mast and rigging work.

The next morning with the weather easing slightly down to 30/35 knots, Audrey spotted Tonga as it appeared through the mist and spray at 07-15 hrs; I was oblivious and catching up on some sleep, why do all these breakages happen at night and just as I go for a nap?

Our destination was the town of Neiafu in the northern Vava'u Group, this little town nestles serenely within a closed in bay tucked well inside the surrounding hills and is called Locally "Port of Refuge". We sailed around the northern tip of the island and altered course to sail close along the western side, the seas calmed down considerably in the lee. As we got closer our track took us back to the east and we left Hunga Island to starboard. The eyeball navigation was easy between the islands and along the channels into Neiafu but our chart plotter had us ploughing the fields and cutting off headlands as our electronic chart showed Cayuco taking a short cut across solid land. This is the problem of relying on modern navigation aids, especially at night, the surveys in this area are just not up to date and electronic charts cannot be trusted, paper charts are the same so daylight entry makes a lot of sense. The entrance passage into Tonga is very pretty, although it was still misty with lots of drizzly rain you could see the islands, channels and bays clearly, it reminded us a lot of Gocek in Turkey where we had cruised in amongst the islands some years before.

It took seven hours from first seeing Tonga to when we were safely alongside the customs wharf, we checked in, grabbed some fish and chips and a beer in the Bounty Bar, then, in the pouring rain, we took Cayuco out and anchored for the evening. The next morning, fine and sunny, we were able to move closer in to Neiafu, pick up a mooring buoy near the Paradise Hotel, blow up the dinghy and go ashore for the day.

Tonga is a delightful place, it is separated into groups of islands over a wide area and we were in the most northern Vava'u Group. The people are very lay back and life has a fairly slow pace. It must be similar to what UK was like 50 to 60 years ago, no-one locks their doors, there is an inherent trust between the residents and there is little or no trouble at all, if only it could stay this way. This was always going to be a chill out day so we checked out the facilities, had a beer and a snack, Audrey after being given a considerable amount of confusing information, found a hairdresser and we got a few stores in. Facilities for any repairs were dire, they will have a go at anything but with only a small boatyard for general slipping and antifouling it is very limited. All spare parts are shipped or flown in and are usually ordered through New Zealand. Our enquires about any rigging work were unfruitful so we resigned ourselves to having to sort something out, we had arranged for a rigger to replace our lowers in Fiji, all we had to do was get there in one piece.

Later in the day I had a look at another rally yachts engine, the yacht whose engine had failed on the way from Raratonga. As I suspected the fuel lift pump diaphragm had become porous and was allowing diesel fuel to pass into the engine, subsequently this dilutes the engine oil. The only cure is to fit a new lift pump or a repair kit. The skipper took all the details up to an importer in the high street in order to fill in the necessary paperwork and obtain a new lift pump; this fault is fairly common on engines.

The next day was a Sunday and in Tonga on a Sunday everything is shut, we pottered about on board and I did a radio net for Richard our rally support organiser. Due to the continuing inclement weather, some rally yachts had been stuck in Nuie and Richard was keen to find out what had happened to them, all was well and they were even now en-route to Tonga. A French skipper and his crew came over in their dinghy and together we replaced Cayuco's broken forward shroud with a length of high strength spectre rope, I joked that with high tech "go faster" spectre rigging, Cayuco would be much quicker now and they would all have a job to catch us. The Skipper told us that in the gale from Nuie, his yacht hit 22 knots surfing down the waves before he shortened sail, I was suitably humbled, but then, it was a high spec racing class yacht so I was not too surprised at her performance.

The rally organised a briefing at the hotel for us with information about the next leg of our voyage to Fiji, we also discussed the agenda for a rally sail around the Vava'u Islands with local dancing girls, a Tongan Feast, a midday BBQ the day after and a visit to some caves on the sail back. The briefing was then followed by a party in the Paradise Hotel with more local dancing and a buffet, afterwards we had our own dancing with more of the local beer and wine, it was well past midnight when we slowly wended our weary way back to our respective yachts.

Internet facilities were good here, had a good chat with our son and arranged another net with the rest of the family members in a few days time. Our stay in Tonga was only for about ten days so it was important to see as much as possible. Because our rig had a temporary repair and we did not want to use Cayuco unnecessarily another yacht asked us if we wanted to join them for the rally sail round the Tongan Islands and the feast. We agreed and Tuesday 17th June saw us all sail off to a nearby island for more local dancing and the evening Tongan Feast. The dancing performed by the local schoolchildren with accompanying music by the adults was more spontaneous and natural; most agreed it was better than the previous show. The feast however was typical open fire cooking with some of the meats cooked in an "Umu", a sort of underground pit, all the food is wrapped in banana leaves first and then covered up with soil or whatever there is to hand, it is then left for a few hours while it slow cooks. It was all very traditional and well prepared although some of the more exotic flavours took some getting used to. The amount of food is gargantuan so some sort of exercise is required afterwards, dancing, walking and even rowing back to the boats were all considered to be acceptable. The next day we set off for another island where we anchored, swam, and went ashore for a pre-prepared BBQ laid on by the ladies of another nearby island.

Some yachts had decided to spend a few days visiting other anchorages and there are over 40 recommended picturesque places around these islands. The position of the large coral reef on the east side of the group and the direction of the prevailing wind, ensure little swell inside the archipelago and the sailing conditions are normally ideal. On our way back to Neiafu we visited the caves and some of them are so large we took the dinghy inside. It is advised to row the dinghy when inside the caves; otherwise there is a build up of exhaust fumes which can harm the wildlife, especially any bats which may be hanging from the rooftops. For the more adventurous among us, there are some caves with underwater entrances opening up into large caverns, I'm told they were amazing but definitely a pastime for the younger and "daring do" set.

In the evening we all went to the "The Mermaid" for a meal, it was the best one since the day of our arrival and the fish and chip supper in the Bounty Bar. Our internet link previously arranged with family a few days before never materialised, try as we may, there was just no connection, Audrey especially felt very disappointed, she looked forward to their chats, small as they were they represented a great deal to her.

I managed to obtain a handy piece of plywood from the boatyard, we had still been experiencing water squeezing through under the washboards and soaking the cockpit when the seas were really bad, I had an idea how to stop it altogether as soon as I could get round to it..

On Friday 20th June we filled in our clearance papers, fuelled up our tanks and bought some more stores; we also obtained some duty free spirits and beer from the shop in the high street. This was a bonus as nobody realised it was possible until the last minute, to take advantage you need your clearance papers and your passport. We had planned to leave on Sunday morning but as the customs don't work at weekends we had arranged to do the paperwork on Friday. Saturday morning we did some last minute stuff and I helped the skipper with the broken down engine, his spare lift pump would not be available for a few more days so he planned to catch us up later.

The next Islands were the Fijian Group; we'd last visited there in 1983 while working in the area so we were looking forward to visiting them again, a quiet Saturday night followed while both of us readied ourselves for the off the next morning.

Figure 21: An odd signpost in the town of Neiafu, Vava'u group, northern Tonga, it has the names of Capitol cities from all over the world with their corresponding mileages

Chapter 9

Tonga to Fiji

Tony

Sunday 22nd June on a very nice fine day we left Tonga at 09-30 hours; it was very calm again so motored out of Refuge Harbour and laid course for Savu Savu in Fiji. This is one of the shortest legs of the rally, 240 miles in a straight line but more like 350 the way we were going to sail it. There are many ways into Fiji from the Tonga direction, a lot of them however are littered with reefs, some charted, some not. They are OK during the day but far more dangerous at night, you may be lucky and pick up the breakers on the reef with radar but there again, you might not, as it was not possible to get all the way through the reefs in daylight we decided to go by the battleship route and stay in relatively deep water.

Our chosen route led us north to a position around 16° 36′ S, 179° 00′ W before turning SE between the islands of Nggaamea and Naitaaba then down the Nanuku Passage. This was a three day sail and as it turned out it was one of the best sails of our whole Pacific experience, day and night was a gentle force 3, we had our fore and aft rig with, main, jib, mizzen and mizzen staysail set up, broad reaching and averaging our 5 to 6 knots over the ground. The only concession we made was to take the mizzen staysail down at night. The staysail was our most awkward sail to set and control and I did not want to be taken by surprise during the hours of darkness. A sudden squall and it would have been difficult to get down quickly. It was manufactured with a lightweight material and would have blown out well before I could get it stowed.

The islands we passed to port were the Lau Group, known as The Exploring Islands; some of these islands are used by the Fijian military and strictly off limits. In any case the Fijian Government imposes strict no anchoring policy in their waters until officially checked in, even then special permission is required to cruise around the Lau group, there is talk of relaxing this rule in the future.

Again we had been at sea without shore battery charging facilities for some time, our last mains electricity for battery charging had been in Tahiti on the 15th May. As we were now able to use our new petrol generator every day when at anchor, or on a harbour wall, it was much easier to keep the batteries fully charged. This was much cheaper but we still saw no reason to use battery power unnecessarily. We didn't use our chart plotter, radar or any instruments unless there was a special reason to do so; I had wired both our radios on separate circuits so could still use these independently. Audrey had also discovered that she did not have to leave the freezer on all the time, a boost twice a day was all that was needed to maintain the minus temperature when the freezer was fairly full. All these little additions to our knowledge made a difference to our peace of mind while we enjoyed the good sailing conditions; the new generator was an added bonus.

While Audrey was on watch the night before closing on our waypoint off the Nanuku Passage, she had a funny feeling that the motion of the waves had changed, she switched on the instruments and was shocked to see the depth meter recording depths of 12 to 18 feet, (4 to 6 metres), as we were many miles away from land she called me up and we studied the situation. I agreed with her that something did not feel right but a check on our English charts showed no problems, turning on the chart plotter I overlaid the radar plot, the display showed nothing untoward except for what looked like some unusual wave action in a large circle around us. I changed course to the east as this was the easiest direction with the present wind direction and shortly it appeared to give us deeper water. By chance we also had a fairly recent New Zealand chart of the area, a quick check of our recorded GPS position on this chart confirmed we were right over a shallow reef recently discovered, not only was the reef clearly marked on this New Zealand chart it also showed the exact depth readings we were experiencing. This very clearly demonstrated the dangers of cruising in these waters, as it is not a commercial shipping route; there is no financial reward for anyone to carry out a survey. Work is being done by the New Zealand Government but it is slow and there is a lot of area to survey. This episode took place between 01-30 and 02-30 hrs, it was a tense time and we were very relieved when we eventually moved into deeper water. I rechecked all the information the next day but I still found no reference to the soundings we had on either the UK paper or our electronic charts, I was bemused as I had purchased complete sets of both brand new systems only 12 months before when we left UK. Once again we were left with the feeling that you pay your money and take your chances. One of my favourite sayings is,

"I don't take chances, only calculated risks", I'm not sure which one of these this comes under, but I know we were very lucky that night, with any sea running it could have been very different. The co-ordinates were 16° 50′S, 178° 35′W, BE LUCKY.

The next morning saw us sailing down the Nanuku Passage accompanied by three other rally boats, as you approach the end of this passage and towards the end of Taveuni Island, you turn to the west to head for Savu Savu, it is just about here that you sail through the 180° meridian, after this we were back in the easterly section and the longitude readings start to decrease and technically, we were on our way back home.

We were now heading for the northern Fijian Island of Vanua Levu and the headland of Lesiatheva Point; it was about 45 miles away, so with our speed of 4 to 5 knots over the ground, we would take about 10 hours to get there. Another gentle night's sail as we closed our waypoint placed well offshore due to a large shoal patch off the headland and then north for about ten miles to Nawi Island. This put us neatly off the town of Savu Savu about 08-00 hours in the morning, some other yachts were hovering off the inlet and one by one we were called in to the lovely anchorage just off the Yacht Club.

Our rally organiser had been busy and most of our check in procedure was carried out in the yacht club, this was just as well because there's loads of paperwork and every department wanted a photograph to accompany the forms. One of the things we learnt very quickly is to always have plenty of photographs available; each department will need one when clearing in and sometimes when leaving as well. It was not unheard of to need six photographs for a check in procedure and an equivalent number to leave, no-one seemed to know what happened to them but we very soon learned not to ask complicated and difficult questions.

Later on when most of the rally had arrived, we learned that the skipper and crew still back in Tonga on their yacht had sorted their diesel fuel lift pump problem and were on their way to Fiji. A cool beer at the bar was in order, our friend John said it would be rude not to, a walk around the small but typically tropical town and a Chinese meal in the evening completed our day.

The stay in Savu Savu was destined to be short but eventful; trips had been arranged to the rainforest, BBQ's at the yacht club and lots of other events arranged for our enjoyment during our time there. Our laptop packed up and refused to do anything, so we handed it over to an "expert". I, together with most of the other rally skippers, raced Optimist dinghies round a course laid off the yacht club on Saturday afternoon and we all had a great charity fund raiser for the young sailors of Savu Savu. Others gambled on the outcome and the favourites took off in fine form with zero wind conditions, all profits went to the young sailors fund plus any other cash that could be prised out of the onlookers.

We also picked up an LED anchor/cockpit light made in a little shed near the yacht club, the electrical power needed to run these units is negligible and we had good use for anything like that.

The day of the rainforest trip dawned, 30th June, we had not signed up for it, having lived in the rainforest areas on islands in the South Pacific previously in our life, we saw no reason to repeat the experience, neither did we relish being eaten alive with man eating mosquitoes. It was just as well, the tropical downpour which greeted the daybreak never stopped for the rest of the day, everyone who participated was thoroughly soaked to the bone and really experienced the rain forest at its worse; the torrential rain did however keep the mosquitoes at bay.

Our laptop given to the local computer repair shop came back working but with the proviso that the unit was on its last legs, whatever, we managed to plug it into the yacht club Wi-Fi link and chat to our sons in England, we also had text facilities again so Audrey was much happier being able to contact family. This difficulty of contact was Audrey's worse scenario and at the time I did not fully realise the importance of keeping and maintaining a regular family connection.

Audrey

I was looking forward to getting to Fiji and to not having to use the dinghy all the time, plugging into electricity, being able to walk ashore, maybe having good Wi-Fi connection, easy access to water instead of having to take the cans ashore in the dinghy every time, but it was not to be, we were out on a mooring and had the same limitations as before. It's all starting to feel like much of the same. The rally schedules were starting to get to me, now heard that two other rallies, World Arc and New Zealand Pacific Rally are in the same area as us and will impose restrictions on marina and mooring spaces. It's all getting like our cruising area in UK, the Solent, too many boats, bloody crazy. I was feeling at low ebb, maybe it's all building up, could do with some creature comforts and some time out. Glad we have the two days booked at the First Landing Hotel Resort for Cayuco's lift out in a few days time, almost don't want to look forward to it in case I'm disappointed again. Would be good to get Cayuco sorted out without any rally distractions, wish we could just run away. I felt better after having this bit of a whinge, I miss family so much, also what used to be normality, whatever that was?

Note.:At the time I wrote this, I genuinely felt better for writing it and getting it out of my system. The traumas we had faced, the difficulties we had overcome, battling half way round the world in the fleet's oldest and slowest boat while still managing to keep up with the punishing rally schedule. I believed that my feelings were fully justified and it's important to share them.

We went shopping to buy a present for our oldest grandson's birthday, I found a Fiji "Bula" shirt, a great little story book and a Fiji pencil case, he would enjoy receiving these from his "Boat"

Nanny and Granddad; this was how we had been labelled. The youngest two were only three to four months old when we left, I was missing them and their growing up and couldn't wait to get back to UK, sometimes we could catch them on the messenger camera, but it was a rare occurrence. In the evening we went up-river in the dinghy to a restaurant on the waterfront, came back late with a wet bum from the condensation on the dinghy, Ho Hum; nothing changes.

On the 1st and 2nd July we cleaned up the boat, stored up again and filled up with as much fuel and water as we required, it was all done from cans again and we only needed enough for two days. Our next leg was only a short sail; we left our mooring at Savu Savu at 07-30 on the 3rd July and set off for the resort of Musket Cove on Malolo-Lailai Island. Some of the rally had decided to go the short way through Bligh Water and then through the coral reefs and channels, this would take them approximately 4 to 5 days as the channels are tortuous and only daylight sailing is recommended, they would also have to find safe anchorages every night.

The distance to go east round the south island of Viti Levu and then along the south coast is much longer but sailing day and night through relatively clear water only takes two days, it also avoids most but not all of the coral reefs. We had many dolphins on this passage and they stayed with us nearly all the time, their silvery fluorescent shapes could be seen weaving and darting about alongside Cayuco at night by the light of the moon, it was a magnificent sight. We passed south of Suva during the second night and went through the channel between Mbengga Island and the mainland, it was much busier than we envisaged with high speed ferries crossing to the island all night long. Our route took us through the Navula Pass in the large outside coral reef and on to Malolo-Lailai Island. Musket Cove is tucked in between these two small islands and has its own coral reef around it, the route through to the marina is strictly daytime only. Even then, with insider knowledge and waypoints to guide us, we still touched the coral reef lightly as we tried to find the deep water. Looking over the side we saw the seabed in the clear water, there were starfish, (real name sea stars), an amazing array of coral and crustaceans and a cheeky black and white sea snake raising its head and hissing up at us.

It's vital to point out here, seeing a coral reef above water is the easy part, most are just underwater and cannot necessarily be seen even at low tide. You sometimes have to find the channel well out from your destination and then pick your way through the coral slowly. With the early morning sun behind you, slow speed and someone high up in the bow to pass on information to the helmsman usually works well, you also get used to recognising the colour of the water, deep blue = good, light blue = bad.

Our arrival at Musket Cove was heralded by a sudden tropical downpour, we still managed a perfect stern to berthing manoeuvre by dropping our anchor and reversing up to the jetty, our stern lines were taken by the marina lads on the pontoon, we were all soaked to the skin but at least the rain was warm, thank goodness for small mercy's.

Musket Cove is a five star marina and resort, the facilities would not be beaten in any marina anywhere, it is just idyllic and beautiful; within minutes we were able to plug in to mains electricity, the first since Papeete in Tahiti. A package arrived from our son containing a DVD with photos of the family and some snooker games of the current World Series, what more could we ask for. It was a nice sunny day until someone mentioned having a BBQ, talk about annoying the weather gods, it turned cold, the wind started blowing and the rain came.

We retired and cooked a quiet meal on board, then spent the night looking at family photos and some games of snooker. The resort had its own airstrip, the only problem was the runway went right across the island from one side to the other, to walk along the beach to visit the other side of the club; you had to walk across the end of the runway. At both sides of the walkway across the airstrip was a sign in big red letters, BEWARE LOW FLYING AIRCRAFT. At least it caused much merriment among all the people using it.

We managed a quick chat on the internet with our family; there was only one machine in the office so due to the demand to use it we were all making 15 minute calls so that everyone had an equal slot.

A BBQ was organised by one of the yachts who was leaving the rally, fortunately the weather improved and we all enjoyed a nearly dry couple of hours. Our time here was limited, Cayuco was due for its lift out at Vuda Point Marina about twenty miles away and we were looking forward to a bit of pampering at the First Landing Resort Hotel.

Figure 22: Musket Cove Marina on Malolo-Lailai Island near Viti Levu in Fiji.

Figure 23: Mind your head when walking around Musket Cove Resort and Marina.

Tony

On the 9th July we rose early and readied everything for the short passage to the boatyard, before we left Musket Cove we also had to attend a rally briefing, these informal chats were used to update our passage plans and acted as a forum to bounce idea's and routes off each other. It was also used this time to ensure we were all up to speed with regards our entry to Australia, our route through the Great Barrier Reef was going to be through the Hydrographers Passage and accurate navigation is required, plus, the Australian authorities like to know who is entering their waters and monitor everyone closely. I think it was the only country where we actually had to have a visa in our passports before arriving.

Briefing over we cast off and headed for Vuda Point Marina, of course, we had to negotiate the passage out through the reefs first and it was low tide, it was a very slow and careful Cayuco which left Musket Cove. As we set off the sun was ahead of us and high in the sky, it was difficult to see the underwater reefs, I had also accidently deleted the track on the chart plotter of our way in, nevertheless we successfully reached deep water and set course. The first thing we saw was friendly dolphins, hissing sea snakes and a big low black cloud on the horizon. Within minutes of leaving the wind was 30 to 35 knots on the beam, a reefed main and jib and once again we were flying along at 6 to 8 knots in relatively calm water, this was great, we could soon make up the lost time at the briefing. It was not all plain sailing, inside of the main coral reef there is a very large area of smaller reefs and islands and it's not possible to lay a direct course, much safer to head for the main dredged big ship channel for most of the passage and then head off to the marina at a suitable point

We arrived at Vuda Point Marina at high water, good for depth to get in but bad in trying to find the very tiny entrance. On a lee shore, in a steep rough sea caused by the reducing depth is not good for the nerves. Knowing there is a very shallow reef all along the shore and around the entrance, which extends a long way out doesn't help. The entry buoys are very small and could not be identified until dangerously close to the edge of the reef, we made it in but it was certainly a bit nerve racking; now we know the arrangement and waypoints it is much easier. This is an ongoing problem, most places you visit all have their little idiosyncrasies, however, as you usually only enter and leave once, all the stored information you collect is probably never going to be used again, at least, not by us.

The boatyard was ready for us and when we had checked in, it was only a matter of waiting for them to organise the boat hoist to lift us out. We had already contacted them earlier and informed them of our proximity; nevertheless, we missed the lift out for the day and had to wait till the next. You are never entered on the lift roster until they see the whites of your eyes, with boats arriving from all over the Pacific to use the boatyard services I suppose they are never really sure if anyone will make it or not.

10th of July late afternoon saw Cayuco on the hard and us safely and comfortably ensconced in a chalet in the garden of the

First Landing Resort. This sounds extravagant and luxuriant given our financial situation, luxuriant it was, but extravagant it wasn't. It may have been expensive by Fijian standards but by European standards it was extremely reasonable, plus, we had a rally discount negotiated for us by our organisers. Anyway it would have been impossible to live on board while all the work which had been waiting for months was carried out. Apart from hull cleaning and antifouling, we had a very worn out stern shaft seal to replace, an engine and gearbox to service and the damage to the rigging and chain plates to sort out, as well as other minor jobs. We had booked in the hotel for two days but it very soon became obvious that we would need longer than that, fortunately we were able to book another two days without any problems.

The rigger who worked out of Suva and was an Australian was excellent; he came aboard almost immediately we were ashore, examined and measured the rigging, took templates for the chain plates and promised everything back as soon as possible. This was not as easy as it sounded, his workshop where all the rigging had to be made up was in Suva and the road was typical cross country Fijian. It was a five hour journey to get there and the same back, so a lot of time was spent in travelling. In the meantime the yard organised a team for the work on the hull and the engineers to do the stern shaft seal, I had taken the precaution of bringing a spare kit with me so that was a good call. To be honest, I had been watching the stern shaft seal for thousands of miles, it was a constant worry. When we arrived in Antigua after our Atlantic crossing I noticed the seal was badly worn, in normal circumstances I would have changed it at that point, but by the time we had completed the work necessary in Antigua to continue we were already late. I knew we only had one spare kit, plus we had already arranged to come out of the water in Fiji, so checking the fitting regularly we continued on. It was one of those calculated risks. I needn't have worried so much about it, it survived 14,000 miles of constant turning and after the initial set-up pressure had been worked out it never leaked a drop.

For four days Cayuco was turned inside out, the hull, stern cabin, main saloon and engine compartment were a mass of bodies carrying out there designated tasks, we watched in amazement. Cayuco emerged from this onslaught looking smarter than we had ever seen her, I for one had a new found confidence in her, the seal and rigging problems had obviously been worrying me far more than I thought.

Audrey

We in the meantime had been enjoying a relaxing stay in the chalet, we had hot showers, a rare luxury, a bed that didn't constantly move, internet facilities and we had found the yacht club next to the boatyard that served excellent cheap snacks and meals. On our final night we decided to have a special meal in the resort, they gave us a ringside seat while we watched a local dance troupe performing in the hotel grounds, it was superb and a complete surprise to us as we knew nothing about the planned entertainment.

The next morning we checked out of the hotel, watched Cayuco slip back into the water and went aboard to sort out the chaos left inside. We bought more stores for our next passage to Australia, fuelled and watered up and generally prepared for the off. The rally had organised a check out with the Fijian authorities for the yachts at Musket Cove, unfortunately with our extra days at Vuda Point Marina we would not be able to get back in time to complete the formalities. We decided to go up to Lautoka only a short distance away and check out from there, this turned out to be a successful trip, we bought more stores and managed to obtain another cheap mobile phone to replace the one I had accidently given a float test to over the side of Cayuco.

Before we left Fiji we returned to First Landing Resort to use their internet facilities, we managed to speak to both our sons, saw some great photos of our two new grandsons and found out that the package we had sent from Suva had already arrived plus birthday gift for the eldest one.

Tony

Leaving Vuda Point Marina at midday for Mackay in Australia, our decision was to by-pass Vanuatu although a lot of the rally yachts were going to visit there on the way. We had been in Vanuatu in the 1980's and worked in the area for three years while I had been involved in developing a diesel engine training course. It is a beautiful place and well worth a visit but our plan was to spend more time in Australia and along the Great Barrier Reef.

If we had known as we sailed out of Fiji what the weather gods had in store for us on our passage to Mackay, we would have changed our plans and visited Vanuatu, a few well chosen days there would have been a lot more comfortable.

Chapter 10

Fiji to Australia

Tony

As usual the weather forecast when we left Fiji was chancy, how often would you willingly set off with a reported 30 to 35 knots of wind, across an ocean, with a prospective 16 day passage and not a lot of signs of a reprieve for a while. Midday on the 16th July saw us leaving Vuda Point Marina and waving goodbye to other yachtsmen, mostly independents, while they shook their heads in disbelief. Whatever, the wind was behind us so that takes at least one force off the true wind strength, the sun shone intermittently between the scurrying clouds and we had another rally boat for company, well, that is for the first 8 hours or so before they pulled ahead.

As we cleared the main reef and out through the Navula Passage the full force of the wind and the Pacific rollers hit us, there was no turning back now; we could clearly see the waves breaking right over the coral banks on both sides of the channel. Our main concern was to head out to sea and put some distance between us and the treacherous reef which continued west for some miles. It was pointless trying to carry the main so we opted for just the reefed jib. Who cared; we were still doing 5½ to 7 knots over the ground. This combination of sail downwind is as comfortable as it gets, the main just overpowers the boat and causes the vane self steering gear to lose control, it can even broach, not good at sea. Sailing across an ocean demands a degree of comfort and care especially when there's only two of you, the need to conserve strength while maintaining vigilance is paramount, no heroics needed here.

Once clear of the hard bits we set course for the southern tip of Efate Island 518 miles away, this track would take us just south of Port Vila the capitol of Vanuatu in case we changed our minds en-route and decided to break the journey. If we did carry on to Australia without stopping, the distance to the Hydrographers Passage in the Great Barrier Reef was slightly less than 1800 miles with another 150 miles after that to the entrance of Mackay Harbour. The good news was, having cleared all the debris and goose barnacles out of the paddle, the log was working again and with a clean bottom we were sailing better. We were happier in ourselves even though the conditions were not ideal, with new shrouds, angled chain plates and the new stern shaft seal working well, we had more confidence in Cayuco than before. The constant threat of living with rigging or prop seal failure out on the ocean had largely disappeared and we were secure in the knowledge that our other essential systems would be OK. This assumption made us feel better in the current sea conditions but it was a bit premature, mother nature, had not finished with us yet.

Audrey

It was great to talk with all the family before leaving Fiji and to find out about the arrival of our grandson's present we sent some time ago before his birthday.

My queasiness returned as we left the shelter of the inner reef and Cayuco felt the large rollers outside, seems every time I have a few days of calm and relaxation, I have to go through the next couple of days feeling sick, at least it's not as bad as when we first started the voyage. Not the most comfortable of nights at sea, the books on the shelves fell off twice and landed on me, have put them in a bag and stuck them under the berth, have a job to fall on me again. Steep and lumpy seas, the motion of the boat is very quick, seems to be jumping from wave top to wave top, then again, we are sailing pretty quick, rain showers and lots of sail changes. Wind is boxing the compass, probably because a low pressure system with associated trough is moving rapidly east over us; neither of us got much sleep. Much better by the 18th, queasiness has gone, wind down a bit in strength and now behind us, far better sea conditions, we're sailing goose wing with main and jib, had a restful sleep on my second off watch period. Good conditions most of the night and carried same sails till daylight, lovely full moon, only faded as the sun came up. Had to revert to fore and aft rig as wind veered to blow from the south again, means the low centre has definitely moved east and passed south of us. Our boat speed through the next night stayed at a good six knots with up to seven on occasions, lots more cloud today, hope it's not all going to go pear shaped again. Sunrise getting later each morning, not surprising, we are moving west fast and have covered over 370 miles in three days, would be good if it kept like this. The weather persisted and we continued on our course, it was tiring but with a steady 120 to 130 miles a day we weren't complaining.

Monday 21st July 2008, Happy 35th wedding Anniversary, never expected this when I married Tony all that time ago, but there you are! We're still doing quite well, 6 to 7 knots average with our reefed fore and aft rig again, some concerns about weather change on the way, picked up a forecast on the net this morning from fellow sailors who have more technology than us, seems there is another low heading our way. It's getting very chilly at night, we are only 18° 20′ south so didn't expect it to get cold yet, but then, it is the winter season in Australia. Maybe the weather pattern is bringing in the cold wind so might have to put a thicker blanket on the sea berth, only been using a sheet so far. Not using the engine very much at all, batteries being kept well charged by our various systems and the petrol generator purchased in Papeete, although a bit noisy, was working well when needed.

Tony

We were making very good time, although it was fairly windy with a difficult sea, the wind direction continued to change every few hours and had gone right round the compass since leaving Fiji. The varied conditions over the last few days had kept us on our toes and disrupted our sleep patterns; we were therefore trying to catch up on our sleep during the day.

On the 21st July we celebrated our 35th wedding anniversary, very fitting as 35 years is Coral and we were just about to enter the Coral Sea. Over our main evening meal that night, we promised to celebrate properly and go ashore for an anniversary meal when we arrived in Australia.

We passed south of Vanuatu watching the island go by from about 10 miles off; foolishly, we decided to carry on straight to Australia and this proved to be the wrong decision, for now, however, we were still sailing well.

A strange thing happened towards late afternoon the following day; we spotted a disturbance in the water ahead of us, what appeared to be a pod of whales going round in circles with a lot of agitation and commotion, jumping and diving. I altered course to give them plenty of room, we did not want to get too close in case they were feeding. It made no difference, wherever we went, after a few minutes, they still seemed to be ahead of us. As they appeared to move closer, we could make out a large whale in the centre with 6 or more smaller black and white whales, (we think they must have been orcas), circling the bigger whale in a tormenting fashion and making regular assaults, charging towards the bigger whale then curving away at speed, it all looked very odd. I was more concerned about them accidently ramming into Cayuco as they all seemed pretty excited, due to this we turned even further away while keeping a close watch on this strange phenomenon. Cayuco sailed by at about 5 knots with the pod of whales on our starboard side and the smaller whales still keeping up their provoking tactics on the larger whale. Shortly after, I was able to return to our original course, but the whales appeared to be keeping station close behind us, still very restless, then, an even stranger event happened. The large whale, at least as long as Cayuco, came up alongside and took up station about 15 to 20 feet away, again on our starboard side. Incredibly, swimming in the water between us and the full-size whale while maintaining the same speed, was a much smaller whale, a baby calf, keeping very close to our hull. I use the word baby very loosely here as the little whale still looked to be about ten feet long. By now it was late afternoon, we continued in this manner with the group of black and white whales now swimming around all of us. The presence of Cayuco seemed to disturb the group of circling whales, they continued this behaviour while making occasional charges at the large whale and her calf, when they did come in, and at speed, we watched in horror as sometimes they swam straight under our keel. We had never experienced anything like this before and although we assumed the large whale was female and trying to protect her calf, it was still a major concern. Both of us are more than familiar with the damage whales can inflict on sailing boats. This stand-off continued for the rest of the daylight hours, we had our evening meal and as darkness came on the situation remained the same. All through the night we could hear the whales snorting and as the moon came up, we could see their silvery sparkling shapes moving around us lighting up the phosphorous, it was a worrying night.

The wind had decreased so our speed slowed slightly, as the fingers of dawn gradually crept over the horizon behind Cayuco, the pod of smaller circling whales gathered in a group astern of us, they seemed to wait for a few minutes, then swam off towards the south. Our two other whales stayed where they were and just continued to quietly swim alongside us, a couple of hours later, with the sun well up in the sky, they moved slowly away. Shortly afterwards, in the direction that the two whales had left, we spotted another group of the larger type whales diving and showing their flukes, we will never know for certain what this episode was all about, but it looked very much as if the adult female whale, had used Cayuco to protect its calf from the marauding orcas. I know afterwards, Audrey and I felt humbled to have witnessed nature in such a raw manner, even now, as I write this, I feel a lump in my throat and I have tears of wonder in my eyes, we were glad the young whale seemed safe for now.

As the day progressed the wind eased until we were sailing at about 4 knots, our course was leading towards the north of New Caledonia, the choice was to give the very large reef to the north of New Caledonia a big detour, or to sail straight through the north passage. I saw no reason to make the detour; the north passage although according to the chart it had not been surveyed, was very wide, with depths of water into the hundreds. Anyway, I reasoned, at our present speed we will be through most of the reef in daylight. I regretted those thoughts later but for now it was decision time, turn north round the top and sail another hundred miles or straight through, save the miles, and take one of those calculated risks. We held our course and decided to go straight through, naturally, over the course of the next few hours, the wind got lighter, our speed reduced and yes, you've worked it out, we ended up sailing through the entire north passage in the dark. By 19-00 hours on the 22nd July, we were north of Petri reef on the east side of New Caledonia and heading for the north passage with our options reduced. If we changed course now and sailed north round the top of the reefs, it would be longer still. Indications were that it was going to be a protracted night, we changed our normal off watch rota and I went down early to get as much sleep as possible, the sky was already showing ominous signs of deterioration.

We held on and approached the North Channel with a lot of trepidation, I had tried to find knowledge of any previous passages through here but with no luck, I'd searched our data bases and various books but to no avail, even the pilot books recommended the northerly route, now I started to doubt my decision and wondered if I'd got it wrong. It was looking as if I would be on duty most of the night, or at least till we cleared the passage, the first third, about 15 miles or about 3 hours sailing was OK, deep water, plenty of room and no problems but by now it was pitch dark.

Then the depth of water started reducing, it went below one hundred feet and less, considering we had been over a thousand feet a few minutes before I was not too happy, I changed course to the north and then to the south, it appeared to be getting deeper further south so that's where we went. We carried on like this for the next few hours; by now we were motoring so I switched on all our navigation aids in an attempt to see if there was anything in our way, not a thing showed up on our radar, normally this would have been good, but not tonight. By now it was 01-00hrs on the 23rd, Audrey had come up for her watch but because of the perceived threat we both decided to stay up and keep a look out, the night was made worse as there was little moon to speak of. We both experienced a few anxious hours while we tried to feel our way through the passage. At some time during the night the wind rose and once again we were able to maintain our 5 knot average with just the jib. Clearing the North Passage we entered the Coral Sea about 05-00hrs while it was still dark, the wind had continued to increase from the south east but it was expected to back to the north as the approaching low pressure passed us by.

A couple of hours later we were receiving weather forecasts on SSB radio from the Australian meteorological office. They were now talking of a complex low pressure system coming across the top of Australia and another one coming across from the south, the forecast was the worse it could be in our present position. There was a passage through the reef behind us that we had no interest in repeating. A reef over 30 miles long coming out from New Caledonia to the south of us, so close we could see the surf breaking on it in the gathering daylight and another low reef with small atolls behind us spreading to the north which went on for about 80 miles. The wind was forecast to go right round to the west in the next 24 hours which would put us on a lee shore, we had to make sea room as fast as possible and we needed quite a lot of it.

From our position as we exited the North Passage early morning of the 23rd, the easiest course to Mackay across the Coral Sea was to go close north of Sandy Island and then the same for Renard and Bampton Islands. They were just over 100 miles away and from there we could shape a more southerly course to our destination. Sailing south of these islands is not a good idea, the area is strewn with reefs for more than a hundred miles, this may be feasible in fine weather and good visibility as you can pick your way through but not with our present forecast. The only sensible thing to do was to go north and west to allow for any wind shifts which may be coming our way in the next few days. At the moment the wind had veered to the east, the forecast was for it to go north east by mid day and north by the evening, we headed north west and intended to keep this course as long as possible, it was no good trying to miss one hazard, if we ran into the next one. We were still sailing well with 20 to 25 knots of wind now on our starboard quarter, even with the first reef in the jib our speed over the ground was averaging 6 knots.

All through the day the wind gradually veered to the north east and we kept heading north west adjusting the sails as required, it was imperative we get really good sea room away from the coral reefs south and north east of our position. By 18-00 hours it was blowing from the north at a steady 25 knots, we had changed to a westerly course but the wind was still backing, by midnight it was worse, 40 knots from the nor, nor west and the conditions were awful. We would have to tack soon as our course over the ground including lee-way was south of west and taking us straight towards the reefs south of the islands, we had given up using the engine as it had little effect on our speed.

The gale continued through the night and by 06-30hrs the wind had gone right round to the west as expected. At some point during the night we had changed course and were now heading north trying to claw ourselves away from the dangers to the south and east. It was an intense time, not made any better by the very confused seas now coming from every direction. All we could do was wait until the wind direction went back to the south, at the moment we were sailing away from Mackay in a northerly direction and heading for the Solomon Islands 1000 miles to the north. The terrible conditions continued for the rest of the day, in daylight it was just a mass of white water, windblown spray and rain. In the last eight days up to the start of the gale we had covered 1100 miles, converted, this gave us over 137 miles a day, an average of nearly 6 knots, by Cayuco's yardstick it was an excellent result, sadly, our daily runs were about to take a drop.

It was Saturday the 26th July at daybreak before the wind direction allowed us to get back on course, the wind speed had dropped to about 15 knots but the sea state was pretty grim, it took another six hours before we were sailing over the waves instead of through them. Cayuco was a mess down below in the saloon and fore cabin, but at least nothing serious had broken, I thought about the new rigging and chain plates we had fitted in Fiji and was glad we had been able to get them sorted before this lot. At noon it was only 348 miles to the start of the Hydrographers passage, we were already looking forward to arriving, it had been a hard few days. Chatting to the other rally members sheltering in Vanuatu on the 18-00 hour SSB schedule, our hopes faded, another low, even more intense and worse than the last one, was heading straight for us.

Another rally yacht was about 100miles ahead of us, he had left Vanuatu as we came past and had gone north round the top of the reefs, he was a much faster yacht than us but had the same problems in the gale, on the SSB he confirmed our fears of another low pressure system. We tried to catch up on the sleep we had lost while at the same time sailing as fast as we could, it was unlikely we would make the entrance passage before the next lot of bad weather came in but we were going to try. When Audrey went to sleep I couldn't wake her up for her next watch, so I left her sleeping and had a cup of coffee to keep me awake, I got a bonus when she did wake up as she let me sleep on when it was my turn. Cayuco was sailing well and it seemed she wanted to get to Australia just like us. The wind started to die down about midnight and by noon on the 27th it was calm again, as we had not been using our engine very much we motored to keep our average daily distance up. We also started to see a lot of shipping, oil tankers, bulk carriers and cargo ships became a regular feature on our watches.

It was definitely the calm before the storm, the sky took on that leaden heavy look and the evening sunset looked very threatening. A slight breeze started from directly ahead about midnight, by 05-30 hours on the 28th it was up to 20/25 knots and the barometer was dropping like a stone. We were hard on the wind making about 225° over the ground with only 117 miles to go to our waypoint off the Hydrographers Passage, we managed to keep this course until the wind backed more to the south west then we changed tack and headed slightly north of west, not exactly on course but the best we could do. The wind direction stayed much the same coming from around the south west but the strength went up to force 6/7, around 30/35 knots, it became apparent we were not going to get in before the next gale caught us. All day we battled to make headway, tacking in appalling conditions towards our landfall, by 18-00 hours we had got to within 60 miles of our waypoint off the entrance to the Hydrographers Passage but by then the wind speed had risen to 45/50 knots, it was impossible to make any headway. We battened everything down for the night, shortened sail even further to a scrap of jib, by now we were virtually under bare poles. Taking the safest option we headed south east into clear water, it was obvious we were in for a beating and I wanted to keep a modicum of control on our general direction. All thoughts of a nice comfortable marina were abandoned; the safest thing to do in conditions like this when it's expected to get worse is to head for deep water. With the Great Barrier Reef to the west of us, reefs and islands to the north and the wind from the south west, our only safe course was close to south east. This put us in clear water away from all the hazards except shipping, even if the wind changed direction we would still be able to get in eventually. In the worse scenario, if we were pushed too far south, we would still be able to get inside the Great Barrier Reef using the wide Capricorn Channel situated at the south end of the Reef.

That evening as we listened to the SSB radio on the 18-00 hours net, we couldn't raise anybody but we were still able to receive the Australian Meteorological forecast, they were talking about force 10 gales in our area. Unbeknown to us, the other rally yacht had managed to get into Mackay just before the worse of the gale, safely tied up in the marina they listened to the wind shrieking through the rigging as the storm increased in intensity, they told us later that they were thinking of us.

All through the night we tried to keep Cayuco moving out of danger, the wind rose still further and the noise as it tore through the rigging reached a crescendo which made conversation difficult. Around midnight we could see nothing at all, keeping a watch was unworkable, sleep was impossible, Cayuco just kept pounding into it and seemed better left to her own devices, she maintained the best course she could while we retired below and shut the hatches.

In reality there was little else we could do; we huddled together on the floor of the saloon in our wet weather gear and tried to keep warm, our gallant little vessel fought the elements all by itself. About 02-00 hours Audrey managed to boil a kettle and make us both a hot cup-a-soup, this with a couple of chocolate bars kept us going. For nearly 24 hours we had to grab what we could, it was impossible to cook anything, the motion was so violent it would have been dangerous to attempt to cook hot food on the wildly gyrating stove. In the early hours of the morning while we braced ourselves sitting on the saloon floor, I was propped up against the cockpit steps, while Audrey leaned against me, she had slipped into a fitful sleep and I was supporting her as best I could.

Normally we kept vegetables like potatoes, onions, tomatoes etc in nets strung up against the ceiling of the saloon. This tactic kept them dry and aerated so they lasted for the maximum amount of time, we had long since removed them from their storage and placed them well protected in the fore cabin. Before we did this, some had escaped and had been rolling around the saloon floor, we thought we had captured them all but no; an onion must have been hiding behind somewhere. As we lay against the steps, jammed in between the galley cupboards and the saloon seats, I felt something knock against my leg, it was still dark and so switching on my torch I was just in time to see an onion roll away and under the saloon table. Initially I ignored this and put my head back to doze, again the onion banged into my leg, having now got liberated, it was enjoying its freedom. With the still violent motion of the boat it was rolling all over the place, time after time I made a grab for it but as I had restricted movement it remained elusive. I started to chuckle, it just seemed so funny, the onion appeared to be joining in the fun, every time I made a grab for it, the boat lurched and it rolled away again, I imagined the onion putting its hands up against its head and going "nah, na-na-nah, nah" and running away again like in a children's comic, was hysteria starting to set in? OK, I was tired and my movement was limited, but I never did catch it, later we found it while having a spring clean, whatever, it did take the seriousness of our position away for a few minutes.

At first light on the morning of the 29th I stuck my head out of the saloon hatch and tried to look around, all I could see was spray being driven horizontally from the tops of the waves, all around the boat was a white wall of aerated water; it was difficult to make out much of anything. Cayuco was sailing blind, with her tiny scraps of sail, well off the wind and balancing herself, she plunged into each sea, over the top and buried her head in the next wave. Everything was soaking wet, sea and rain water crashed noisily against the doghouse and the cockpit cover; I wondered how much longer the canvas cover over the cockpit would last. As I scanned what little horizon we had Cayuco rolled over the top of the next wave, to my horror I glimpsed the top part of the bridge of a ship and a funnel steaming north about 200 metres astern of us, whoever it was had already gone past the danger point of collision, I hoped he had seen us on radar but I doubted it, I quietly said a little prayer to St Elmo, the patron saint of sailors.

The wind had backed further to the south and showed signs of going round even more, as we were well to the south of our original waypoint, it became beneficial to put in another tack and head back for the entrance channel. To help us manoeuvre I started the engine, very slowly I put the head into the seas and used the auto helm to steady the course, as we tacked I quickly released the scrap of jib and winched it in on the other side, it thrashed wildly and complained loudly about being treated in this way. Once again I balanced the tiny jib so that Cayuco sailed off the wind but without needing much help from anything or anyone. That's the joy with owning an old classic long keel well balanced boat like the Salar 40, when you need it to perform without you, it just gets on with it. The course may not have been a straight line, but the bonus was, neither of us had to stand and steer by hand for hours on end, in fact, we went back below and made another cup-a-soup. For the rest of the day Cayuco slowly clawed her way back towards the Hydrographers Passage.

By noon we were only 28 miles from the start of our entrance through the Great Barrier Reef, the wind had eased to 30/35 knots from the SSW, the barometer was rising and we were making slow progress, unfortunately the log had now stopped working again but it would have to stay that way until we got in.

It took the rest of the day for us to approach the passage and it was after 20-00 hours just as it was getting dark before we entered the outer part of the channel. I was watching the lights of a large commercial ship, he was heading straight out through the reef at about 15 knots and his course was going to take him extremely close to our position. Cayuco was sailing up from the south which meant we were on the wrong side of the channel, obeying the rules of the road we should have crossed over to the other side of the passage. I was concerned, he was closing our position fast and with our slow speed we would be unable to make it to the other side before he was on top of us. Our VHF radio, always on channel 16 when at sea, crackled into life, it was the ship heading for us and he was also concerned about our proximity. The MV Petani, I think it was a large coal carrier, was requesting a response from the white sailing yacht entering the Hydrographers Channel, I replied instantly that I thought we were the "English" yacht in question, let's face it, who else was going to be out there after the conditions of the last 36 hours, just how many idiots are there. I explained that because of our slow speed, it would be impossible for us to get to the correct side of the channel in the time available and allow us to pass red (port side) to red (port side) as the rules of the road recommend. He was not concerned about this and also expressed surprise at seeing us entering after the conditions of the last few days. He suggested that as he was constricted by the draft and could not deviate from his course that we pass each other green (starboard) to green (starboard) and keep each other informed of our actions should there be any problems. I agreed to this and thanked him for his use of the radio as it had eased my uncertainties as to what action to take, the manoeuvre went smoothly and after safely passing each other we continued on into the passage. It is probably worth a mention that the Hydrographers Channel through the Great Barrier Reef is less than a mile wide. After sailing nearly 1800 miles and having 13½ very gruelling days at sea, all we wanted to do was get inside, the trouble was, we were now entering an area unknown to us and at night, what the hell, darkness or not, we were going in.

We also faced other difficulties; it was 23-00 hours and at high tide before we arrived at the start of the inner channel. Even though the rise and fall of the tide is small by comparison to the waters we were used to, the current at this part of the channel can run over 4 knots during the middle part of the tidal range. It was also a spring tide; this meant that as we entered and approached the narrowest part of the channel a few miles further on, the current was going to be at its maximum. We had no reasonable alternative, the gale had delayed us and upset the timing of our arrival, to wait offshore in the still poor conditions was not a desirable prospect, it was blowing hard from ahead and we were inside the part of the entrance where random reefs stretch for many miles outside the main barrier. Anchoring was an alternative, but I had checked the chart and pilot books for suitable anchoring places before entering and found nothing. I was seriously in need of local knowledge, as the gale was abating we decided to carry on in.

Battling to continue, we reached what is called the "Bond Entrance Channel" about three miles inside the reef at around 01-00 hours, this is where we nearly stopped making any headway over the ground, with the engine pushing us at 4½ knots and the current at 4 knots we barely moved against it. This channel is between two islands and the water rushes between them, as we got to the narrowest part, remember our log had stopped working the day before, our GPS now began recording a minus speed and although we were still pointing west, we were in fact travelling slowly backwards.

To add to the problems, our hydraulic steering system now decided to stop working. Air had somehow got into the system, the only thing to do was to try to top up the reservoir and then bleed the system again. This was surely the worst time and place to start playing up; I chastised myself for not checking it earlier as I should have done, why do these things always happen at night? I managed to work Cayuco into the tidal lee of one of the islands at the edge of the channel where the current was not so strong. Then, with the control console tied up with a bit of string, Audrey holding a torch in one hand and a funnel in the other, I poured some more oil into the steering system reservoir. At the same time I was trying to keep the boat steering in a straight line with a rudder that was only partially working. Somehow, amidst this whole ordeal, we managed to refill the reservoir, rotate the steering wheel quickly from lock to lock 20 times to bleed air from the system and miss the ship coming through between the islands. With the steering more or less working, albeit with a bit of free play in the system, we had another go at getting past the islands and into a more favourable but still adverse current. It was dawn before we got well clear, daylight saw us south of Bugatti

Reef at slack water with another 6 hours of favourable tide, oh sheer joy.

The rub was, it had taken the last six hours to travel about twelve miles with the engine.

We had headwinds for the next 30 miles as we motored in-between the reefs and islands, the channel was too narrow to tack effectively and we had lots of shipping coming down channel so continued to motor. We found out later that all the shipping had been held up in the anchorage due to the bad weather and had recently been given permission to leave. Due to the environmental sensitivity of the Great Barrier Reef, the port authorities who control the sailing and arrival of commercial shipping cancel all movement when conditions dictate.

During the night it had been necessary to pass other ships green to green as they came down channel, after a little chat I found out that it was quite normal for this to happen in these confined and restricted channels. The pilots are familiar with small sailing boats and the use of VHF radio is the norm to communicate with them, the radio usage is a lot more relaxed than in UK where it is more formal.

As I said earlier, it is 150 miles to Mackay after entering the channel through the Great Barrier Reef, this is another day and a half at our usual speed and we expected to get in at daybreak on the 31st July. However, once we had negotiated the first 30 miles of headwind and turned to sail west, the persistently strong southerly beam wind gave us 8 knots under sail. The engine went off and all day we sped across the relatively calm inner passage, we passed numerous islands, the sun came out and it turned into a brilliant sail. After the ordeal of the last few days, we, with Cayuco chuckling away to herself at the bow were really enjoying it.

Australia is very protective of its borders, as you approach it is more than likely you will be over-flown by the customs plane, they spot all boats from above, commercial and leisure, then call up to chat on channel 16. Sometimes they inform small fast surface vessels of your location so that further checks can be made. It is essential to have a visa registered before arrival including estimated date and time of entry, this data is then logged into their system and you can register up to a year beforehand. We had completed the formalities months ago but when leaving Fiji we had updated the information and supplied new approximate dates. The authorities are insistent on proper formalities being observed and they are adamant on this, there are no exceptions. Heavy fines have been imposed when these requirements have not been met.

At 03-00 on the 31st July 2008, we slipped into the quarantine berth in Mackay Marina, we were exhausted but after tying up, that did not stop us sitting in the cockpit and reflecting on the last passage. Both of us were ecstatic; we just sat and had a beer, one of our last cans of Fiji Gold. We hugged each other and were so relieved to have made it, the adrenalin was flowing, we'd sailed over 1900 miles in 14 days 15 hours, not always in the right direction, at an average speed of over 5 knots, in the conditions of the last week we were pleased with this. Australia was our own personal half way mark, from here as far as we were concerned, it was all downhill, or so we hoped.

Audrey texted our lads and she received replies almost immediately, well, it was only 5 pm the previous day in UK, but it was wonderful to be where modern communication systems actually work. We finished our drink, thought about the voyage so far and went below to grab a couple of hours sleep.

Up early before the Australian Customs and Immigration/Quarantine came aboard, we finished off the last three eggs for breakfast. Australian Quarantine regulations are some of the toughest in the world and no organic produce is allowed in without prior checks. All meat, fruit and most food products will be removed and destroyed, only some canned items are allowed in and it is worthwhile studying the documentation on the internet before arrival. We ourselves had stocked up in Fiji with this in mind and used up our stocks accordingly, it had worked well, after a thorough search, only some dried cloves and bay leaves were removed. We would certainly have lost the eggs had we not consumed them minutes before they arrived, actually, I was still eating mine when they knocked on the cabin, but by the time they had got on board, the last delicious remnants of succulent egg were disappearing down my gullet. Oh how sweet are little victories.

Audrey - The Pacific, on Reflection

I have just had to double check the pages of my journal; I cannot believe we sailed across the Pacific in 6½ months. Some of our fellow ralliers left the group to take more time to cruise their chosen areas, a few decided to go further south to New Zealand.

When I first looked at the sheer enormity of the Pacific Ocean as an area of water to be crossed by a small sailing boat, it looked an impossible distance. We spoke to other yachties who have sailed a similar path as our own; many have taken years to complete it. The rally is a schedule of less than two years and fits in with the natural trade wind routes over this period. From my point of view I was prepared to give up two years for this trip, after which I wanted to catch up with the progress of our grandchildren.

My initial response was modified after looking at a world map, with the many island groups across the Pacific, the ocean can be divided up into more easily managed passages between the islands. With little Cayuco it was certainly a gruelling pace, bear in mind she was the oldest and slowest boat in the rally fleet, then take into consideration all the problems we had to solve on the way. We enjoyed our island visits as much as we could in-between repairs, refuelling and replacing stores and water. It could also be an expensive operation when we eventually had to launder towels and bedding, not very practical to do them with our limited facilities, it was best to ask around first, costs varied enormously.

Home comforts during this period were sadly lacking. Several months could pass before we had the benefit of mains electricity. Marinas became a thing of the past and most of the time grocery and chandlery shops were miles from the boat. Fuel and water normally had to be transported in jerry cans by dinghy, a long and back breaking business especially in the baking heat. All these things are acceptable for weekends away and the annual holiday on board, but after months on end, it starts to lose its attraction. I found an entry in my journal as we were approaching Fiji, we had just received a radio message suggesting that due to other rallies and lots of boats converging on the same areas in the Pacific, space would be limited just about everywhere we went, this did not help my composure or my feelings that this was the final straw. As it turned out we were not inconvenienced at all. At the time, it coincided with an anxious feeling that we would never get there.

This was after all a sail round the world; challenge first and foremost with any tours or sightseeing experiences a bonus which had to fit within our limited budget. Fortunately for us, due to the diligent work of the rally organisers, lots of the tours were laid on as part of the stopovers and therefore free of charge or otherwise at very reasonable cost. Moreover, in our earlier life, we had lived and worked in the Pacific Islands and visited many of them as a requirement of the position. This former period had given us the opportunity to explore the islands at our leisure and because of this, we did not miss much.

Before we started I reckoned on crossing one ocean, I had now sailed across two major oceans of the world! The feeling of relief and euphoria as we sat onboard, tied up in Mackay Marina was overwhelming, it was time for another poem.

The Story So Far, or, The Ballad of "Cayuco"

So, now we've arrived down under,
We're in the land of OZ.
I never thought we'd get this far,
When we set off first for Kos.

We left our berth in Turkey,
The Greek Islands to explore.
We reckoned it was loads of fun,
So thought we'd do some more.

By and by, we sailed the Med,
Till we ended up in Spain.
We bid farewell to Cayuco,

And went home on the plane.

But, our sailing wasn't over,
After winter we'd be back.
Returning to our little ship,
To have another crack.

We sailed her back to England,
Our trip for now was through.
Time for friends and family,
And fitting out to do.

But, what's this about a rally?
They call themselves "Blue Water"
And a journey sailing round the world,
Beginning from Gibraltar.

We went to the London Boat Show,
Met Peter and Annette.
They explained about their rally,
Though we had our doubts, as yet.

It was quite an undertaking,
The problems could be many,
But if there was a time to go,
Now was as good as any.

There's not a lot to add here,
The rest you're surely knowing.
We're past the point now of return,
It's only forward going.

But our little ship is holding fast,
And keeps us safe and sound.
While we circumnavigate the world,
All, the way round.

Tony

We were both content to have finished the Pacific crossing, apart from some very pleasant interludes; the weather and the conditions had not been anything like expected. It was an El Niño year and although not a notable one, it had been bad enough for us. The South Pacific Convergence Zone had given us and a few others a hard time, we have since chatted to people who had perfect conditions nearly all the way across and hardly even took any spray onboard. It also highlights some of the decisions I made which were not all they could have been, I should have used the radio more for weather information and fitted e mail facilities to it connected to a computer. Having said that, we did continue sailing sometimes when we should have sought shelter, sailing past Vanuatu and on to Australia was a classic example of getting it wrong. Cayuco is a superb sea boat and we never felt that she would let us down, even in atrocious conditions, life on board was still manageable.

Australia and the Great Barrier Reef promised a new dimension to our sailing experience and we were both looking forward to it.

Chapter 11

The Great Barrier Reef, and Over The Top

Tony

Mackay Marina is superb, not only does it have all the repair facilities required by the cruising and racing yachtsman, it also includes most of the leisure pursuits enjoyed by them as well. The marina restaurants are very good and the yacht club welcomes yachtsmen from all parts of the world. As usual, we found a little cafe/snack bar come grocery shop round the back which produced very good breakfasts and meals, plus, was also a good source for vegetables, canned goods and fresh milk.

It was about this time that we learned of the accident concerning two fellow yachtsmen who had been moored next to us in Tahiti. During the storm we had encountered a few days earlier as we closed the Great Barrier Reef, they had apparently been about 300 miles north-west of us and heading for Cairns. The same night of the gale, in atrocious weather, they had unfortunately run up on a coral reef and the boat had been a total loss. After sending out a mayday and setting off their EPIRB, they escaped from the wreck in the life raft and were picked up within hours by a commercial ship. It brought home to us just how careful you have to be and how lucky we had been.

Since the repair to the roller furler spar in the Marquesas I had not been unfurling the jib completely but leaving one turn of the jib around the spar, my thinking was, if the glue holding the joined sections parted again, the screws, not being able to slide out, would hold the joint together. So far the philosophy had worked very well; however, the roller furling gear had developed another fault. It had started to stick when the jib was set, such that when trying to furl it, the roller part jammed completely. The only way to get it to work, was to go up to the bow and forcibly turn the drum with a big lever, in this case, a long jemmy bar, when the sail was shortened enough, it was then possible to pull the rest in by hand from the cockpit. The cause was traced to the bearings in the roller drum which had worn to such an extent that the drum was jamming on the base. Clearly we would need to change the bearings but to do that it looked like we would have to remove the whole furling gear.

After investigating the mechanism I thought I had worked out a way to change the bearings without removing the spar, but it would need two people, as there was a rigging guy working in the marina I asked him for his advice. He agreed with me that he thought it could be done in-situ and although busy due to the local race week coming up he would be able to fit it in.

The next day saw him going to the top of the mast to secure the spar from sliding down the shroud, when he came down there was further bad news. On the way up, being a professional, he had automatically checked the other rigging fittings, both lower shroud tangs port and starboard on the mast were in a dangerous condition. I climbed up the mast to see for myself, I went cold, both fore and aft lower shroud tang fittings were hanging on by a wish and a prayer, they had split across on the mast through bolt and on the clevis pin end fittings. How the hell they had held up the mast a couple of days previously in the gale was beyond me, we were going to have to have major surgery to make it safe again. The rigger who had his own workshop complete with a machine lathe etc agreed to make up the fittings and sort out the roller furler gear, once again it all had to be tailor made.

I then made an attempt to cure a water leak from the rear of the engine exhaust heat exchanger, as I undid the rear plate and removed the water hose, the cast iron fitting crumbled in my hand. At least I'd found the cause of the leak but I now had to get a new plate made up. At the same time and as the engine had been smoking a bit, I removed the fuel injectors and sent them to Brisbane to be overhauled. Another job was to change the fuel lift pump, there had been a tiny nagging fuel leak which I could not stop, as I had a spare pump, I decided to change it and cure the problem, I also managed to fix a water leak from the loo. With all this going on Audrey decided to do some work on the teak decks, she had tried in Fiji but ran out of time. The daily temperature in Mackay was 12° to 20° so it felt cool to us after being in the tropics for so long, whatever, for the next few days we were both gainfully employed.

We enjoyed the social life and had a couple of meals ashore, one of our little fleet had decided to leave the rally here so he arranged a party in a local hotel, as they were an Australian couple we had a pre party taster of crocodile and kangaroo hors d'oeuvres, tasty and very different.

By the ninth of August all the fleet had arrived, a lot of them had been sheltering in Vanuatu when the storm hit us, they had left afterwards so their arrival in Mackay was a bit delayed. During this time I managed to get the computer working on board through a Wi-Fi link, had a good chat with family back in UK and also cured a leak from the fore hatch which had shown itself during the gale, all in all, a good day.

It was a busy time but the rigging was repaired, the water leak cured from the engine, the injectors refitted and all other jobs put back together We sent postcards and some presents home for the grandchildren, fuelled and stored up and made ready to leave, both of us were looking forward to the next stage. Sailing up The Great Barrier Reef and through the famous Whitsunday Islands had got to be one of the main highlights of the whole voyage

Well, we left Mackay to start our Great Barrier Reef experience but Cayuco decided against it, no sooner had we left the harbour than the engine started to lose oil pressure, there was a thud, the engine started chucking out black smoke and we turned back. I quickly radioed the marina to inform them we were returning and we slipped straight back into the same berth. The initial diagnosis looked serious but it didn't take long to work out what had happened, the new fuel pump was faulty, thinking I was curing one fault I had caused another one. The diaphragm in the pump had split and diesel fuel was pumping straight through to the engine sump. This diluted the engine oil, hence lack of oil pressure, the heat from the engine caused diesel fumes to vaporise and burn instantaneously in the sump; this caused the thump we heard. Then, with the engine oil higher than usual, neat diluted fuel rich oil made its way to the cylinders via the breather tube and burned with the fuel causing the black smoke. This was not a disaster, just a setback; all I needed was another new fuel lift pump, some engine oil and a new filter

It was our lucky day, the local Perkins dealer not only had a new lift pump and a service kit on the shelf, he also delivered it to the marina less than two hours later. All I had to do now was change the pump for the new one, then renew the engine oil and filter as this was now ineffective in lubricating the moving parts. The hardest part of the whole job was removing the old fuel rich engine oil, there was a lot of it and the waste oil vat was the other side of the yard. By the end of the day we were all ready to set off again, however, the next day it was blowing another howler outside so we decided to enjoy the comforts of Mackay Marina for a bit longer.

Audrey

When we returned to Mackay it was a depressing few hours, the problem initially showed all the signs of being serious and could have put us out of the rally. Tony knew that the symptoms were indicating a possible piston ring problem as a worse scenario but was hoping it was only the fuel lift pump, knowing he had just fitted a new unit did not help his diagnosis. However, a check on the oil level with the dipstick soon showed up the problem, unfortunately, the new unit he had fitted proved to be a faulty one, he was soon able to get us back into working order. It was really a blessing in disguise, the weather turned nasty again, so we teamed up with our friends John and Jane from Penelope 3 who had hired a car and together we toured the area taking in the sights from the land for a change. We drove up through the mountains to Eungella National Park, it was very picturesque and a good photography session ensued. We had been told that this was the place to see the Australian platypus in the wild so we hot-footed it down to the observation platform built alongside the river. All the advice was to keep quiet and still while watching for ripples on the surface as they are very shy creatures. After a few minutes the ripples appeared, tension was high, we were not the only ones trying to catch a glimpse of this rare mammal, the ripples came closer, oh, what a letdown, it was a turtle. As we changed places throughout the day, taking in a walk, more photos and another drive to a forest hut for lunch, mostly liquid I'm afraid, we still saw no evidence of Mr or Mrs Platypus. We saw more turtles, a moorhen, other bird varieties, a long beaked thing and even a kingfisher but not a sign of our quarry.

Towards the end of the day as we took one more gaze along the river, again being very quiet and seeing nothing, a shout went up further along the bank towards the road bridge. All our neighbours start to run towards the bridge, everyone had forgotten about being quiet, as we got to the bridge, not only was everyone shouting, taking photographs, leaning over the parapet, sliding down the banks etc, but a large coach was also rumbling slowly over the bridge. There, below us in the water, was the platypus, swimming slowly along, splashing and diving for supper, occasionally coming up chomping a meal of shrimp or a small fish, it was completely oblivious to the cacophony of noise all around it. Shy little creatures my Aunt Sally, this platypus almost posed for pictures and seemed to enjoy all the fuss he or she created, anyway, I got my photo. Our biggest surprise of all was the size of it, didn't really know what to expect but thought they would be larger; it was about 14 to 18 inches long, just short of half a metre and apparently this is about as big as they get. Whatever, he was very cute as he continued to hoover up food from the river seeming to paddle along the surface. Think they should print a "T" shirt though, along the lines of "I've seen the Platypus of Eungella Park".

The weather was still bad the next day so we took off again with John and Jane, this time to the Hillborough Nature Reserve. We went for a fairly long walk along an organised nature track, at various places there were boards explaining what each tree was and what it was used for, the trees also had little explanations tagged onto them. The notice boards explained that many years ago, (and probably still now), how the tracks were used by the Aborigines to travel from one hunting ground to another. The walk finished at the animal sanctuary with perfect timing, we arrived just as they were about to give the wallabies and kangaroos their afternoon feed. The sanctuary is an open area where wild and fairly tame animals co-exist. Some are baby joeys rescued when their mothers were killed by vehicles on the road and others are wild animals who have just got used to when the rest are fed, all can come and go as they please. We were told which animals were used to being petted as they had been there since they were born and this made another great photo opportunity. When we returned the evening was finished off with a meal at the yacht club and plans were made to leave the next day.

Tony

With a period of good weather forecast for the next few days we left Mackay at 10-00 hours on the 24th August 2008. As far as Australia is concerned August is the middle of winter, the equivalent of UK's February so I suppose we shouldn't have been too surprised about the colder wind and the occasional gale, it was still pleasantly warm during the day with temperatures 15° to 20°C. We were heading for a group of islands called the James Smith Islands about 30 miles away, the names of the individual islands included Silversmith, Tinsmith, Anvil, Hammer and others, all have good night anchorages in settled weather. We dropped our hook in a small bay on the west side of Goldsmith Island in about 8 metres of water, our friends Hugh and Shan on the rally yacht Stargazer were about 150 metres away. It was a windless night, there was a beautiful sunset. Cayuco rolled a bit while we slept, the recent gale had caused a large sea to run and it had not yet calmed down, the swells were creeping round the corner of the point and spreading out across the bay. The next morning after a leisurely start we sailed north past the small islands of Thomas, Shaw, Mansell, Lindemans and Pentecost, again, all have good anchorages but we didn't have time to stay. Our plan was to anchor overnight somewhere in the Whitsunday group, our first choice of Hamilton Island was quickly ruled out. As we approached there were yachts everywhere, we discovered the annual Hamilton Island Regatta was in full swing, it was just like Cowes week in the Solent or a busy summer weekend. We sailed up the Dent Passage between Dent and Hamilton Island dodging all the yachts milling around, then continued north through the Henning Passage and along the west shore of Whitsunday Island. Just round the westernmost point and slightly north along Whitsunday Island there is an anchorage called Cid Harbour, this was the one we had picked out, a further 30 miles north and another stunning anchorage. It was a much calmer bay and a good sleep was had by all. The next morning we went ashore with Hugh and Shan to walk a nature trail on Whitsunday Island starting in Dugong Bay and going north, while we were there, a more adventurous group from another yacht came ashore and started to walk the Ngaro Trail, this climbs right to the top peak of the Whitsunday Island and takes a couple of hours. After our return we had a quiet beer in the cockpit of Cayuco, spent a relaxing day just doing nothing and then had another good sleep before setting off north again next day.

Leaving the anchorage at 07-00 we headed for Bowen, this used to be a thriving fishing village but is a bit quieter now, still a few commercial vessels working but like fishing all over the world, it's a changing scene. Not much wind in the early morning but a good breeze by 11-00 hours, we sailed along the shore of South and North Mollie Islands and on past Armit and Gloucester Island which is now a National Park. We could have sailed between Gloucester Island and the mainland but it was low water, there would not have been much depth in the channel, we carried on and went round the north point. From there it was a short sail towards Stone Island and up the channel; we were still too early to enter Bowen so anchored off the entrance and waited for more depth of water. On our way up the channel, large whales had been jumping out of the water only a few hundred yards to our starboard side, it was like we were watching a TV documentary, right out of the water they climbed before twisting in the air and falling back in, we supposed they were trying to stun small fish in order to eat them. Many dolphins were also seen swimming along with us, leaping and diving alongside Cayuco, riding our bow wave and charging underneath the boat, it was wonderful to see them again. Stargazer had sailed on to another anchorage so we had said goodbye to them for a while.

When the tide had risen enough we entered Bowen Harbour, arranged a berth in the small marina for the night and treated ourselves to a run ashore. Bowen is a wonderful place; larger than we thought and with all the facilities you could need, we availed ourselves to a fish and chip supper in the Irish Pub with a pint of beer, our trip up the Great Barrier Reef was living up to expectations. The next day we heard John and Jane of Penelope 3 talking on the radio, they were heading north, so after a chat they agreed to try and make Bowen. By early evening both of us were tied up in the marina so again we went ashore to show them around. No guesses where we ended up and it was another lovely evening, I think the expression, "It's a hard job, but someone's got to do it" comes to mind and sums it up.

Our progress due to the attractions of the Whitsunday group had been slow, we really needed to cover a few miles so both Penelope 3 and ourselves decided to make a 24 hour overnight run to Townsville, this is just over 100 miles from Bowen so fitted in with our plans. Leaving Bowen at 11-00 hrs just after high water we managed to sail between Bowen Island and the mainland, this saved a few miles and set our course north. As soon as we got into deeper water, there were the whales again, just 200 yards away a huge one came vertically out of the water, 2/3rds of the body was in the air, it did a huge belly flop and we heard the crash as it hit the water, it repeated this several times, we tried to take a photograph but unless you have something like a camcorder it is very difficult to catch the right moment, it was certainly amazing.

We had a relaxing sail for the whole trip, a pleasant 12 to 15 knots from abaft the beam, lots of stars all through the night; this is what it's all about. Entering Townsville around 11-00 hours the next morning we tied up on the free temporary local authority berth while we negotiated with the nearby Townsville Motor Boat and Yacht Club. Having sorted out a berth for us and Penelope 3, Jane then cooked us all a nice English breakfast. The Townsville Motor Boat and Yacht Club, (TMB&YC) is a very friendly club, we enjoyed their company and their home cooked food, they also advised on the points of interest in town. We all went to the very large aquarium, it was built as a working coral reef and is a vast building, it is temperature controlled and includes an artificial tidal water flow through the tanks, all the coral fish imaginable are in there including large sharks. There are huge plate glass tanks where you can walk alongside but even better there are tunnels which go underneath the tanks and you can see up through the water. They even have a shark feeding show at 4pm in the afternoon up on the top level. It is a fantastic place with teaching rooms, regular talks throughout the day, film shows and guided tours. We were told it is the biggest aquarium in the world; we'll have to take their word for it.

Back on board Audrey tried the computer to see if the internet was possible but we were too far away from the base station, never mind, off tomorrow, another overnight run to Cairns.

Up early for a 08-00 start, 1st September so it was "White Rabbit" time, supposed to be lucky if that is your first words of the new month, anyway both Penelope 3 and Cayuco left Townsville MB&YC for another 100 miles plus. This was another excellent sail, no wonder the Great Barrier Reef is renowned as a sailing area, A 15 knot wind once again just abaft the beam for the whole trip. Clear sky throughout the night, shooting stars as well this time. We started with just the jib but we had the main up shortly after and were able to hold both sails full nearly the whole time. The main shipping channel here is well marked; in fact there are two or three different tracks you can take to sail up and down the reef, as we were not familiar with the area we stayed to the edge of the battleship route especially at night.

Large ships use the inner passages 24 hours a day, by Australian regulations they must carry a pilot all the time they are within the reef, their professionalism is first rate, often they will talk to you on the radio to confirm your course and intentions. There are pilot stations at regular intervals along the coast where one pilot will finish and another takes over, this ensures any ship always has someone who has local knowledge for that area.

There are heavy fines for anyone who causes pollution of any kind; even small yachts have to be fitted with holding tanks for their black water.

For safety every leisure craft has to carry a folded plastic orange sheet called a "V sheet" these can be spread out on the vessel or in the sea alongside, it is about 3m x 3m square and visual from the air in case of emergency.

As you leave Townsville to sail north, the Great Barrier Reef tapers in towards the Australian Coast, at Mackay it is 150 miles before you get outside the reef, at Cairns, it is only 40 miles to the open sea. This has the effect of narrowing all the channels the commercial ships use, with care there is still plenty of room for small sailing boats to navigate north or south just outside the shipping lanes with safety. You are expected where possible to observe the correct side of the channel, even if you are just outside it.

The many islands and shallows also cause the direction of the channel to change regularly so careful navigation is the key. Night passages are not recommended, but we found no trouble sailing during the hours of darkness, the clearly lit channels, the buoyage system and our usual navigation instruments worked well all the way. By day it is possible to take short cuts between islands, this not only shortens the route it also makes reef sailing much more interesting.

Again we had a brilliant sail, just a bit more overcast than usual, the trip took just over 31 hours, leaving 08-00 and arriving at Marlin Marina, Cairns 15-15 on the 2nd September. A word of warning, as this area is a very busy sailing region, we had taken the precaution of telephoning the marina the day before in order to reserve a berth; it was a good call. Another local marina is the very friendly Yorkies Knob Boating Club Marina a few miles north of Cairns, it was popular with a lot of yachts but you may need transport to town.

Both Penelope 3 and Cayuco were still sailing in company and as Cairns is a popular tourist area we had both decided to spend a few days here. John had also arranged to lift out Penelope 3, he wanted to change the anodes, clean the bottom and check the folding propeller. I would also be able to help as John wanted the boat out and back in the water within the day. It was one of the easiest places for this work to be carried out before Thailand and Cairns is also a good place for obtaining boat spares of almost any description.

Audrey

Our first day in Cairns was spent cleaning up Cayuco, doing some laundry, investigating our surroundings and arranging a trip inland with John and Jane for the next day. We found the Yacht Club a short walk along the beach, it was just what you would expect in the tropics, lovely place complete with balcony, al fresco dining and a very good reasonably priced menu.

Our outing next day was to the Kuranda National Park, this was quite an amazing place; we started our trip by taking the airborne sky rail. This is a suspended lift over the treetops, you sit in your own little pod with windows all round and literally fly over the top looking down onto the forest below. All manner of birds and wildlife are down there somewhere, we saw white cockatoos and plenty of red and green parakeets. The lift stops at two destinations on the way up, there you can disembark and follow marked nature trails through the forest, these have plates describing the flora and fauna at regular intervals, there is also a viewpoint lookout over the surrounding countryside, it is a truly magnificent experience. On the way up there are comfort breaks and a place for a cup of coffee although we took a bottle of water with us as it was a hot day anyway. At the top there is the small village of Kuranda which is completely surrounded by rain forest, it is possible to have lunch in one of the many hostelries and visit the numerous tourist attractions. This is where I fulfilled one of my ambitions in life and actually got to cuddle a koala. We also saw kangaroos, wallabies, wombats, crocodiles, snakes and many more animals in what appeared to be their natural habitat. Of course the dangerous ones are kept safe from the public, wouldn't be popular to have a few tourists on the croc's main course menu. From the village you can return on the sky train, or make your way to the Kuranda Scenic Railway, this travels slowly along the 34 miles of track down the gorge and back to the start. We had already decided to return by train and had purchased the tickets with this in mind. The railway is very traditional with authentic bench seats which has to be said are not the most comfortable, in compensation, the trip is outstanding, with stops at viewpoints of natural beauty, definitely not a day to forget the camera.

Figure 24: The authors in Kuranda Park, Australia, with Audrey cuddling a Koala, one of her personal dreams.

Tony

The next day was scheduled for Penelope 3's lift out; I went with John to help with the work while Audrey went shopping for presents to send home for the family. The work on the boat went well but it was a bit of a rush towards the end to get it finished in time for the re-launch, we made it with minutes to spare. It was a happy group of people that ended up in the Yacht Club that night for a meal and a few bevies, all ready for the next leg of the trip.

We had a bits and pieces day next, getting ready to move on, after the festivities of the night before no-one was too keen on an early start. We had a good internet connection with the lads back in UK so had a good long chat, this always cheers Audrey up, we were a long way from home and it was going to be a long time before we saw them in person again.

Off to Port Douglas, just a short day trip, cloudy and not much wind so having to motor, set off at 08-00 hours and thought it may clear up later and get better but it didn't, had some wind before lunch but the rain came with it. It was hot when we arrived in Port Douglas about 16-00 hours on Sunday 7th September, managed to get two berths in Mirage Marina for the night. Port Douglas is a pretty place, the marina is small but friendly, a flock of green and red lorikeets roosted in the trees alongside the mooring in the evening. They are like English starlings in volume and numbers but with different colours and lots of noisy attitude.

John noticed his stainless steel foredeck fitting which takes all the rigging strains of the jib had started to crack, the welds and the plate were nearly split all the way through. Couldn't risk sailing any further until it had been repaired, that's what holds the mast up, luckily, there was a welder working on a fishing boat nearby. He looked at the weld and said he had seen these fittings break before, reckoned it was caused by lots of downwind sailing, the continual working of the rig causes the fitting to fatigue and eventually it would have snapped. John and I looked at each other in a knowing way when he mentioned 'caused by downwind sailing'; we didn't have the heart to tell him we had done almost 20,000 miles in this fashion in the last 12 months. Basically, with the right equipment, it was a simple repair, he took some measurements, removed a fitting, took it away then re-appeared next day to weld it in place and reinforce the weld further across the plate, a most successful outcome. This welding work delayed us so we stayed here a bit longer; this meant we were able to explore a bit more. Port Douglas is a quaint little town, Olde world and a bit like you would imagine a Wild West town to be like, it was very colonial looking and the hotels and bars had definitely seen better days. Having said all that, it was a very friendly town, we enjoyed our stay there and our evening in the local sailing club which seemed to cater for everyone and everything.

We had filled in our paperwork for Indonesia in Fiji and Mackay; this takes some months to process so it's essential to get it done in good time. New rules adopted in some Indonesian island groups regarding entry and the cost involved were putting a question mark on where our first landfall would be. Kupang province were apparently adopting the rules, while Bali had decided not to, the difference in cost for us was enormous, several hundred dollars between them finalised our decision and Bali was where we were going to check in. For us this also meant we had extra time to get to Darwin where the support team would meet us next, with our relatively slow progress this far, any extra time was a bonus.

In the end, we didn't get away from Port Douglas until Thursday 11th September; we left at first light with the intention of making Cooktown 70 miles away by nightfall. The weather was overcast but we had a good quarterly wind again so were making more than 6 knots over the ground. With our delayed stay at the marina in Port Douglas I had once again got the log working which had stopped on the way there, also found the fault on the spreader lights which had not been working properly for months.

The Great Barrier Reef was closing in on us, the distance to the open sea was now only about twenty miles, from here the channels would be much smaller and we still had a lot of shipping so care had to be taken when sailing. Penelope being bigger than us was always faster, all day we followed her while we both picked our way along the channels and between the coral islands. We anchored in the river at Cooktown off the fishing quay late afternoon, it was a good job the anchor went in first time and held, as we tried to pull the anchor up a few inches the anchor winch motor failed again. Once again I had to bury myself in the anchor locker and dismantle the electric motor mechanism, at least after our problems in Tahiti; I knew how to strip it down. The problem was easy to diagnose, in the gale on the way from Fiji, water must have got into the brush gear, the brushes were sticking in their holders and as they wore down when the motor worked this caused an air gap between the brush and the armature, we could keep it going but eventually I would have to strip it down and overhaul it.

The initial remedy to the anchor winch was easy to apply, while Audrey raised the anchor from on the deck; I had a new task to perform, apart from flaking down the chain in the anchor locker as it was raised. I took a hammer in my hand and wacked the electric motor every time it stopped working. This shock to the system caused the brushes to slide back onto the armature under the pressure of the brush springs and hence the motor would work again for a few minutes before requiring the same action. This rather brutal procedure was to be the butt of a few jokes later on in the trip.

Captain Cook repaired his ship Endeavour in Cooktown after running aground on Endeavour Reef, named after the incident, this happened at 11pm on 11th June 1770 while he continued to sail north through the night. His voyage north after this event was continued during the daylight hours and an anchorage was sought every night. There is a statue in his memory on the south side of the harbour wall as you enter the Endeavour River, also named after the ship; Cooktown itself is probably named after Captain Cook. This was allegedly the place where the first kangaroo and an Aborigine were spotted by the crew of the Endeavour, although Joseph Banks the famous botanist onboard was reputed to have spotted another Aborigine near where they first landed in Botany Bay.

Cooktown is the northernmost town on the east coast of Australia and is in far north Queensland, there's not a lot more civilisation between here and Cape York. It is another pretty town, very lay-back and again colonial looking with reasonable price hotels and restaurants although we did most of our eating on board. It was almost another 400 miles to Cape York which we had to round before heading for Darwin, so after a day working on the winch and sightseeing we up anchored and headed for an anchorage in Watson's Bay off Lizard Island.

This was an excellent sailing day, leaving Cooktown at 06-30 we headed slightly east of north to miss the next headland some twenty miles distant and with a beam wind of 25 to 30 knots we fairly tramped along. Sailing at an average speed of 8 knots nearly all day we followed the now narrowing channels, taking extra care in the busy shipping lanes and short cuts between the islands when we could. For once, Cayuco, having left Cooktown first was ahead of Penelope 3 and with the prevailing conditions it stayed that way until we reached Lizard Island. This island is off the main north/south channel and is on a link that comes down through a different route; commercial ships pick the fastest passage that their depth dictates, so not all ships use the same channels all the time. Also there is a one way system in operation on some sections of the inside reef passages so it all makes for interesting course work.

Lizard Island is a National Park, it has a small resort on its west side with a tiny airstrip, the swimming, snorkel and scuba diving are superb and as it is part of the Great Barrier Reef, access to other dive sites is straightforward. The island was so named by Captain Cook on 12th August 1770 as all he found on the island were lizards; the highest point is 'Cooks Look', where he is supposed to have climbed in order to see if there was a way out of the shallow channels. He was not happy sailing into what he thought may be a bottleneck and worse still with the prevailing wind behind him, in the end they were using longboats ahead of the Endeavour to find the best way through the reef system. As it turned out he sailed on and eventually found the way out north near Escape River.

For us it was a windy night but we had a comfortable sleep anchored right into Watson's Bay. We were up early and off again by 07-00, we knew from here the anchorages got a bit sparse and as it was important to cover some miles we were going to sail as far as possible before anchoring. By 18-00 it was obvious we would not make our next chosen anchorage so decided to stay the night tucked around the corner of Cape Melville and close in to Bathurst and Melville Bay. It was an open anchorage and as it had been quite windy during the day we thought it may be a bit on the rolly side, in actual fact, close in and out of the direct line of wind it was very comfortable, it reminded me of coming along the south coast of England and tucking in behind Beachy Head. A comment in my log regarding the night reads,

"Blowing a hooly, but calm in here".

Audrey

Another early start saw us motoring out of Melville Bay trying to miss the fishing boats beam trawling across our path as there was now no wind at all, not to worry, by lunch time the wind was back and we were sailing well once more. It had been decided to try to head for St Margaret's Bay 180 miles away, this meant another nights sail but it would cover a lot of distance, in any case anchorages were in short supply unless you happened to be a catamaran. It turned out to be a very pleasant sail, a constant south east wind of 20 /25 knots, a full moon nearly all night and next morning we were well on course for a late afternoon anchor drop in St Margaret's Bay. This bay has a lovely long mangrove lined white sandy beach, the sort you imagine turtles hauling themselves across to lay their eggs, or crocodiles visiting at sunset. We watched with binoculars during sundowners and while eating our dinner, right up to nightfall, but never saw anything looking like either. As it was going to be a very early start next morning we turned in shortly after dinner. John on Penelope 3 and Tony had chatted on the radio about our next leg to the Escape River; it was nearly 80 miles so would be a long day sail for us. It was essential we arrived at Escape River with plenty of time to spare; there are not too many good anchorages on the way and reading up on the entrance it was best negotiated after half tide as there is a shallow bar at the entrance.

Tony

Our early start was 04-00 Hrs on 17th September, fortunately we had a good wind from early on and made good time, the wind started about 15 knots but very soon it was blowing 25 to 30 knots, we covered the logged 80 miles in 12 hours, an average of over 6.6 knots so by 16-00 we were trying to find our way over the bar. This had to be given a bit of thought, the onshore wind was 25 to 30 knots and the water over the bar was only about 12 feet deep (4 metres). Even if we could find the channel it wasn't much deeper, we also had 2 metre seas running and there were no buoys or leading marks visible, with our near two metre draught it didn't look like it was going to be easy.

It was half tide when we arrived and Penelope 3 who had set off a bit later than us were approaching fast, they needed a bit more water than us so we tried a place where the outgoing stream is supposed to scour out the channel and keep it open. Watching the depth metre closely while trying to find the deepest water we slipped across the bar in a surge while keeping in touch with John. Other problems here are that the bar and channels can move, warnings on the chart tell you that depth readings may be inaccurate. It's a bit suck it and see and not made any easier by the fact that as it's so far north and rarely used by anybody there are no sea marks of any description. There are some transits on the land using headlands that are useful but only approximations, we were glad to get safely over the bar.

Going on the information we had managed to obtain, we felt our way in slowly using the depth sounder and entered the river, it was deeper inside so we conveyed this to John. Our problems were not yet over, the bay is used for commercial pearl production and there are pearl rafts everywhere, we slowly negotiated the rafts, mooring ropes, haphazard channel markers which seemed to have no bearing on the channel and unmarked underwater rocks and sandbanks, it didn't feel as though we were being made welcome. The end result was a memorable anchorage off another mangrove tree lined shore, in the flat calm river it was tranquil, very picturesque and another good photo opportunity. The shore looked like a mixture of mud and sand and at low water was the ideal place to watch crocodiles slither down to the water, although we watched closely we never saw any. However, next morning, there were clear suspicious sliding marks down the ooze and disappearing into the water, just in case, no-one went for a pre-breakfast swim that morning. We had been warned that we were now in shark and crocodile country.

Audrey

There was little sign of human life, only a small shed structure that we assumed was something to do with the pearl industry but we saw no people at all while we were there. This was a real out of the way place, absolutely miles from anywhere, if you got yourself into trouble here, it could be a problem getting help.

The silence of this place prompted me to put pen to paper once again, this next poem was the result.

OZ – The Outback

There are certain Places
Along the way.
Which, to put it mildly
Make your day.

And situations
There are but few,
That make you look
Inside of you

The silence speaks
With gentle voice
You have to listen
You have no choice

It is only then
You can hear the sound
Of this ancient land
Which is so profound.

Tony

A fairly early start as we left our anchorage and picked our way tentatively down the river, it was already blowing strongly so it was quite a rough ride over the bar, but at least I had the track on the chart plotter from yesterday. Our objective today was to sail north heading for the Albany Passage, this is a short cut between the Australian mainland and York Island, then round Cape York known as the top of Australia. After that we would sail down the other side of the Cape York Peninsular to another anchorage called Red Island. Here we could have a few days rest, store and fuel up, before our next long sail, a thousand miles along the north of Australia and sailing west along the Torres Straight to Darwin.

We made a fast passage and two hours later we approached the Albany Passage, it was a great feeling to be approaching the top of Oz, this is another one of those memorable times of your life, not too many people actually get to sail round here in their own sailing boat. The current was with us and we sailed quickly through the half mile wide passage taking photographs as we went. Very soon we were out the other side and heading for Cape York, it looked just as barren as we expected.

Sailing along here we were only a short sail (about 25 miles) from Thursday Island in the Torres Strait, this Island at the top of Australia has a pub called "Australia's Top Pub" and is reputed to be the most northerly pub in Australia. A look at the chart confirms you are less than a hundred miles from Papua New Guinea and it is possible to cross the Torres Strait using the many islands between the two countries. The current and tides are not very regular here and can run strongly, they are affected by sea conditions on the Pacific and Indian Ocean ends of the Strait, there are also many coral atolls and shoal patches so care is needed.

We jibed round Cape York and set off on our new course parallel to the coast for our Red Island anchorage. It was a really fast sail and we were off Red Island by 14-30 hours, picking up the leading marks we made our way through the small entrance channel watching the depth sounder. The anchorage here is very tight and there is only room for a few boats, we picked a spot where Penelope 3 could anchor alongside us and a few minutes later we were both safe and secure lying to the now warm and light offshore breeze.

Ashore we met up for a drink in the local Fishermans Cafe and reflected on our trip up the Great Barrier Reef. All of us had really enjoyed the experience and wished it could have gone on for a bit longer, the regular strong beam winds made for great sailing. Anchorages, apart from the extreme north, were generally plentiful, the scenery and townships were stunning, what a shame we all agreed that it was over. Soon we would be back to days at sea and out of sight of land, taking everything as it came. The next voyage to Darwin, eight hundred miles away, was along the Torres Straight, due to the amount of time we had spent on our trip so far, it was unlikely we would be able to stop anywhere else.

We investigated a stop at Gove, a small mining town at the southern edge of the Wessel Islands with a fascinating onward passage through the "Hole in the Wall". This is a narrow short cut through the group of islands where if you get the tide right, you can be shot through the gap at fifteen knots over the ground. It looked interesting but we knew we would spend more time in the friendly club there; it has a reputation for the kind of hospitality that causes your legs to give up working, so we decided against it. Time was marching on, it was already getting late for our arrival in Darwin and the preparation for the onward passage to Indonesia, we were all going to be very sad when the time came to leave Australia.

Next day was the same round of storing and fuelling up, filling up the water tanks and generally getting ready. We wondered about taking a taxi to Garling about three miles away which has a larger shopping centre, in the end we obtained all we wanted from the main store. The fuel and water, in cans of course, we bought from the local garage, he even drove back to the beach with all the cans in the back of his pick up for us, he explained that he was used to it, all the cruisers that came in had the same problem. Fortunately we had managed to sail most of the distance from our last fuel stop so did not need a tremendous amount.

Red Island was a very friendly place, everybody was willing to help and nothing was too much of a problem, it's much the same in small communities the world over.

The Cape York Peninsular, where we were, is not that wide, a quick check on our charts confirmed that in fact we had sailed about 45 miles round the top but were only about 11 miles from our anchorage in the Escape River the day before.

Another good night in the local hostelry and back on board, we lifted the dinghy back on deck before turning in, this ensures it will be dry when you deflate and put it away in the morning, once again, we were off.

. Saturday September 20th at 11-00 hours saw both yachts pulling out of the Red Island anchorage heading for Darwin, we waved goodbye to friends we had met on another yacht anchored nearby, they were waiting for a window in the weather to go the other way. The route across the Gulf of Carpentaria was due west, we had a fresh wind of SE force 4/5 although the long range forecast was not good, after the first couple of days the wind was destined to die down and stay calm for the next week, we wanted to get as far as possible before we lost our favourable wind.

As predicted the wind held at the start of the voyage, our noon to noon runs were 123 and 133 miles for the 48 hours after leaving but then the wind gradually died and we started drifting. The bonus for us was the current mostly flowed west, so trying to catch every zephyr we slowly covered the miles. When it was really light we motored for a few hours leaving the main up to act as a steadying sail, as soon as any breeze came up we sailed.

On Tuesday 22nd we past Cape Wessel which was just under our half way mark, OK so far but after that we had mostly light conditions. Penelope 3 was well ahead of us by this time and we had lost radio contact on the VHF, we chatted where possible on the SSB schedules but generally they were experiencing the same calm conditions. A couple of squalls gave us a few more miles for 2 to 3 hours at a time but why do they always strike at night?

For the first time since leaving Gibraltar it started to get boring, all we could do was sit there or use up our precious diesel, this is where we realised that boring was good, if we were bored, it meant nothing was happening and best of all, nothing had broken. Our plan was to take a short cut through the Clarence Strait about 150 miles before Darwin, this would save us a few miles but it was essential we got there at the right time, if the tide was against you, nothing moved forward until it was with you. Our luck held and apart from a couple of hours of adverse current at the beginning we held the tide nearly all the way to Darwin. This channel is east of Melville and Bathurst Islands but is treacherous for its shallows and is mostly unlit; I undid the anchor and had it ready to drop in case of emergency, one cannot be too careful when in strange waters. Our wind came back for the last 24 hours and once again we were able to sail. This was alright during the day but we had to negotiate several island passages during the night with lots of shipping about and those shallows as well, it made for interesting navigation and a few more grey hairs.

We arrived in Darwin early morning shortly after dawn and anchored in Fannie Bay near John and Jane who had got in the night before, Richard our rally organiser came out in a boat to meet us on arrival and took Audrey and Jane ashore to do the necessary paperwork. He had also arranged for the divers to do the Mussel Treatment, this is a requirement for any vessel arriving at Darwin and before entering a marina. The Black Striped Mussel is a pest and very prevalent in the Torres Straight, it is also very aggressive; it grows very quickly and blocks the inlets to engine cooling and toilets. The Australian authorities are trying to control its progress so spray all hull openings with a deterrent and even run the fluid round the engine cooling and toilet systems. This is a free service paid for by the Australian Government which we were pleased to hear, their thinking is that it's in their own interest to ensure it's done. You are given a clearance certificate when they complete it which allows you to enter a marina. We received permission to moor in Tipperary Marina but it was not possible to book in till the next day, so we blew up the dinghy and took a run ashore, it was nice to be back in civilisation again.

Early next morning well before dawn and in complete darkness, there wasn't even a moon, we up anchored and headed round to the Tipperary Marina. The first part of the trip was alright although the many lights of the town shrouded all the navigation marks until we were right on top of them. As we had to go outside three yellow quick flashing cardinal buoys marking hazards inshore there was no room for mistakes and the tide was falling. Dawn came and we could see where we were going, round the corner and up the river. Following the directions we found the marina entrance and had to go through a small lock one boat at a time. They gave us a temporary berth so we were unable to plug in to electricity, however, true to their word, we moved into a permanent berth with all facilities two days later, it was also much more convenient for toilet, showers and laundry. We found the Dinah Beach Club just along from the marina and enjoyed a few social occasions, great food, reasonable prices and really cold beer, what more could you ask.

If only life was that easy, while in Darwin I had to investigate why the engine was still overheating and would not rev above 1600, then do an engine service before the long Indonesian trip, Another job to do here was our anchor winch, it still needed urgent surgery, every time we used it I was still hitting the casing with the hammer to free off the brushes to make it work. I stripped down the winch motor again, the brushes as suspected were sticking in their holders and also badly worn, I would have to find a supplier to order a new set. Oh well, nothing changes then!

Chapter 12

Darwin, and on to Indonesia

Tony

Didn't take long to find a supplier for our winch motor brushes, the marina manager had a list of marine services and dealers, the only problem was getting to it about 5 miles away. Fortunately our friend John had hired a car for a few days and also needed some parts picking up, within a few hours all bits were ordered and I hot footed it back to Cayuco to start stripping down the exhaust system. Our problem with the engine cooling system was persisting, although I had changed the impellor on the raw water pump, checked all the hoses, cleaned out all the heat exchanger membranes, it still would not run over 1600 revs without overheating. I decided to check the exhaust system for a blockage; it had probably never been cleaned out since new.

Darwin is a very hot place, probably the hottest we had yet encountered, working on the engine exhaust system was tortuous. It took two days to strip it down and rebuild it, I cleaned the internal parts of the cast iron water traps with acid, leaving it for a couple of hours before washing out. It has to be said; I found nothing convincing that would be causing the overheating problem, after a meticulous reconstruction, checking all the exhaust passages were clear and cleanliness of all the items, a trial of the engine showed little improvement. I even checked the inlet and exhaust valve clearances in the unlikely case one of them had closed up and was holding a valve open, the injection timing was spot on; any engineer would discern from this I was desperately clutching at straws. I knew the inlet manifold was clear because there was no air filter, in 1971 when this engine was fitted, air cleaning devices were not deemed necessary, the intake manifold was just a curved tube allowing air straight into the cylinders, so discounted that as a source of the problem. As far as what else to do I was losing it, to me, at the time, there seemed no logical explanation, I even thought about fitting a new raw water pump, but after removing it, hiking around the suppliers, even trying to find a second hand one from the fishing marina scrap dealer, a check on the flow rate revealed it was in excess of what was required. My friend John, from Penelope 3, would have a suitable expression for this type of situation, he would solemnly declare that:-

"He was losing the will to live" and that's about how I felt.

Anyway, I had done everything I could on the engine for now, the new brushes were ordered for the winch, we had a few days left, it was time to take in the sites, scenery and check out our environment while having some fun.

Audrey

John and Jane had invited us to a day out in the car they had hired, so armed with a couple of tourist brochures we headed for the rivers and wetlands all around Darwin. We also wanted to combine the trip with some shopping and storing up for the next passage using the bigger out of town supermarkets. Driving along we went through Palmerston and headed further inland, on the way I was amused to see a town called Humpty Do and thought only in Australia, what an arresting name, it was lovely. We continued on into the bush and came across a turning down a lane into a visitors centre, we decided to take a river cruise to see the salt water crocodiles but first, as it was getting near lunch time, a bite to eat was in order.

The river trip was extraordinary, the setting itself is photogenic but when they started attracting the crocodiles around the boat it was daunting, they were not babies but full grown 15 to 18 foot adult crocs and we were feet away from them. OK, we were behind a glass window but they did look big and awesome, I could be forgiven for wondering just how strong the glass was. The skipper stopped the cruise boat in mid river, the crew had a long pole with a piece of meat dangling from it, they dunked this in the water and then pulled it up to two or three feet above the surface, they kept doing this for a few minutes. Eventually a huge crocodile swam out from the reeds on the riverbank; it tried to grab the meat but the crewman pulled it up out of its reach. After a bit more teasing the crocodile jumped right up after the meat with only its tail section left in the water, it was a spectacular sight requiring more photos, we were glad of the protection offered by the window. This technique was employed at various locations along the river and we were left in no uncertain terms as to just how many crocs there are in the rivers around Darwin, no wonder there is a proliferation of "No Swimming" signs. In fact all along the northern coast of Australia is a known crocodile danger area, the long pristine white sand beaches are devoid of holiday makers and sun worshippers, what with the crocodiles on land and the sharks in the sea, it could be an unhealthy pastime except in known protected areas. Whatever, it was a good day out and we both relaxed for a few hours, we finished off the day with a good meal and a couple of drinks at the Dinah Beach Club.

Next day towards evening in the Darwin Sailing Club there was a briefing for the subsequent leg of the rally to Indonesia; we heard how our visas were progressing and most of the rally had a get-together in the Club afterwards. The information regarding Indonesia was somewhat worrying; the recent changes in the rules regarding sailing boats entering the country were confused. According to information that some of our rally friends had received via the internet, yachts on a previous rally which had left some days before had been impounded and held until the paperwork was sorted out. This was in fact true but after a few days they were released and apologies all round ensued, it was a case of over reactive authorities, but it didn't help our thinking about going to the place at all. On a cruise of this nature, due to the length of time it takes, lots of things can change in different countries while on the way round, one just has to keep one's ear to the ground and not get caught out. We were lucky, our rally team were very experienced in these types of problem and they communicated all up to date news as and when necessary, they also negotiated on our behalf for the various permissions needed to sail in Indonesian waters, it was good to have them on our side.

While waiting for our winch motor brushes to arrive we found a good internet cafe to chat to family, Darwin is a very busy centre for bush and outback activities, young and old constantly came and went in search of the real outback experience, due to this influx of people, internet cafes and chat rooms were flourishing.

I had an energy spurt and during the cool of the early morning on two successive days I managed to wash down the boat and give the bright work a polish. Tony got hold of the winch motor brushes and some new fuel filters for the bosun's store, it was nearly time to be on our way again.

While we were tied up in Tipperary Marina, Tony heard of a Japanese guy along the pontoon who could fix computers, as ours had now died completely he thought he might as well give him the computer and let him do his worst. The next day, computer was returned working in all respects. We were both amazed, it had been written off by two separate companies who had tried to get us to buy a new one. We were told it was just the motherboard battery which needed replacing, what do you know? Three dollars for a new battery and a six pack for the guy and we were back in business. Turns out he was a computer programmer, been in the business for years, writes his own programmes, builds his own units and was taking a sabbatical to enjoy his other passion of sailing, you just never know who you are going to meet next.

Tony

When the winch motor brushes arrived, a quick check confirmed they were too long, too wide and too thick for the holders, no problem, a small sheet of emery cloth, a few rubs up and down with the brushes on the sheet and hey presto, perfectly fitting set of new brushes, don't you just love it when a plan comes together. With the motor rebuilt we had a working anchor winch again, I even wrapped thick plastic sheet around the motor and taped it on with duct tape to ensure it would not let sea water in again.

All the paperwork for leaving Australia and entering Indonesia had been completed, it was with a sad heart we left Tipperary Marina early morning on Thursday 9th October 2008 and headed for the fuel jetty on Fishermans Wharf, it was hard to leave Australia. After refuelling we continued out of the harbour and sailed down the channel, there are lots of shoal patches around Darwin so we kept to the main channel until in deeper water and then set course for Bali. As we left Darwin an unusual sight met our gaze, on the way in was a huge oil rig being towed by an ocean going tug, very odd seeing an oil rig on tow, not something you bump into every day. I entered the details into our log and took the requisite photo of the unusual event; I remembered I had only seen this twice before, once along the south coast of UK and before that in 1981 approaching Singapore Harbour.

Along the route to Bali are the small coral atolls of Ashmore and Cartier Islands, they are about 450 miles out of Darwin and can in calm weather give a unique anchorage for a night. They are only slightly off the track so we had decided to sail close by them and make a decision whether to stop for a rest at the time.

This turned out to be a very windless passage; we had not had anything as calm as this since the Panama to Galapagos voyage. We always tried to sail whenever there was wind but there was precious little of that.

Ever since leaving Darwin we had also been over flown by the Australian Coastguard planes, first they would fly past us and ask us all the required questions then a few minutes later we would hear them calling up Penelope 3 some miles ahead of us and asking the same questions all over again. It must have rang some bells when I answered Cayuco from Portsmouth, England and then John answered Penelope 3 from Portsmouth, England, although we had not met before the rally, both yachts were registered and sailed from the same port. I understand the need for the Australian authorities to take care in their coastal waters, but when this happened five or six times, day and night, it got a bit much, especially when less than an hour after the last call we also got questioned by the Australian Coastguard Vessel Harvey Bay. To make matters even more hilarious, we were heading away from Australia, so heaven knows how much more concerned they would be if we were heading towards it.

During this trip there were lots of dolphin sightings and the quiet conditions meant you could see the wake they left and the splash as they re-entered the water. We also saw sea snakes and birds, a small bird landed on board for a rest and quite brazenly sat on the stern cabin completely ignoring how close we were, always amazes us how friendly and confident these little birds are when you're at sea. We have had them in the cockpit with us, even sitting on Audrey's head and shoulder while I took a photograph.

By the 12th October we had given up the idea of anchoring on Ashmore and Cartier Atoll, we sailed slowly past and just kept going, it was to be a slow passage anyway.

Gradually we sailed, then motored, then sailed again, before we knew it we were in the Indian Ocean proper, the depth came up to 700 feet (250 metres) as we crossed the Scott Plateau or the shoals near to the reefs. The temperature was still well over 35°C during the day and it didn't drop very much at night, we didn't bother wearing any clothes, didn't need anything to keep warm and it saved on the laundry. To keep cool and have an air flow through the boat we had left all our hatches open, one night a flying fish jumped straight through the fore hatch and landed on the floor, unfortunately for the fish, we didn't find it until the morning.

We drifted, motored, drifted again, sailed a bit, this was getting boring, but boring is good, it meant nothing had broken and nothing had gone wrong, the weather was calm, we could relax, read a book, let Cayuco drift along all by itself, it was great.

We drifted past the island of Sumba some 50 miles off, there were still large pot like buoys floating on the surface with tall flags on them, we thought there may be nets hanging below so sailed slowly past, we saw nothing in the water but they may have been marking lobster pots or such like, so carried slowly on.

Gradually we closed our destination, the night before we got in there was a sudden squall, wind and lots of rain, took me by surprise on watch, had to dash round closing all hatches, shortening sail and crouched under the cockpit cover sheltering. It was surprisingly cold rain but it refreshed the whole boat and cooled everything down, got quite a good sleep after. There was an increase in commercial traffic as we approached Bali; this is one of the major routes through the Indonesian Islands with shipping heading for Singapore and the South China Sea. There were also more whales, we saw a pod of them with an occasional burst of spray from their blowholes; it always fascinates both of us when we see this happening.

As we approached Bali early morning on the 18th October the current in the Lombok Channel was very strong and against us. At this time of year, the current almost always flows south through the passages between the Islands, it flows from the South China Sea to the Indian Ocean. Any respite from the current in this channel is only for an hour or two at most, if at all. It was the north east monsoon season and our onward passage was through here, we knew it would be difficult to motor against this current when the time came, so we were going to have to use a bit of cunning. For now we just kept pushing on against it until the current eased enough for us to get into Benoa Harbour in Bali, we located the marina and slipped into our waiting berth. The officials were ready for us, the charming and helpful Harbour Master organised all our paperwork and was the first to make a joke about the amount of it.

We were both pleasantly surprised by Bali and Indonesia; it is well worth making the effort to obtain visas and CAIT (Clearance Approval for Indonesia Territory). The really great thing on this passage was that Cayuco had not broken anything, nor had anything gone wrong, even the engine was fine as long as we didn't exceed 1500 revs. As 1250 revs gave us 5 knots, there was not much point in going any faster and using more fuel than necessary, I just kept wondering what the problem could be.

Audrey

The day after we arrived and as we had nothing else to do, we joined John and Jane and hired a taxi for the day, works out very cheap with four of you. It was still very hot but as we climbed up above sea level it became more comfortable. We were all heading for a local park with scenic walks, the highlight of which would be a ride on an elephant. Arriving at the park we all bought a ticket; this entitled us to an elephant ride and included a local lunch together with all the beauty of the walks around the park.

The elephant ride was unusual to say the least; we both sat in the chair on the animals back while the Indonesian rubber man, the driver, clambered round the elephant as though he was a trapeze artist. He balanced on the elephant's neck swinging round and underneath, alongside and over its head and all over the place while it was walking along. We did the long elephant walk round the park, took more photos and had a good view of all the gardens from our vantage point. At the end of the ride, the elephant, with us still on its back, walked into a large pond, the water came half way up its body which the elephant loved; it enabled him to cool off and throw some water about, (it enjoyed this bit as well). It then walked out of the pond and proceeded to perform a balancing act with all four feet standing on a small handy tree stump about a foot high, the elephant then sat down on the tree stump causing all of us to fall backwards but not quite out of the basket. Following this we were allowed to get off and after unceremoniously dismounting bought some mangoes and fed them to our friendly steed. Of course the whole ride was punctuated with a photo session so some fantastic photos were obtained by both parties on elephant back. The handler explained that the elephants name was Tony but we supposed he might just change it to suit the circumstances.

Then it was another walk through the picturesque gardens and into the hall for a really well prepared lunch all washed down by a couple of Indonesia's finest brew, a wonderful half day out so far. Back in the taxi the driver took us the long way round and showed us as many of the sights as possible, there is so much to do in Bali, it's impossible to do it in one day. We visited the monkey park and accidently arrived during a feeding session so they were very active, more photos. We drove through a main commercial area and had a little time for some retail therapy; I managed to purchase some very well made and unusual cotton garments, all individually handmade and at an extremely competitive price, I vowed to come back again in a few days when we had more time. It was like having your own designer label.

The trip round Bali was truly a fascinating journey, everything so different from Australia, everywhere we went reflected local culture and traditions, there were little shrines everywhere and all the establishments no matter what it was had a little flower basket at the entrance. The final part of our taxi ride took us to an area of large temples and shrines right on the beach, there were a number of them, some perched on the top of little islands just offshore, it was possible to walk to them when the tide was out. They were all highly decorated and covered in murals depicting various religious carvings, we were told it was a very revered area, some places had restrictions on actual entry and the complex had been in existence for many hundreds of years. After a wonderful day we returned with our driver back to the Yacht Club and finished the day off with a chat and a glass of wine.

We had started to realise that Indonesia is a much underrated country, the paperwork trail before arriving is tortuous and it was fortunate that our experienced advisors dealt with most of it. The attractions were starting to outweigh the difficulties, having now seen just a small part of Indonesia, we realised it was well worth the effort and we looked forward to seeing as much as possible while we were here.

The next day while Tony did some work on the engine trying to find out why it still wasn't performing as well as it should be, I went shopping to renew our stores. Bali being a main tourist centre is very well subscribed with shops, supermarkets and all other retailers abound, sometimes their enthusiasm to get you into the shop can be a bit overwhelming.

At least the computer now worked well which enabled us to chat to our family at home, these regular little updates kept us in touch and were a welcome break.

Figure 25: lets go elephant riding in Bali.

Tony

All I could do with the engine was to keep on looking, there had to be something wrong, I hoped there was nothing serious developing that would eventually delay us, not being able to keep up with the rest of the fleet was not an option. All the major parts appeared to be ok so I felt a little bit re-assured by that. While I toiled away, Audrey ordered some large bottles of water, the type that sit on top of water machines in offices and slowly she proceeded to fill up our stocks of bottled water one by one, it was a lot cheaper to do it this way..

An assortment of rally boats were now arriving; some had checked in at Kupang on the south west tip of Timor and then cruised through the Spice Islands, visiting the islands of Komodo, Sumba or Sumbawa on the way to Bali. It was all systems go while they all tried to fuel and stock up for the next leg to Nongsa Point Marina and then on to Singapore. Some local men on the quay wanted to clean and polish the hull and topsides; although normally this is work we would have completed ourselves we were tempted to let them do it. First of all they work very reasonably, but secondly, as one of them explained to us, there was very little work for them locally. One man in particular convinced us to let him loose with our tin of polish and a couple of dusters; he did an excellent job and worked through the heat of the day. He was meticulous, in the end he worked for two days and Cayuco gleamed brightly at the finish.

Over a snack lunch he explained that he lived on a 50 foot sailing boat just along from the marina with his wife and family, his dream was to prepare it for the tourist trade and then licence it for trips out to watch the whales, dolphins and take dive tours out around the islands. We wished him well for the future and gave him a little extra for his good work on Cayuco plus a large bag of rice purchased especially for him and his family, I only wish we could have given him more.

Time was marching on and we were getting close to leaving, there was no rally information here, we had been briefed for the whole run to Nongsa Point Marina before leaving Darwin, we did however, manage to get hold of some updates of the new marina and more importantly the entrance with a shoal bank right outside it.

We all did one more shopping trip around the market in Kuta; Audrey managed to put together a few tops and trousers, all at very good prices and unusual designs. In retrospect she wished she had been a bit more adventurous and bought more. The evening before we left we all went ashore again to the Yacht Club, I had decided to try the delicious Nasi-Goring again before I left, it is a lovely inexpensive meal, cooked in a stir fry method and the main meat can be chicken, lamb, prawns or more probably what is available. It contains egg noodles and various local vegetables like bean sprouts, water chestnuts, carrots, in fact anything to hand and is mouth-watering as a vegetarian option as well. It is all lightly cooked together in a local sauce, with the natural flavour and juices from the ingredients, plus a helping of rice and maybe a dash of soy sauce, prepared properly, it is absolutely delicious.

John and Jane in Penelope 3 left Bali early on Saturday morning; they together with some other rally boats wanted to stop off and visit the Orang-utan reserve in Kalimantan Province on the Island of Borneo. Leaving Bali Marina in the north east season is probably the best time of year weather-wise but it poses a problem in getting north up the Lombok Strait, the current flows south strongly nearly all the time, when the tide changes to flow the other way it only has the effect of slowing down the south going current. If you catch the tide right, it's possible to get nearly half way the first day and anchor in a very picturesque bay on Lembongan Island, this was our plan. Our departure was timed for two hours before low tide slack water when the current in the channel should have been at its weakest for the next four hours; we would be out of the marina and into the strait before the weaker current started.

At 09-30 hours on Sunday 26th October we slipped our lines and left, the water in the marina was very dirty, a recent heavy rain storm had disturbed a lot of debris where it had got caught up between the moored vessels. As a result I had not started the engine until we had removed all but one line which we had doubled up as a slip, it was then a case of, start the engine, move into gear and pull the last line in as we left, I wanted to minimise the risk of getting a blocked water inlet, we already had enough problems with engine overheating.

Our plan worked fairly well, we negotiated the channel out through the reef and waved at the fishermen. They stand for hours, up to their waists in the water, fishing poles dangling over the coral, catching anything big enough to eat. We kept well inshore to escape the last of the south going current, even had a little back eddy which helped us along till the first headland, had to be careful of the inshore reef, there was already one large local fishing boat stranded on it and we did not want to be the second. Round the headland and into the next bay gave us another slight lift, but not as much as before, we clawed our way north of Lembongan Island before turning across the current and heading for the anchorage picking up a local mooring about 16-00 hrs. You are allowed to use these moorings in the evening; they are for tourist boats which come across from the mainland during the day and are only used between 10-00 and 16-00 Hrs.

An analysis of our route showed we had probably used the right tactics, the fifteen mile passage had taken nearly six hours and we had over thirty miles on the log. In fact a bigger yacht than us left Bali at the same time, he stayed out in mid channel, an hour after we were safely moored we observed him slowly motoring north past the point about a mile off the island. For the next two hours he was almost stationary against the current and anchored near our position just before nightfall. I silently patted myself on the back for our use of tactics which had probably been honed during years of sailing around the Channel Islands and the South Coast of England, if you don't get it right around there, you go backwards fast.

A very peaceful night with the added bonus of a good sleep, we were up at the crack of dawn and motored away from Lembongan Island, we ate breakfast on the hoof with the sun coming up over the horizon. By noon we were in position $08°\ 22'S$, $115°\ 42.4'E$, if you plot this position on a chart, it will give you an idea of how close we hugged the shore to get up the Lombok Channel. There were times when we could have thrown a stone onto the beach and were in less than 6 metres of water, whatever, our strategy worked and by mid afternoon we were sailing offshore with a 15 knot breeze from the north- west.

During this close encounter with the shoreline, we passed row after row of small local fishing canoes pulled up on the beach, there appeared to be hundreds of them and every little village we went by was the same. Shortly after ten a.m. they all took to the sea, skimming across the waves at surprising speeds, we supposed they were fishing but it looked like they were having great fun, some of them shot by very close and we got some lovely pictures. They have three very slim hulls are about 5 metres long, extremely light weight with a triangular brightly coloured lanteen sail, each with one person aboard and obviously suited to the generally light wind conditions of these parts.

With a nice breeze we sailed along just offshore of Bali Island heading for the Karang Channel, a gap south of Saubi Island between Goa Goa Island and the Karang Takat Reef, this leads from the Bali Sea into the Java Sea. A lot of care needs to be taken sailing between all the islands in Indonesia, a great deal of the near 1000 mile passage is around a hundred feet deep (about 35 metres) and there are reefs, low lying atoll type islets as well as high volcanic islands. It has an extremely varied topography and it's the ones you can't see that cause the trouble. Many sailing boats have come to grief in this region, as well as the shoals there are also the fishing traps and the local fishing boats to contend with, a lot of them when steaming at night do not bother with navigation lights. Others have extremely bright lights to attract the fish, when sailing through a fleet at night it is very confusing, there is no respite from this, wherever you sail it is the same, fishing is a main source of income here and there are thousands of boats engaged in the activity. It is unlikely any of them will move for you, it's a case of keeping out of the way of them at all times, you are the trespasser and there is no relaxing on watch day or night through these waters. The fishing traps are static structures floating on the surface and anchored to the seabed. They have few distinguishing marks, are sometimes difficult to see, some fairly big, others quite small, they are all over the place, shallow and deep water, unlit, don't show up on radar at all well and are a real hazard at night.

It is also a very busy commercial shipping route, the South China Sea is to the north, Malacca strait and Singapore to the west, with Australia and the Pacific Islands to the east it is a preferred short cut. We saw many large ships at random times, one night three ships all converged on our position simultaneously at a branch of two channels. They passed close on both sides all intent on each other, our AIS worked admirably, although none of them had taken the time to enter their name on the transmission, I wondered afterwards if they had seen us at all. As we sailed offshore of Java, I considered whether to pass close to the island of Krakatoa which has resurrected itself and is known locally as Anak Krakatoa, (Baby Krakatoa), it started erupting again in August 2008 and was still active in October as we sailed nearby. We decided against taking a detour, the wind was light and the current there is worse than the Lombok

Channel, with our existing engine problem still manifesting itself, it was not a good idea.

We continued heading on our course to pass north of Pulau Belitung, an island 200 hundred miles north of Jakarta, it is a major crossroads for shipping and the shallow sea makes for good fishing so there is an abundance of boats. The island has a chain of reefs and islets stretching nearly 50 miles to the north east, currents are strong and unpredictable, the weather pattern is fickle with sudden violent squalls giving extremely reduced visibility, i.e. less than 50 metres and including thunder and lightning. By the time we reached here, the two of us had been doing a watch and watch about system for seven days and we were getting tired, need I say more.

Having successfully negotiated the perils of Pulau Belitung's reef and moved into the Java Sea our next 300 miles was fairly straightforward, all we had to contend with now was the commercial shipping, fishing boats, the occasional fish trap, squalls and yes of course, I'd forgot, fog, and an adverse current, Oh well, mustn't have it all our own way I suppose!

The wind remained very light but we sailed whenever it was feasible, our fuel reserves were also good so we were relatively happy with our progress. As we sailed we were gradually being set north, not really a problem as the wind, what there was of it, slowly backed from north-east to north-west and made it more like a beat. Drifting north would help us sailing west when the time came and as we approached the channel up to Batam Island our intended landfall.

We developed an unusual way of sailing, instead of trying to avoid the squalls, we searched them out, we had discovered that if you let a squall overtake you, the wind gave you a boost for between half an hour and up to a couple of hours. With the correct trajectory you could slingshot from one squall to the next and keep sailing for much longer than you would normally be able to. There were a lot of squalls, at any time they could be clearly seen sliding majestically along the skyline; it was not unusual to see five or six even more at any one time. Before the end of our passage we had perfected this technique quite well, OK it meant sailing a greater distance and the course was a bit unpredictable but it saved a lot of fuel. As you approach the Equator squalls get confused and can be erratic in their behaviour so any wind generated can come from almost any direction, you just have to be ready for any changes.

All went according to plan until we were further north of Pulau Belitung than intended and well off our rhumb line to Batam Island. We were hit by a really big squall, we'd seen it coming by eye and tried to check its size on the radar without success, we tried to move out of its way, it looked huge and mean. I'd reefed down well and it was inevitable that it would hit us, the first front roared over us with an intensity that we had rarely encountered, lightening was hitting the water simultaneously all around the boat, the noise of thunder was deafening. Cayuco heeled over to the violent gusts and sped off while we tried to regain some degree of control over our direction, the rain was intense, a real tropical stair rod rain, visibility was reduced to no more than 20 metres, if that. The radar had blanked out entirely even on the 12 mile scale, the whole screen was pink, I adjusted the contrast but all that did was to cut out everything else, this was a really bad one and it did not relent, an hour later we were still in it. Before the squall hit I had checked the radar and horizon for ships, this gave us a little confidence as usually you are through the squall before too long and minimise the risk of collision when visibility is seriously impaired. This squall lasted much too long, we had not seen more than a few feet for over an hour and we were still well heeled and hurtling along. I was reluctant to reduce sail further as for once we were sailing fast in the right direction, nevertheless, it started to get worrying. We both took up positions on either side of the cockpit and started to do a continual 360° sweep of our tiny world. A short while after we started this lookout, a large ship appeared through the haze directly in front of us and very very close, it was steaming past our bow no more than 50 feet away and most of it had already gone past. Shooting across its stern Cayuco gave a shrug and came upright momentarily as the wind faded around the ships structure, within seconds we were back sailing and the ship had disappeared.

It all happened so quickly we never even saw the name, perhaps it was the last thing on our minds at the time. Checking the radar gave us no assistance, the screen was still a blank mass of pink, I tried different ranges from a quarter to 12 miles to no avail, the squall had shut down the entire screen and even the AIS had not picked it up.

I'm told that small ship radar, due to the band frequency it works on and the relatively low power of the unit, can suffer from this problem in extreme conditions. By maritime law commercial ships use two different radar sets, both of which have different band widths and use a lot more power, this, in theory should alleviate them from having our kind of situation, I only hope that's true and he did see us, but I have my doubts.

Our intermittent sailing and motoring continued for the next few days, we watched dolphins and the occasional sea snake while commercial traffic became more and more frequent as we approached Singapore.

The next milestone was our 2nd crossing of the Equator, remember, remember, the 5th of November, well that's the day we crossed back into the northern hemisphere, 05-40 in the morning 83 miles south of Singapore. A new cocktail was made-up, we called it "The Equator", apologies, but we were severely limited on mixers, it consisted of Woods 100% rum, ice and apricot juice, this was only because we needed to toast King Neptune but couldn't handle neat Wood's rum at that time in the morning. Neptune got his neat though just as the sun came up to start the new day. Audrey took some photographs to remember the occasion but as I was still sailing naked their inclusion has had to be prohibited, it was over 30ºC even at that time in the morning and much too warm for clothes.

Later in the day a small swallow landed in the cockpit, it was quite tame and sat on the hatch top before deciding the top of Audrey's head was a much more comfortable place. After a while it hopped down to her arm for a photo shoot. A few hours later, nicely rested, it flew up above Cayuco, circled for a few minutes and took off carrying on with its original journey, we wished it well.

On Thursday 6th November at dawn we were 25 miles from our destination and entering the channel between Bintan and Batam Islands, with the adverse current our prediction was to be in Nongsa Point Marina by around lunch time. By 10-00 hours we were only about 6 miles from the marina, still with a light wind we were motor sailing, the engine started to run hotter even though I throttled back to almost tick over speed, it was no good, I would have to shut off the engine and sail the rest of the way in. A Dutch yacht "Prue of Holland", also on the rally came up behind us and volunteered to tow us in the last few miles. I have to admit, I was at a low ebb, a lifetimes experience with diesel engines and I was unable to determine the fault, it was the first time I could remember when I had not been able to solve a mechanical problem with any engine. I had forgotten that feeling of failure, the emotion of inadequacy was hard to bear; I swore to myself that when we got in, I was not leaving until our overheating problem was solved.

The marina was informed of our predicament and as we approached gave us a temporary berth on the outside finger pontoon which made it a lot easier to moor up.

After checking in and completing the usual paperwork, the temptation was to start stripping down the engine straight away, fortunately I voted against this and with others who had recently arrived, forgot all about the work and decided to experience the quality of the local refreshment in the bar. A meal later on in the evening finished off the day and we both retired happy to our berth, my mind however, had not retired and the thought of trying to find the problem tomorrow haunted me for most of the night.

Waking up next morning I felt more positive, going through all the symptoms so far encountered in my mind I had come to the conclusion it had to be caused by a blockage somewhere in the inlet or exhaust system. I had checked and rechecked all the usual remedies and had found nothing conclusive, it was time for a thorough strip down until I found something tangible.

Audrey decided to go shopping with Jane and keep out of the way, I arranged all the tools needed to strip down and remove the inlet and exhaust manifolds as a start to bigger things later. The night before I had been explaining what I had to do with Peter our

Nongsa Point and Singapore rally co-ordinator, he said he knew of a local diesel man who might be able to help and would try to contact him in the morning.

As I returned to the business of dismantling the manifolds, I heard a knock on the side of the hull; it was our local diesel man. It was a hot morning so a cool drink of fruit juice was in order; while we drank I explained our dilemma and what I was doing to attempt a cure. He was a Perkins man from way back explaining that when he started in the business as a lad, Perkins engines were used in the local tractors and he had developed his company from there to the marine side of today. He recognised our engine as an old standard Perkins 4236 model immediately and clearly knew all about them, let's face it, they are used worldwide on any number of applications and have a reputation for reliability and long life. Listening to my diatribe of woe, he also explained how these symptoms were synchronistic with an air flow problem with which I agreed, hence my current work schedule.

We put our drinks aside for a moment and together we undid the bolts and removed the manifolds, as we separated the inlet manifold from the engine a large wad of hard black oily fragments dropped from between the two items. We just looked at each other, it was clearly obvious what had been causing the problem; a smile grew across my face. The inside of the inlet manifold was almost completely blocked with debris; it looked like a bird's nest had been sucked in and stuck across the inlet tubes. I thumped the air with my fist and cried "EUREKA", or maybe it was "GERONIMO", whatever, I had found the problem. I was ecstatic. By the time Audrey returned from her shopping trip, the engine was back together and running, no overheating, maximum revs, no black smoke and full power. As we had to move from our temporary berth I cast off and took Cayuco round the marina and gave the engine a blast outside and back in again then moored up on our new berth, at last everything was working correctly.

Audrey

When we arrived at Nongsa Point the engine had almost given up on us, I knew Tony was depressed, he took it as a personal slight that he could not solve the problem. He had overcome all the situations that this voyage had thrown at us, his specialty had always been engines and mechanical thingamajigs of any description. In all my life with him for the last 37 years I had never known him to fail in sorting out problems with an engine or anything mechanical and one hell of a lot of other things. When I went shopping with Jane to get out of the way, I was dreading returning, I knew Tony would not move until he had sorted the engine out, nothing will waver him from what he has focussed on doing. I walked down the pontoon to where Cayuco was tied up, the marina attendant tried to tell me to walk to the left but I knew Cayuco was to the right, he kept on and I tried to ignore him, he chased me and said

"That way, that way",

I knew better and said

"no, this way", I walked down the pontoon and Cayuco was not there, I started to listen to the attendant, to be honest, I was so lost in my thoughts regarding the problem that I was not really concentrating on what he had been trying to say. As I walked back to the other pontoon, Tony approached me, he was all smiles, I dare not think that anything had been sorted, it would not be the first time he had kept the full reality of the situation from me by showing a happy countenance, as yet I had to be convinced. It didn't take him long however to explain what had happened, this was really good news for us, we were approaching the part of the rally where it was more essential to have a reliable engine. The short crossing of the Singapore Strait alone was next, although it was only about 6 miles across, there were four shipping lanes which dealt with the larger ships and two inshore lanes for the smaller ones. With ferries, ships entering and leaving and some rushing straight by, it's probably the busiest stretch of water in the world. That evening to celebrate our success we joined a group of about 15 others from the rally and took a taxi round to the nearby Turi Resort, here there is a selection of restaurants catering for a wide variety of tastes, it was wonderful having solved the engine problem, we both relaxed more than we had for a long time.

Most of us were leaving soon but I went into the local town centre with a few others to refresh our stores, what an experience, biggest collection of unrecognisable fruit and vegetables that I've ever seen! We have lived and worked abroad in developing countries for years and it took me by surprise, there were big tanks of live goldfish and catfish for sale; puts fast food into another category. I purchased a few basics, the trip across to the Singapore Yacht Club was only a few miles and we would have to stock up again before leaving there. On our last night the marina put on a BBQ for all of us, it was a fitting end to our Indonesian experience. It included BBQ kebabs, chicken legs, fish steaks and various meats it may have been prudent not to ask what they were, no matter, it was very good grub with local salads and rice all washed down with the local beer and wine, a good night was had by all.

Tony

On the 9th November we left Nongsa Point Marina for the Singapore Yacht Club, our paperwork for clearance out of Indonesia had been completed the day before and a group of rally boats left just before 09-00 hours. It is a very short passage; I think the shortest since the start in Gibraltar when we crossed over to Morocco ostensibly to carry out a radio check. The Singapore Strait was very busy as usual but we all crossed safely, it was a matter of cruising slowly along the Batam shoreline while watching for gaps in the shipping, gauging their speeds and then making a dash for it, even so great care has to be exercised. We crossed over without having to avoid too many leviathans, our engine now behaving better and able to hold full revs without problem. Sailing past Sentosa Island and the Singapore Merlion still spouting water on the seafront we were moored in our berth in the Singapore Yacht Club by 14-30 hours.

Both of us were looking forward to Singapore, we had not been here since 1981 and at that time thoroughly enjoyed the experience, we had a cup of tea and contemplated the next few days while waiting on board for the instruction to proceed to the office and complete our entry formalities.

Chapter 13

Singapore and Malaysia

Tony

The marina at the Singapore Yacht Club is a bit of a disappointment, the club is a fantastic complex but the marina itself is right next to a commercial port and is not the cleanest of places. An oily film on the water pervades the moorings while the frequent 24/7 fast ferries and crew launches using the facilities alongside cause an incessant wash rolling through the marina, requests from the club to come and go at a more leisurely pace have been ignored. Warps need constant attention, fenders and topsides take a beating and the continual snubbing makes life onboard uncomfortable, as somewhere to relax it didn't work.

We moved three times trying to find a more comfortable berth but in the end we gave up and left, this was a shame because the club itself is marvellous and has wonderful amenities. If we ever sail into Singapore again it would be to another marina, there are others nearby at similar prices, more peaceful and most are nearer the centre.

Enough of the moaning, I had to finish off the engine service, change both fuel filters and check the gearbox oil level plus all the systems for our next passage, I was happier with Cayuco now, we seemed to have got rid of most of our engine problems although the heat exchanger still had a tiny leak on the cooling system. I cleaned out the bilge again as we were still getting rubbish into the bilge pump strum box, this was causing an intermittent fault and kept stopping the pump working. We had wiper motors and blades on the doghouse windows, these had not been working since the gale in the Coral Sea so I freed them off, greased them up and got them working again.

Figure 26:The Singapore "Merlion" as you sail along the front towards the Singapore yacht club

Audrey

The Singapore Yacht Club Marina did not live up to expectations and it was more than a bit below par. It was next morning just before a violent thunder storm that we managed to hook up our electric lead; sometimes this takes a bit of time when sorting out all the different types of connections that various marinas use.

At least the internet worked well, this was a bonus since we had not had a lot of success since leaving Australia, the internet service in Indonesia was still patchy, we even had a quick msn type written conversation with family at 2 pm, in Singapore this time it coincided with them getting up for work in UK.

Tonight it was John and Jane's turn on Penelope 3 to buy dinner, so a good evening was had by all, we ate in the yacht club bar on the first floor of the club; this gave all of us a wonderful view of the sunset.

On the 11th we all went into town for the day, did the popular river trip but these days there are no sampans or river dwellers, however the photographs still picked out the old town and we went down as far as the Singapore "Merlion". After a liquid lunch we visited Raffles Hotel for afternoon tea and sampled their "Gin Slings", all a tad extravagant but with every possibility we would never be in Singapore again it just had to be done. Another photography session in and around the hotel plus an excellent snap of the quite elegantly dressed doorman, turban and all, when we faxed a copy to our lads later he immediately became known as "Turban Dude", rather apt we thought.

Next day we moved berth to try and find a calmer spot, wasn't very successful, reminded me of our berth in Gibraltar; that was pretty awful as well, it's fair to say that it was worse than most anchorages we had used in open bays. The constant wash from the commercial ferries just caused us to sway and Cayuco kept snatching at each fore and aft movement. Tony tried many different combinations of warps configurations but none were successful.

Across the nearby West Park we found a local Chinese supermarket, had everything including the proverbial kitchen sink and all at reasonable prices so started our store up routine for the forthcoming passage to Malaysia. Had a fish and chip lunch in the Yacht Club on one day, excellent meal and very good value, thought we may try that again before we left.

The rally briefing for the next section to Thailand was on the 14th November with a party afterwards courtesy of RSYC, this included Chinese Lion and Dragon Dancers, all very spectacular. Other dancers performed their own local versions of displays, the colours of the costumes were vivid and the movements incredible, their levels of fitness were quite extreme. I was glad I took the camera, it was an amazing show and the pictures turned out well. Before the meeting I had also been able to take some good shots of the club from the balcony including the marina, the sunset and a rain cloud in the distance with a rainbow right across the sky, unfortunately the rainbow in the photograph never quite looked as impressive as it did on the night.

The next few days were spent fuelling and storing up; going through the usual checks, laundry and making lentil loaves, chilli con carne, lasagne and other simple foods to put in the freezer, this preparation makes life easier when sailing offshore.

The internet allowed me to chat with family although we never succeeded in getting the mike or cam facility to work; it was always by typing the conversation into the box and sending, a bit slow but better than nothing. We had a lot of thunder storms during our stay here, it was a continuation of the weather we had experienced all the way from Bali and we didn't think it would get much better in the near future.

The evening before leaving we took a last excursion into town and visited "Little India", sari, jewellery and souvenir shops abounded, we had been recommended to a restaurant and had a superb meal as only the Indians can produce. A wonderful relaxed atmosphere pervaded the whole evening even though we were the only white faces to be seen, Singapore really is a very safe place to walk about alone any time of day or night. In some ways we were not fond of the changes that have taken place in the last few years, the old character haunts like Change Alley, (an old bazaar street where real bartering took place), Boogey Street and the dock area has been "cleaned up" to the extent that it is now pretty much sterile and worst of all; modernised.

Our previous sojourn in 1981 while on a stopover in Singapore was much more exciting, Raffles was nearer the sea, Change Alley was famous for its cheap goods of any description, Boogey Street and the night life was more risky but exhilarating and colourful, we went back to the hotel in the early hours of the morning sitting in the back of a trishaw while defying the lanes of traffic on Orchard Road. The changes have not all been good and we both felt some of the life force had been strangled out of the city. Anyway, whatever we thought; it is a vibrant, exhilarating and safe place to spend a few days.

The time in Singapore was up, we had to move on and continue our journey along the Malacca Strait, a few years ago this area had its own piracy problem, but the authorities and the devastating 2004 Boxing Day Tsunami took out most of the bases that they worked from. Our next destination was to be Port Dickson and Admirals Marina in Malaysia, this is where we would check in, the excitement built as we were looking forward to this and the onward passage to Langkawi Island and Phuket.

Tony

On the 18th November we motored out of the Singapore Yacht Club and negotiated around the Low Island breakwater and anchorage just off the entrance, the weather was overcast and heavy, threatening another thunder storm. Leaving Singapore Island is the same as entering, you need eyes in the back of your head, large ships are restricted to very small channels and cannot move out of the way. Leaving in daylight with plenty of time to get clear is best; observe the correct side of the channel and keep on the edge or just outside of it. Being well marked and the major port there are no hidden dangers underwater unless you get a long way off course. As you leave there is the deep drilling oil rig manufacturing and fit out base close by on the starboard bow, it is an immense operation and is very impressive. Another half a mile and you pass the Pasir Panjang large container ship terminal on the port side, we kept to the starboard side of the channel and crept along the shore of Jurong Island. All the while there are ships, ferries, supply and crew launches, pilot boats, tugs plus lots of small fishing and private vessels charging about all over the place. It didn't get better as we made our way into deeper water, there was a huge land reclamation scheme going on in the vicinity of Jurong Island. Not only did we have all the other craft mentioned to contend with, now we came across tugs towing barges with material for the development and some returning empty to pick up more along the coast in Malaysia. The sheer volume of traffic was a nightmare, my log just reads, "shipping horrendous", thankfully we were leaving in daylight.

The passage was a short one of only 145 miles but it was north westwards along the Malacca Strait, due to the amount of shipping neither of us got much rest during the night. We left with Stargazer and as darkness fell we both realised that some of the barges being pulled by the tugs did not carry any lights, as it was a very dark night with no moon this was very dangerous for us. In the pitch black with no horizon it was impossible for us to pick out the silhouette on the skyline, all you heard was the water bubbling past the flat fronted craft as they slid past in the blackness well after the tug had gone. Stargazer had a very close call with one and actually bent their pulpit as it slid past in the dark, they were very lucky to get away without more serious damage, the main problem was that the barges were not towing straight and were careering to the right and left of the main tow. Just because you successfully negotiated the tug did not necessarily mean you would miss the barge, we had to give a lot of room as the tugs went past. The passage was further hampered as we were going west right on the edge of the main shipping channel i.e., in correct position, the tugs were coming up against our direction but just out of the main west channel and travelling east. Empty towed barges travelling only slightly faster than us also passed returning for a refill, it was all very fraught. Our one help was the huge thunderstorm raging all along the Singapore/Malaysian coast, every time the lightning flashed we tried to identify the shapes of the barges and ascertain exactly where they were and their direction, there seemed to be a hell of a lot of them.

It was a tired couple of crews that welcomed the daylight in the morning, we could see the tugs and barges earlier now but visibility was not good, with the overcast clouds and the humid conditions we still only had about three miles visibility.

Getting into Admiral Marina around 15-00 hours was a relief, by now we had realised that we were not going to be let off the hook that easily, the tugs were picking up somewhere along the Malaysian coast and we thought we may have the same problem at night for some time to come.

What a treat it was to be safely tied up in the tranquil marina, it is truly beautiful, very reasonably priced, clean, calm, no hassle, easy access on and off and after the bustle of Singapore it was really appreciated.

Audrey

We did not get connected up to the shore electrics until the morning after we arrived, it wasn't a problem, we had motor sailed for the last few hours to get in when the wind dropped and the batteries were all charged up. In the daylight hours of the previous day we had managed to catch up on our lack of sleep sailing down the Malacca Strait, the night passage through there was dreadful and I was glad we would not have to do that bit again.

With our marina paperwork completed we took a taxi into Port Dickson to complete the formalities, fortunately Customs, Immigration and Port Authority are all close together, very friendly and efficient. We stayed for a Malaysian lunch, rice, bean sprout, chicken and chilli sauce with clear soup, just what the doctor ordered. After a while exploring the town we came across a stunning Hindu temple, ornate carvings covered every square inch of the building, it was decorated in many different pastel shades. I took some photos and marvelled at the intricate workmanship, the same care is observed inside and out, we were invited to have a look inside so removed our shoes and entered, the whole building was a work of art. Tony wondered how long the outside of the building would look so marvellous if it was sited anywhere in UK, the graffiti artists would have a heyday.

The next day, 21st November, we, together with Rob and Phoebe from the yacht "Mani" hired a taxi and took a day trip into Malacca, the old capitol of Malaysia. There were more temples and we walked all round the maritime museum, had another Malayan lunch and took a trishaw ride around town, these are all individually decorated with different kinds of flowers and again are all brightly coloured. The roads in Malaysia are not renowned for their comfort or quality, the taxi driver wanted to return to Port Dickson in daylight so all too soon our visit was called to a halt and we started on the 100 kilometre ride back to the marina, as a matter of fact, returning along the roads in daylight was a good call.

The next two days were chill out days on the marina, boat cleaning, laundry, etc; Tony had another go at the screen wipers which had stopped working again and we had a nice long chat with family on the internet, this time with a good cam connection as well. The forecast was strong winds from the direction we wanted to go, so another chill out day was on the cards, never mind, there were much worse places to get stuck.

Figure 27: A stunning Hindu temple in Port Dickson, Malaysia

Tony

It was the 25th of November before we ventured out again heading for Langkawi, sadly the conditions had not improved, we left with three other rally boats and started beating into an uncomfortable sea and just to make it worse, we also had the current against us. At least we had said goodbye to the tugs and their attendant barges, we discovered as we sailed past that they were loading from the quay in Port Dickson just a couple of miles further on from Admiral's Marina.

The first night spent at sea was not good, we tacked inshore to try and get some respite from the battering, the waves were short and steep and kept breaking over Cayuco gradually soaking everything, except of course our wonderful sea berth. As we worked our way inshore the waves reduced in size because the wind was blowing slightly offshore, this tactic had other dangers, the coast all along South Malaysia shoals out to sea for many miles, shallow sandbars come and go depending on weather conditions.

Going inshore turned out to be a mistake, although the seas were a bit better the water was shallow and the depth varied between 100 to 30 feet, it was dark by this time so I started the engine and headed back out to sea. The batteries needed a top up charge anyway and running the engine meant I could also switch on the radar and chart plotter. This navigational aid for once did not help my composure, by accident we had strayed into a large region of sandbars, there was no moon, lights or distinguishing features of any description, not even a fishing boat, a bad sign indeed in these waters. I mentally berated myself for putting us in this position, during the day it had looked good, we were well offshore or so I thought, I'd let my guard down and had not been updating the charts enough for coastal waters.

As I tried to motor sail into deeper water the red light on the instrument panel came on indicating a problem with the engine, I switched the engine off and reached for the torch.

A quick check revealed it was only the vee belt driving the alternator which had snapped, we were still sailing but the only course we could make with the greatest time before tacking was back inshore, Audrey sailed Cayuco while I once again disappeared down into the engine compartment. Of course, the engine compartment light chose this moment to stop working, so with torch in teeth and a handful of spanners I fitted a new belt. It didn't take long, less than 30 minutes; I had long since arranged this job so it could be carried out quickly. I finished, started the engine, checked all was OK, tacked Cayuco back to our original course and we were off again. Mind you, Audrey was getting increasingly worried by the rapidly approaching sand bank on the plotter screen and had been trying to slow us down for a good few minutes. By the time we tacked back offshore, the depth was down to 30 feet, we had to wriggle our way out to sea using the depth meter to find the deeper water, it was a black night, we sailed blind and it was not fun.

Common sense dictated we headed out to at least the 20 metre line; the wind was still blowing directly from Langkawi so made the best course we could and continued to thrash our way into the seas. It was another uncomfortable night and it didn't get any better, we'd left Admiral Marina early morning on Tuesday 25th November and had to beat all the way to Langkawi Island. Three hundred miles in three days and hammering into the seas the whole way, it was a relief to get in to a nice calm berth at 09-30 on Friday morning, we checked in at the Marina Office and went to sleep.

Audrey

It was not a pleasant passage to Langkawi, the unseasonal strong winds had been persistent for three days and almost on the nose, it was hard work, we had got used to the following trade winds and the rough conditions had been a wakeup call. I had been reduced to producing one pot stews with the pan permanently fixed in the fiddles and we ate it in mugs or deep bowls. The galley by this time was quite well modified; I had a place to secure all the daily needed items. Tony had rigged up, screwed in place and fitted little racks everywhere he could. There were wooden frames with different size holes for mugs, cups, plates and glasses etc, these kept all to hand without having to move very far, the sink also became a good place to pour hot drinks. The whole layout had a sliding strap along its length to support anyone working in the galley in rough conditions. Most of the time it worked well, only occasionally distributing itself all over the saloon floor, Tony knew when this happened without having to investigate, a torrent of verbal abuse would emit from the region of the galley in the saloon.

In deeper water there were lots of fishing boats, their lighting system was hap-hazard, some brightly lit, some not at all, others with odd lights all over the place and then some with brightly flashing coloured lights. It was very difficult to determine which way they were moving or in fact whether they were moving at all. Forget all about the well ordered disciplined system we're used to in Europe, this lot bears no resemblance to anything we had ever seen, it was just a confusion of random lights, or in some cases not, doing whatever they liked.

We arrived off the Langkawi Island Group about midnight, the channel between Pulau Beras and Pulau Tepor was not clearly marked, only the main shipping lights were visible, so we sailed up and down outside all night in 30 knot winds. First light saw us sailing up the channel with another larger yacht who had been doing the same thing, what a good call; the channel was littered with unmarked rocks sticking up like the fingers of death, we were glad we had waited, of course we could have gone round to the east side of the island and entered by the main channel, but what's the fun in that?

Langkawi Yacht Club is a beautiful place, very switched on and professional, the usual round of good bars and restaurants and even an extremely good duty free shop. Customs, Immigration and Port Authority are half a mile away at the ferry port so all necessary procedures are easy; the whole island is a duty free zone so it's a good place to stock up. The sundowners we purchased here were the cheapest anywhere; we were still enjoying them in Crete months later. The other thing we purchased in quantity was cigarettes, neither of us smokes but they would make good bartering material at sea with the fishermen and in Egypt while transiting the Suez Canal.

Food in the local restaurants was of a high standard and very reasonably priced, we enjoyed our stay in Langkawi. It was relatively easy to stock up with a whole range of unusual and more exotic canned goods, water chestnuts, bamboo shoots and mixed stir-fry accompaniments were everywhere. The Wi-Fi connection was good so chatted to family again and surprise, surprise, watched a football match on Sky TV between our local town football teams in UK, Havant versus Waterlooville that was a surprise.

Our friends Rob and Phoebe arrived on their yacht Mani so we spent the evening with them at the yacht club, during the conversation it was decided we would hire a car between us the next day and explore the island. Tony drove us around and we had a fantastic day, went to a viewpoint, then a waterfall up in the mountains and took some photos of monkeys on the way down, I got too close to one of them and he chased me off, I didn't wait about to argue, think he thought I was after his food.

While we had the car it was convenient to drive into town and pick up some stores for the next passage to Phuket, we went to what is known as the wet market and bought some large prawns, a sea bass and a bald chicken. It came complete with its head and giblets but was plucked completely. It looked like ET (Extra Terrestrial) on a bad day or our son's rubber chicken toy when he was younger which he named "Stretch"! Thankfully my previous overseas experience had accustomed me to buying fresh meat in this way so I was not traumatised by having to behead it and clean it up before cooking.

I also went shopping and bought a nice Batik wrap- around skirt to add to my depleted wardrobe.

Tony

Before we could leave I had to sort out some electrics, the starter motor had been intermittent for some time and examining the system I found a bad connection on the starter solenoid. Audrey had been amused for some time as I used the small hammer to tap the starter motor when it failed to work, like all temporary solutions, eventually you have to execute a permanent repair. It was no good just repairing the terminal because the whole electrical leads from the battery needed work as well. I obtained some large splitter terminals and electrical components from the chandlery shop, then made up and fitted a complete new wiring loom, while I was at it, I also adjusted the fan belt that I had fitted a few days earlier. The next morning we paid a visit to the Customs, Immigration and Port Authority to check out. It was the 3rd December and we were going to spend a bit of time cruising up through the islands of Thailand before reaching Phuket where we had planned to spend Christmas.

Like most places Langkawi allows you 24 hours to leave after you have checked out so we headed for an anchorage called "Hole in the Wall", it's only 20 miles from the sailing club even if you go the long way round. The anchorage is not easy to find and the entrance is well disguised, it is only visible when really close to. You have to go through a short narrow channel between high cliffs and it opens up into a large inland lake, there is fairly deep water for a couple of miles up to a small village. We chose to anchor about half a mile inside, it was the most beautiful peaceful place we had seen for a long time, just to sit in the cockpit and listen to the birds in the trees onshore was calming. We felt we had found one of those secret little places that most people never see.

This was to be our final memory of Langkawi and Malaysia, after leaving tomorrow, we would shortly be entering the territorial waters of Thailand; both of us were looking forward to a peaceful night and the next part of our adventure.

Figure 28: The anchorage of "Hole in the Wall" on our last night in Langkawi, Malaysia.

Chapter 14

Thailand

Tony

It seemed a shame to leave such a beautiful anchorage so quickly, if an anchorage like "Hole in the Wall" had been on the south coast of England it would have been totally ruined by "development" years ago, as so many other examples have been. The inevitable and escalating tourist industry would have capitalised on it to the detriment of all concerned. Here, in Langkawi, "The Hole in the Wall" was an almost unused part of the local infrastructure, just a stunning inland mangrove lined inlet, a few fishermen, some small fast tourist launches from further up the channel, it was such a peaceful spot, we wondered for how long it would escape the inevitable tourist invasion.

Around 08-30, after a breakfast of scrambled egg, bacon and beans we slowly motored out of the narrow entrance channel and said goodbye to Langkawi. It was Thursday the 4th December and we had a rendezvous to spend Christmas in Phuket, our intention was to day sail and cruise slowly up through the offshore islands hopping from one to the other all the way to Yacht Haven Marina on Phuket Island.

We'd had enough of night sailing for a while, all the way since leaving Bali on the 8th October nearly two months ago, we had been dodging fishing boats, floating fish rafts, lobster pot buoys and all manner of flotsam, daylight was bad enough but night-time was dreadful, it was a constant ordeal trying to stay out of the way. There are literally thousands of fishing boats and always some are in view, rarely can you relax for more than a few hours before having to weave your way through the next melee of vessels. The ones with lights are bad enough, they have total disregard for any international regulations, but the unlit ones are just plain dangerous, you end up hoping they will keep out of your way as you have no idea whatsoever where they will turn up next.

It was 135 miles to Ao Chalong in Phuket which was where we wanted to check into Thailand, by day sailing slowly zig zagging from island to island we could use the available wind to sail rather than motor. We were not in a hurry anymore; for once we had plenty of time, we were heading for the island of Ko Bulon about 25 miles away so it was a gentle day sail. One of the problems of sailing in Thailand is when you eventually leave the country; you have to check out at the place you checked in. This can mean travelling hundreds of miles extra retracing your steps to complete the formalities before continuing your voyage; we wanted to clear in and out of Thailand at Ao Chalong to avoid this problem. The authorities are aware that yachties coming up from Langkawi rarely sail all the way to Phuket, they are fairly liberal about yachts taking a few days to get there before checking in; of course they won't take kindly if you arrive two weeks later to do the paperwork. Your check out date in Malaysia is clearly marked on those documents which you have to produce in Phuket; it's just a matter of being sensible and not pushing the system beyond the boundaries of belief. In our case, we were happy to stay onboard at the islands we visited and didn't go ashore until actually arriving in Ao Chalong.

Ko Bulon was a typical Thailand Island anchorage, "Ko" being the Thailand name for Island; we decided to drop our anchor in a bay on the south side of the island in five metres of water. At first we were alone but by early evening three other boats had joined us in this lovely peaceful bay, there were one or two small fishing boats plying their trade around the shore, but other than that it was calm, quiet and tranquil. After the last few weeks it was soothing to the soul, we sat on deck, relaxed and enjoyed our sundowners. As the sun dropped below the horizon, a million stars twinkled in the clear sky, this was another moment to savour and the memory will linger on well after our sailing days are over. We had no interest in taking a photograph, it could never capture our feelings or emotions, or indeed the vision unfolding before our eyes, just being there, was enough.

After a restful night we were off again, planning to head for Ko Kladan we could not lay the course with the wind direction so a quick reconnoitre of the chart showed another little group of islands which allowed us to sail all the way, they were the oddly named Ko Rok and Ko Nok. It was a good choice, the wind was free, there was plenty of it and we rolled off the 42 miles in eight and a half hours. On the way we passed lots of fishing boats just anchored, as they fish all night the crew sleep during the heat of the day and start fishing with powerful lights as soon as it is dark. As the water all around this area is quite shallow, wherever they finish, they just anchor and sleep, indeed, if they find a good fishing spot, they just stay where they are.

The other unusual phenomena in these waters is the amount of fairly small uninhabited islands, what can only be described as lumps of rock, they rise vertically out of the sea to around 50 to 100 metres high and they are everywhere. When sailing you just pass one after the other, they all have names and must be a good fishing ground as there is always a small fishing boat or two circling round the base of them. Our anchorage this time was in the channel between Ko Rok and Ko Nok, again it was peaceful and quiet; a small camping resort was hidden away behind some trees on the beach. We heard on the radio that some other larger sailing boats had been asked to pay 400 bart (about £8 each) for every person on board in order to anchor for the night, or maybe this was a charge to go ashore. Anyway, they declined to pay as no-one in the dinghy that had come out from the island had any authorising documentation and refused to give any receipt, the result was that all the yachts which had been asked for money moved off to another island. The people in the dinghy never came to see us for any money, they probably took one look at Cayuco and thought better of it; I fear they would have been disappointed in any case.

Another very pleasant night, but on waking there was a lot more wind than the day before, it was overcast and as we wanted to get under way we picked up the anchor and motored up the channel between the islands watching the depth meter very closely. As we emerged and continued out to sea we set the sails, the strong beam wind laid us well over to port and it was in this fashion that we headed for Phi Phi Don. Breakfast was taken on the hoof in the cockpit, while Cayuco, sailing herself, was hard on the wind for our destination. We managed to sail most of the way, covering the 32 miles in seven and a half hours, the sail was harder than the day before and we had to put in some short tacks, the 32 miles as the crow flies probably meant we sailed more like 40 but it was exhilarating.

South Bay on Phi Phi Don was a disappointment, very touristy and commercialised, we discovered later there were many other quieter places to stay the night, after our almost deserted and tranquil islands of the last few nights we were totally disillusioned. We didn't even bother to go ashore, the incessant thump thump of loud disco bars on the seafront convinced us to moor as far away as possible, needless to say we had no interest in staying there the next day.

Audrey

The sail up from Langkawi to Phuket was outstanding, perfect sailing conditions, wind almost always was good for us, temperature day and night was pleasant, I can't remember if we wore any clothes at all on the entire trip, except maybe when we were anchored and a boat came too close. Saved loads of fresh water and had very little to launder on arrival, there was no rain until leaving Phi Phi Don and then only a short shower. Hit my knee on the granny bars while I was taking a photograph of the very picturesque vertical rock formations and gullies through the hillside, this put my patella out of joint again so I collapsed on the fore deck, luckily I saved the camera from going over the side. I have had this problem for some years but it always takes me by surprise, just have to be careful with it, a gentle tap on the side and it slid back into place, say la vie. Shame about Phi Phi Don, must have been a beautiful place before man found the potential to make money?

7th December in mid morning saw us sailing quickly with a beam wind the 27 miles to Ao Chalong bay in Phuket, we only used the main and jib which prolonged the joy of sailing as long as possible, we knew we would not arrive in time to check in today anyway so might as well have the benefit of it. When we arrived it was surprising how busy the bay was, finding a clear anchorage position near the landing pier was not possible, so we ended up about a quarter of a mile away in 8 metres of water. This is a very popular place at the festive season and of course it is a natural stopping place on a circumnavigation, after Christmas and New Year celebrations you still have ample time to continue across the Indian Ocean in the better north east monsoon weather.

Early the next morning we blew up the dinghy, went ashore at the pier and completed all the formalities, this chore is relatively easy here, all the relevant officers are in the same building and they just pass you from one room to the next. By 11-30 hours we were motoring out of the passage between Ko Lone and Cape Panwa on the south east corner of Phuket en route for the Yacht Haven Marina, this is about 30 miles from Ao Chalong so it was 18-00 hours before we were safely tied up. Yacht Haven Marina is a very pleasant and inexpensive marina about two miles east of the New Sarasin Bridge which links Phuket to the mainland. It is up a fairly shallow channel between Phuket and Thailand and it boasts most of the necessary facilities needed for a modern yacht, anything that can't be done, the Harbour Master can arrange, we were here for Christmas and intended to enjoy it at all costs.

Tony

Yacht Haven Marina for us was a real "Haven", we were very nearly 20,000 miles into our voyage, we had left England in mid August 2007 and it was now almost mid December 2008. This was over 1250 miles a month for sixteen months, given that most small boat sailors average about 1500 miles or less a year, this was about 12 years of normal sailing; it's not surprising that a few things had broken.

To check out our surroundings we went for a walk, the marina complex had the usual array of chandlers, charter operators and cafes where simple meals and a drink could be obtained. Venturing out of the marina we walked along a small lit path through the trees and bushes to check out some colourful lights glittering someway along the shoreline. It turned out to be the Haven Bar, a separately run and privately owned restaurant and bar run by an Englishman called Mark. We chatted away and over the evening discovered that Mark was putting on a

Christmas day dinner, I said I would see if any other yachts in the rally were interested in joining us for the day celebrations.

While chatting away a couple on another table noticed us, the guy came over and said,

"Weren't you the bloke in Antigua at Christmas last year with your arse hanging out of your pants?"

I said, "Yes, that's right, at the time we'd just got in from crossing the Atlantic."

He replied,

"Good on yer sport, last time I saw you, you were wondering if you'd be able to carry on with your voyage; your boat looked a wreck."

"We repaired it and carried on," I laughed.

"Well I never expected to see you again," he admitted, "especially not this far around the world, I'm amazed that you've both come so far in a year in such a small boat".

It was Dave and Ricki, skipper and hostess of the large motor sailor we had met in Antigua last Christmas. It was almost a year ago when he had bought us both a beer on the pontoon the night we had got into Antigua after our eventful Atlantic crossing. We both reminisced about it being a small world but Dave was full of praise for us, he said it was difficult enough in the huge motor yacht he was skippering but in Cayuco no way would he attempt anything like that.

We chatted about our experiences so far, being Australian they were especially interested in the Great Barrier Reef. They asked about our plans for the next few months and we discovered our timetables were roughly the same. The other main topic of conversation was the escalation of pirate activity in the Gulf of Aden, he was very concerned as we all were and the discussion revolved around the various tactics employed to deter the pirates from getting on board.

The next few days were spent getting our bearings. We discovered we could hire a car cheaply for a day from a man who ran a shop across the road; this also doubled as a laundry, a further convenience if somewhat quirky! We set out to explore the island, buy stores and check out the best places to buy boat bits.

Of course we had to have a rally briefing for the next leg to Sri Lanka, this was held in the Haven Bar followed by a wonderful rally party, more photos, this time of the Thai dancers, both male and female in full local costume, quite exquisite. Wi-Fi was good and we both chatted to our family back in UK on a regular basis, even able to book a time to link up and mostly it worked.

Audrey

Our friends John and Jane on Penelope 3 also hired a car and while Tony and John got on with some boat maintenance work, Jane and I decided to drive into town, find the local Carrefour supermarket and have some retail therapy. All went well on our drive into Penang until we reached the bit where they had erected a new temporary one way system, it was all right driving this way the other day so Jane drove straight on, realising her mistake she stopped, reversed out and went to drive off the way indicated. It's not the making of a mistake that matters, it's the getting caught bit, even though the fault had been rectified and we were now ready to safely continue on our way, the eagle eyed local bobby in uniform was not pleased, as far as he was concerned an offence had been committed and we were guilty, I suppose they have to increase the funds in their coffers somehow. After a suitable telling off, Jane's driving license was taken from her and we were told to go to the police station to pay a fine of 300 bart, about six pounds sterling. This was not quite as easy as it seems, alright if you're a local etc; poor woman stood no chance with me as navigator. First turning past the "Irish Bar" he said, ended up driving along a narrow alleyway full of souvenir vendors with no exit, had to reverse all the way back again. Eventually found the correct "Irish Bar" and subsequently the police station, then joined the queue of all the locals who had been given a ticket, seemed as if half the island had got caught. About two hours later, got to the window, paid the fine, drove back to police bloke on duty and retrieved driving license. This in itself was funny, as the license was from the island of "Nuie" in the Pacific Ocean; it had been obtained while visiting there a few months ago, handy for situations like this. By the time we had concluded all this messing about, we just gave up trying to find the supermarket and went back to the boat for a cup of tea, decided next time we go looking, we'll take a cab.

Thailand is very take it as you find it, as Yacht Haven Marina is a long way from town, getting hold of fresh fruit and vegetables was not always easy, that is until I heard of the fruit and vegetable man who appeared every morning in his pickup truck along the road near the marina. As long as you turned up just before nine o clock every morning he would be there, all his wares were laid out in the back of the truck and you just helped yourself to what you wanted and then negotiated a price, simple, straightforward, very entrepreneurial and a godsend to us on the marina without regular transport.

Next day the 13th December we walked along the road outside the marina about a quarter of a mile until it ended up in a very tiny village, the road just finished at the water's edge and there stood two local open air restaurants. Well, this was an opportunity not to be missed, so we had a beer and ordered a local stir fry dish in the one called "The Coconut", it was delicious, so we tried the fresh caught local deep fried prawns, they were heavenly, I would have to say, I've never tasted such delicate flavourful prawns in my life. Tony agreed, so you can guess where we went for a simple low cost snack while we were on the marina.

The lovely lady who ran this establishment was called Penn, one notable evening we really pushed the boat out and ordered Penn's lobster special, there are not very many times in your life when you remember with such clarity, but this was one of them, we promised ourselves to come back someday and see her again, I sincerely hope we are able to. Thailand would make an ideal place to charter a boat for a few weeks and enable us to see all the places we didn't have time to see this visit. We wanted a break, knowing some of the next legs were going to be more difficult for one reason or another made it even more important for us to be well prepared and rested.

Tony

As we were here for some time we purchased a local Sim card for our mobile phone, these make everything a lot easier and cheaper, especially when making local phone calls to find out where to obtain bits for your boat. The real reason was so we could ring some friends and family at Christmas and New Year, our mobiles would have been more expensive, plus, if other people ring you on a local number, it costs you nothing, our UK mobiles charged us whether we rang our family or they rang us.

On the 17th we hired a car for two days, went to Patong shopping and we both had a full Thailand massage including the feet, lovely, came out all tingling and tranquil, was going to say all "flolopy" but don't think it's a real word. On the way back from Patong in the dark we got lost and ended up right at the opposite end of the island, never mind, it made it all the better when we eventually found our way back. Phuket was suffering from the downturn in tourists due to the 2008 financial crisis and the traders were all struggling to get you into their shops, the hassling was some of the worse we had seen, the trick is to ignore them and just keep walking by, shame, because it spoilt an otherwise good day out.

Made a much better job of map reading next day, never made a wrong turn, well almost never, found the place for batteries and ordered a new set for the boat, managed to get deep discharge type, best for the use they are getting. Another interesting point about Thailand is, we were able to replace all our medical supplies without having to see anyone in authority or obtaining any doctors note. Just went to a pharmacist and ordered what we wanted to replace over the counter, this is true of many countries in the world, it may not be good in all circumstances but it made our life easier. During our day I even managed to replace a couple of my shirts which to say the least were going home, they looked like they would fall off my back if I wore them much more.

Over the next few days we took delivery of our new batteries and fitted them, finished off the other odd jobs and basically got Cayuco ready for the next voyage to Sri Lanka after the

Christmas and New Year break. This year, I was determined not to have to work fifteen hours a day on the boat between the holiday periods.

Audrey

Mark, at the Haven restaurant had more or less finalised his plans for the Christmas day bash, I had passed the word around the fleet and quite a lot had indicated their desire to be part of the celebrations, it was starting to look like it would be a good day. It was going to be held in two sessions, an early dinner at 13-30 mostly for local people and a later one at 16-30, for which 14 people from the rally had booked. The reason for this is so we could stay on for drinks afterwards with our own dancing session. Mark had all the ingredients for the meal which was going to cost 1100 bart, about £22 a head, for this the menu included:- melon and Palma ham, lobster bisque, turkey with loads of vegetables, Christmas puddings, cheese board or fruit, coffee with one glass of red or white wine included in the price. For us this represented excellent value but Tony had noticed one very important omission, there was no mention of brandy butter with the Christmas pudding. When he tackled Mark about this he said that it's not traditional in Thailand and nobody knows how to make it, Tony's reply was simple,
"Give me the ingredients and I'll make it"
Mark being British and knowing the importance of brandy butter agreed incredibly quickly and replied,
"I agree, but only if you show my chefs how to make it"
With that the deal was done, Tony picked up the ingredients a couple of days before Christmas and the meal was complete. For information I include Tony's very simple family recipe for brandy butter, courtesy of and handed down by his Mum. It really is delicious.
Take a 1kg bag of icing sugar, ½ lb butter, soften the butter in a largish bowl, add icing sugar and mix together until a thick paste is formed, (in a cold climate warm the butter first), Add brandy to taste, about 5 tablespoons and stir until all blended together, voi'la, enjoy. Good on mince pies as well.

Good Tip, Hold a bit of the icing sugar back in case you pour in too much brandy, then you can add the remaining icing sugar and thicken it up. Stir the brandy in continually until the sugar will absorb no more, (called "solid saturation") if you want to really enjoy it.

Tony

After our disastrous Christmas day dinner in Antigua last year we wanted to get this year's right, in fact all the fun started on Christmas Eve. Audrey made sure everything was prepared for our early morning Christmas day revelry before the dinner and then we, together with John and Jane walked down the road to "The Coconut" restaurant for more of those sizzling prawns and chicken stir fry with noodles that Penn prepared so well.

The big day started on Cayuco with Audrey's pre-prepared nibbles, these were small warm pork and chicken rolls with plenty of bucks fizz to wash them down. Once again John and Jane joined us to start the day off, around lunch time we were all invited to one of the rally yachts with more room onboard. It was a big catamaran, compared to Cayuco it was more like a country cottage, everyone who was going to the dinner and a few others were all accommodated in the huge saloon area. We all enjoyed our hosts hospitality whiling away a pleasant hour or two before it was time to walk along to the Haven restaurant, outside it was a bit damp and for Phuket slightly chilly, down to 25° centigrade at midday!

The evening was as good as expected, Mark and his team had pulled out all the stops, everyone enjoyed the meal and impromptu dancing afterwards, it was all very professional and we all congratulated Mark and his staff on their organisation. Audrey phoned all the family back in UK and even managed a chat on the internet with our two lads and their families. Some of our little fleet who were out cruising the islands, returned to Yacht Haven for the day to join in and embrace the jollifications.

Boxing day was a normal day in Thailand so we went into town with John to pick up a couple of replacement batteries for Penelope 3, batteries take a lot of abuse on a voyage such as this, they work hard and rarely last more than three years, some last a lot shorter time. We were also starting to store up the boats; soon we would be off again. Some more camera shots showing various aspects of Thai life, another meal at Penn's, more pictures, some internet chats with family, also sent pictures to our son for distribution around family and all too soon it was check out time again.

We hired a car to drive to Ao Chalong and checked out of Thailand, took some more photos from the viewpoint, found a place for lunch and did some last minute storing up on the way back in the Carrefour supermarket.

On the last day before leaving we had to go round all our new friends and say goodbye, no-where on our circumnavigation was this more poignant, Mark at the Haven, Penn at The Coconut, we were really sad to be leaving so soon. This is one of the facts of life on a rally with a group of yachts keeping to a schedule, I'm sure if we were by ourselves we would have been tempted to stay longer. Problem there is, if you're not careful, you miss the slots to make later weather windows, perhaps this is why some world girdlers take many years to complete their dream. Would you believe we had a last meal in the Haven of fish and chips, then finished off with the remaining Christmas puddings and the now famous brandy butter sauce, we even had two more puddings with a bit of sauce left in our fridge on board for consumption on New Year's Day. Strangely enough the last night there in the restaurant, we once again bumped into Dave and Ricki who we had met in Antigua the Christmas before, so we had met them on our first night and on our last night in Phuket, we exchanged pleasantries, told them of our plans and found out they were due in Egypt about the same time as us, although no-one really believed we would see each other again.

Early morning on the 31st of December 2008, Audrey paid an early morning visit to her fruit and vegetable man in his pickup truck for fresh stores and we left Yacht Haven Marina. What a peaceful haven it was and what a wonderful place to chill out and spend Christmas. Our plan was to sail round to Patong Bay on the west coast and anchor for the night ready for a start to Sri Lanka early on New Year's Day. The sail went without incident and we virtually circled the island, sailing 44 miles around, to anchor only 18 miles in a straight line across the land from where we started.

The bonus of anchoring in Patong Bay is the fireworks; many yachts had arrived and were secure in this large bay. All were getting ready for one of the biggest firework spectaculars in the world, few places can rival this magnificent display held every New Year's Eve. It starts as soon as the sun sets, Chinese lanterns are set off in their hundreds, maybe thousands, the night sky is full of them and they drift slowly upwards, disappearing away into the blackness. Fireworks big and small are set off it seems all around you, the bay is a half circle so anchoring in the middle it is a quandary to know which way to look, this goes on all night until just before midnight, then everything goes quiet. As the bells ring out the start of the New Year, the whole bay lights up, rockets, explosives, light shows, it's all there, it is a truly magnificent sight, once seen, never forgotten.

We had left some minutes on the mobile phone so rang all our friends and family before it ran out, the whole bay seemed to explode for about half an hour. Gradually, it all quietened down and we sat in the cockpit, finished our drink and contemplated our next passage. To be honest we were not looking forward to leaving Phuket, we knew it was nearly 1000 miles to Sri Lanka which meant approximately 10 days at sea, the forecast for the next 5 days was for more squalls and thunderstorms. Sri Lanka had been through a fairly difficult period, Galle our port of entry had recently been attacked by government rebels and the port was shut down at night with barriers, we were told not to approach too close in the hours of darkness. As we went to sleep I had a picture in my mind of the Andaman Sea, we had to cross this and sail between the Andaman and Nicobar Islands, the Nicobar Islands in particular are not renowned for their friendliness. The New Year promised to be as eventful as the last one and we were not to be disappointed.

Figure 29: The superb Yacht Haven Marina in Phuket where we spent Christmas 2008

Figure 30: Spectacular costumes at the Christmas 2008 BWR dinner and dance in The Haven Restaurant, Phuket.

Chapter 15

To Sri Lanka

Tony

New Years Day 2009 dawned overcast with 10 to 15 knots of wind from the north, there was also a slight drizzle, we were in no particular hurry so after a leisurely breakfast we got underway around 09-30 hours. As Cayuco sailed out of the bay, a ray of sunshine streamed between the clouds and lit up the sleepy town of Penang, the beam of light then progressed slowly up the slope of the hills behind before disappearing altogether, that was our last sight of Thailand, within a few minutes, Penang and Phuket Island had vanished into the murky weather sliding down from the north.

Phuket had been a very memorable visit, sadly we sailed further and further away, but not to worry, it's 2009, this year, all being well, we'll be home. We quickly fell back into our daily routine, it was second nature now, just an automatic reaction, our course was almost due west, we were heading for the Sombrero Passage between the Andaman and the Nicobar Islands 270 miles away, this bit of water is called the Andaman Sea and Galle, our destination in Sri Lanka, was only 1064 miles away, I say only lightly of course.

The weather continued to deteriorate and by noon it was a constant fine drizzle, never mind, we were sailing albeit slowly, visibility was down to less than half a mile, if in fact it was as good as that. Before evening it cleared up temporarily and we saw another sailing boat well astern of us, unfortunately all around us on the horizon the clouds had that oppressive look, there were many squalls marching along the skyline; it was only a matter of time before one of them came our way. After thousands of miles of ocean sailing you develop an instinct, the colour of the clouds and the surrounding sky, the shape, the frequency, all give you clues as to what to expect, it didn't look good and we were right. The first squall hit shortly after dusk, the rain started and that was how it remained all night, wet and miserable. It didn't bother us too much; we zipped up our cockpit tent, stayed underneath in the relative dry and kept sailing quite fast. There was an uncomfortable sea running, the main waves coming from the starboard quarter, this was made worse by a cross sea coming from the south, Cayuco bucked and crashed through the water, sleeping was difficult but by now we were used to this adversity, tucked up in our sea berth with the lee cloth rigged, we made the best of it.

Audrey

Leaving Phuket was hard, the next 24 hours just made it worse, even some visiting dolphins didn't really cheer me up, told myself I must stay positive about the conditions, right, they're positively crap!! Rained all night, loads of squalls, Cayuco rolling her decks under, I imagine it feels like being in a washing machine but it goes on and on, it's better to sleep on your back when jammed in the sea berth with lee cloths fitted, less wear and tear on your knees and elbows when trying to relax. Dolphins came back for an early morning visit at dawn as they so often do, a bit later the sun poked through the clouds for a few minutes, maybe not so bad after all, still rolling but sailing fast, averaging six to seven knots continuously, oh well, Tony will be awake shortly, then I can try for some breakfast and a cup of tea.

By the 4th January the conditions had improved, as the sun rose the dawn was beautiful, looks like a hot day on the way. Sailed through the Sombrero Passage last night between the Andaman and Nicobar Islands, no sign of fishing boats, which was a bonus, had our usual dawn visit by gregarious dolphins again, at least they seem to be enjoying themselves. Saw the moon last night, first time since leaving Phuket, it came out between the rain showers and when it cleared later in the night, even saw the good old "Plough" star formation, that means we're really in the northern hemisphere, actually feels like we are on our way home. Had loads of flying fish on deck last night even a baby squid, must have scooped it up during one of our more aggressive rolls, managed to throw a lot of fish back while they were still wriggling but there were a lot of fatalities lying on deck this morning, just can't get to them all at night.

The next two days were the same, fairly good conditions and good sailing, 120 to 130 miles a day and using the petrol generator to charge the batteries, Tony had once again got the twin jibs working, that was, after a bit of maintenance. The starboard spinnaker pole had not been used for some weeks as the normal fore and aft rig was preferred in the prevailing conditions, salt spray had seized the releasing pin and liberal use of WD 40, a hammer and screwdriver were needed to free it off, Tony greased it up again and we charged off downwind. The wind didn't stay from behind, by the evening we were back to genoa, main and mizzen, we nearly always lowered the mizzen for the night though, especially if there were squalls about, we had been caught out once too often. On the 6th we spotted another yacht a couple of miles behind us. It slowly overtook us and past to port just before nightfall, it was larger than us and at the end of the day, in any given conditions; you can't beat waterline length. Never mind, we were happy, not using any diesel and only 445 miles to go, at noon we had covered 143 miles in the last 24 hours under sails, great!

Tony

Our wind started to die by early morning of the 8th so decided to motor for a few hours, we had done well since leaving so justified using a bit of fuel, could be our honeymoon is over. By mid morning we had started to roll again, an unusual beam sea had come in from the south, I put the main back up and sheeted it in hard, that dampened some of the roll but it was odd to have a motion like this in flat calm conditions.

By noon we were sailing slowly again but looking around the horizon there were a lot of squalls all around us. It did not take long before one of the squalls rolled up behind us, the wind speed rose to 30/35 knots for about two hours during the squall so we had to shorten sail; we were back to the full sail, reef and full sail syndrome. This was not too serious during the day when it was easy to eyeball them, at night it was a different matter, our radar would pick them up and then we could track the associated rain to see if they were coming our way, trouble was, we just didn't have the battery capacity to use the radar all the time. Turning it on for a couple of minutes every hour helped to pin point where the squalls were, but we still got caught out many times.

Before dawn on the 9th January, an impressive squall rolled up quickly behind us, it was travelling much faster than we were and a check on the radar confirmed it was a big one, even expanding the screen size to 12 miles did not give any hope of getting out of the way. I took all the hand held electronics and placed them in the oven, as you do during thunder storms. Then, as it was just coming up to one of our watch changes I thought I would leave Audrey sleeping for a bit longer, no point both of us awake during it. This made no difference, the first clap of ear splitting thunder felt like it shook the boat, the lightning bolt hit the water just behind Cayuco and everything was lit up like daylight for that millisecond while your eye adjusts to the sudden brightness. Audrey was up and alongside me in seconds, don't really blame her, it was very loud, there followed a few more in rapid succession but thankfully none as close as the first one. There was nothing we could do; I had already shortened sail so it was just a matter of riding it out and trying to position ourselves so that it would pass over in the shortest time.

The day broke with total cloud cover; it was so thick it delayed the dawn for some time and all around looked very angry. At noon we were only 86 miles from Galle and closing the coast of Sri Lanka, I was hoping this weather would clear up before getting too much closer, it had been raining for nearly 24 hours, didn't fancy running along the coast at night in this lot. Just after lunch time another big squall with attendant thunder and lightning, lasted about two hours but after it showed signs of clearing up, by 15-00 hours the sun was trying to come out and it all looked good.

As we only had about 60 miles to go at 18-00 hours I took the mizzen in, I would have probably done this anyway as it was evening but I wanted to slow down, with the warnings about arriving at Galle in the dark it was better if we didn't get there until daylight, I also took the opportunity to put up the courtesy flag and the "Q" Flag, didn't want to upset anyone even before we arrived.

We could already see the high ground of Sri Lanka before nightfall but Galle our objective was on the south west corner so we had a night of sailing along the coast, the lights of the various towns twinkled as we sailed along. By midnight we were already too close so took in most of our sails and virtually drifted with the current, Cayuco barely had steerage way but I didn't want to drift past Galle and have to backtrack. There were many small fishing boats out during the night, few of them carried lights, it was so quiet as we drifted along that we could hear them talking to each other. Sometimes they shone a torch to let us know where they were, sometimes we just drifted silently past them, with no moon to speak of we only saw the shadows of the ones inshore of us, they slid past like ghosts in the night. At one stage I heard excited chattering and then concerned voices, I heard an engine start up, move out to sea a little way, stop and start fishing again. As we had our lights on and they didn't, it's feasible to surmise that someone saw us drifting down on them and decided to move out of the way, I heard them but saw very little, it appeared to be a small vessel with an outboard motor.

By dawn we were off Galle Harbour which has a large military presence, yachts are allowed to enter but only after scrutiny by the authorities, as we were still too early for processing we anchored about a quarter of a mile to the west of the entrance near the marker buoys in the bay. It was then only a wait until the Naval Launch came out to check our papers and allocate a time to enter the harbour, plenty of time for a relaxing breakfast before all the paperwork trail starts again.

There were two other boats anchored with us all waiting for clearance to enter, about 09-00 hours a launch came out to us, two burly Naval types with efficient looking rifles and two civilians with briefcases jumped onboard, can't say the experience was friendly, they were officious and did their job. We had been pre-warned on radio by another yacht who was already moored in the harbour what to expect so it held no surprises. Having completed the initial paperwork to enter and undergone the routine search fiasco, it became obvious to the officers that it was not possible for us to fulfil all their requests; our sundowners locker was mysteriously seriously depleted, as I said, we had already had a heads up on essentials. Eventually when the other two yachts had also been cleared, we were all led into the harbour to moor up. We dropped anchor where requested and tied up stern to on a small temporary looking pontoon, once there, other officials came onboard and gradually all the paperwork was produced and completed. Nobody we talked to was very impressed with the manner or the content of the formalities, everyone had their own stories to tell and I won't repeat them here, suffice to say, some of the more expensive looking yachts had more reason to complain than us, we were let off lightly.

Audrey

The final part of the voyage from Phuket had some scary moments with thunder storms and fishing boats at night, the worst part was entering Galle Harbour. Many years ago my mother said to me,

"If you can't say anything nice about someone, then don't say anything at all", that about sums up our experiences entering Sri Lanka. It's a shame because first impressions are very important and count for a lot; the officers were unnecessarily intrusive and indicated voluntary gifts would help them to overcome recent difficulties. This disturbing episode while entering port left a lasting sense of unease with all the crews and it must be stressed immediately that this attitude is not normally the case. Once we got ashore, the ordinary people of Sri Lanka were very helpful, happy to assist in anything asked for and went out of their way to oblige. Sri Lanka needs tourism and the trade this generates, yachties are part of that business and the activities of the officials did not help.

The Port Authorities and the military are concerned about some of the tactics used by the officials and are actively engaged in preventing their continuation. We were told that once the new marina is constructed, it will be much easier to police the procedures and they should be able to control it completely, we can only hope they succeed, Sri Lanka is a diverse country which has a lot to offer.

Figure 31: In Sri Lanka you have to dodge the cows as well as the traffic

Tony

Having booked in and looked around the harbour, it was clear there were no facilities we would be interested in so obtained a pass from the exit and went exploring. The pass is an essential part of the security and it is needed to get back into the harbour complex, so has to be kept safe, once obtained it can be used for multiple exits and entries.

Outside you will find a row of tuk-tuks; these are motorised open carriages with a canvas roof and look like a large pram. They are powered by a motorcycle engine in the front, the driver sits on a single seat and steers with motor bike type handle bars, two passengers sit usually terrified in the back and hang on. These machines are noisy, fairly uncomfortable and yet the greatest fun. You get whisked round town and the surrounding countryside becoming quite unperturbed when you have adjusted to the unconventional method of transport. Naturally they are extremely cheap, the drivers know all the right (and wrong) places to go, all the shortcuts and will accompany you on shopping trips, indeed you are advised to go with them when purchasing anything. The drivers take it on themselves to look after you, ensure you see all the places of interest, keep you from getting mixed up with the wrong suppliers, get the best deal and protect you from any local disturbances. Listen to them and take their advice is all I suggest, the ones touting for business outside the naval base have to be above suspicion and will lose their spot if there is any hint of indiscretion.

Audrey

First impressions were not good; we parted with some cheap cigarettes, a couple of beers and a Bali polo shirt that Tony didn't like anyway. Outside the Naval Base it felt as if we had been kidnapped by a tuk-tuk driver, he drove us to a bar along the beach and persuaded us to drink beer, even though it was a religious holiday. Shame, another rod to bear, apparently every full moon is a religious holiday and the sale of alcohol is forbidden, to be fair we did ask him. We had to keep hiding the beer bottles under the table every time a police car went by as we were sitting in full view of the main road. We also shared a plate of very tasty noodles and promised to come back for more, it was a lovely restaurant on the beach and the atmosphere was very relaxed and lay back, we had started to chill out again.

The return journey, slightly imbibed, was better than when we had been totally sober, plus, we had started to get used to the local driving standards which is basically, every man for himself. The tuk-tuk driver very skilfully missed all the buses, trucks, push bikes, normal traffic and all the other tuk-tuks which were coming from every which way. As there didn't appear to be many if any rules, nobody expected anyone to do the right thing or obey any protocol. Because of this, everyone treats everyone else as a raving imbecile and expects the unexpected, therefore everyone moves out of the way of each other. It was a real heart stopping drive both ways witnessing the near misses and everything weaving about all over the available road but still missing everything else. By the end of the visit we had got used to it and just ignored them, or better yet, joined in the cheers when they narrowly missed an obstacle. Hire cars are cheap, but one look at the chaos called roads and the driving standards and Tony decided to let the local drivers take the strain. He's a good driver and used to driving on both sides of the road as well as in strange places but Galle was beyond his theory of a "calculated risk" or "taking a chance", it was not too clear what side of the road they were supposed to drive on anyway.

Tony

It would be easy to enjoy Sri Lanka now that their internal conflict is over; it is a beautiful country in culture and history and deserves a lot more consideration than it currently receives.

The mosquito population was very active so we rigged up our mosquito screens over the cockpit; this made sleeping a more pleasant experience without that irritating buzzing noise you get in your ear just as you are falling asleep. The screens were a bit awkward to fit and complicated exit and entry but with our hatch cover screens as well it kept the mosquito annoyance to an acceptable level.

The other bug (as in creepy crawly thing) problem which the netting solved were cockroaches, these disgusting insects you just do not want on a boat as house guests. To prevent this, where possible we never bring cardboard boxes or any similar material aboard, but always unload them on the pontoon and just bring the contents up to the boat. Cockroaches lay their eggs in the folds of the cardboard material and there can be a lot of them. Once on board and established, they multiply very quickly and it is extremely difficult to get rid of them. The other way they can get aboard is by flying, while I was busy one day I heard a commotion from below, Audrey had spotted a rather large cockroach which had flown in and was trying to find a nice spot to hide away, she hates the damn things anyway but realising the importance she was frantically chasing it around with a fly swat, it had two choices, leave or die. Before I could give assistance she had cornered and dispatched the beast with a vicious blow to its body, the corpse was given a sea burial where no doubt it became part of the food chain. Remember, if you ever have to do this yourself, cockroaches leave a very strong pungent odour behind them.

Next day it was a matter of sorting out how to get all the stores, fuel and water arranged. On the pontoons there was no electricity or water supply, in fact the pontoons were only plastic floating drum type units linked together. They were very unstable, kept drifting away from the rocks so that we had to climb up to get ashore, they were held in place mostly by the yachts own anchors on either side of the floats. The harbour master had to keep sending his staff over to re-tie the structure to the shore, it was all a bit Heath-Robinson, in the end we tied it up ourselves as the staff seemed incapable of tying a knot which didn't come undone. We're told the authorities have agreed a new small marina complex in another corner of the harbour, as far as we were concerned, the sooner the better.

The evening was finished off with a meal at the Closenberg Hotel just outside the Naval Base; we were joined by several members of the rally. Most of the rest had taken a five day coach trip around Sri Lanka, they returned with stories of stunning beauty and horrendous roads, but they all enjoyed it immensely. The next few days were spent sorting out the boat and taking delivery of fuel and water. Fuel came in a big drum on the back of a lorry, getting it into our diesel tanks was accomplished by repeatedly filling up our 20 litre cans from the drum, man handling it down the rocks and rickety pontoon, then sliding it up the passarelle and onto the boat. It was then emptied into the tanks using the siphon method, we all completed the operation but it took two to three days to sort out each boat. Water came the same way and it also took a long time to organise and complete. As it was very hot in the middle of the day, we tried to do as much as possible in the early morning or late evening.

Audrey

In general we had a fairly good stay, I hated the pontoon, it was just too insecure for my liking and the walk to the gate was pretty awful as well, took about twenty minutes and was very dusty and dirty. Large commercial ships unloading bags of cement dropped the dust everywhere, it was inches deep and the breeze blew it all over the place. It then congealed around your feet and ankles and started to set with the sweat of your body, not at all pleasant. Tony got repeated requests to give up his nice new cap but he eventually convinced them they were wasting their time, he always kept a packet of cigarettes for them instead though.

We took another tuk-tuk trip into town for some photocopying and to find an internet cafe to send a quick message home, there were no facilities in the Naval Base for this. Also had to have some more photographs for the entry papers made, everywhere we went they seemed to want more photographs, must have needed 50 to 100 each during the whole voyage. Afterwards we visited the local fort for lunch and watched the big monitor lizards wandering about all over the place. On the way back the driver took us to a batik and lace factory where I bought a batik wrap around skirt and a lace top which was very reasonably priced. Even watched the nimble fingered girls making bundles of lace with a wooden frame, they obviously become expert but it looked quite complicated. After a bit of grocery shopping we returned to the boat; a rally friend in his yacht had still not arrived and Tony wanted to turn on the SSB at 18-00 hours to see if he could pick him up. After a successful radio link it was established that Mani was only 100 miles away and would arrive tomorrow, they'd had to return to Phuket for repairs so had been delayed.

All the time in Galle we kept looking for stores, there were no big supermarkets so had to purchase items as we saw them. While out foraging for one day and sitting in a small cafe, we saw a number of gibbons in the trees across the road, they were cavorting from branch to branch at astonishing speeds and jumping from tree to tree, it was an amazing sight to witness. I attempted to photograph their antics but they were far too quick, without a camcorder it would have been impossible to convey the agility they were demonstrating.

Tony

Gradually we were storing up for our next passage, the owner of a local store offered to bring in goods from the capitol which had a bigger range of stock, he supplied us all with a list of everything obtainable and their prices and agreed to deliver to the boats. It worked well; we all got a larger selection of goods of all descriptions although some were a bit on the expensive side. Never mind, we were starting to prepare ourselves for the trip to Oman, this was going to be in two parts, Galle to Uligamu in the Northern Maldives, then on to Salalah in Oman. The first part was nearly 500 miles and the second part about 1200, the problem was, we would not be able to stock up in Uligamu, the island is only two miles long and half a mile wide, any stores obtained there would be very limited.

I serviced the engine again, changing engine oil and filter, renewing the fuel filters and generally checking over all the systems, my concerns were the normal engine related ones, we had been using the engine a lot more since Australia and I wanted it to remain as trouble free as possible.

Audrey loves a surprise so I decided to try and treat her to a night off the boat; we had only been ashore for four nights since leaving England in August 2007 and this was during the fit out in Fiji. I planned a night in the Closenberg Hotel just outside the base and did my best to keep it a secret; I also had to ensure the room had a bath as this is one of the things Audrey misses the most when on board. I arranged it all for Saturday 17th January 2009 and didn't tell her until the morning so all she had to do was take an overnight bag and something to wear for the evening.

The Closenberg Hotel is a lovely old colonial building over 150 years old full of antique furniture, round columns supporting the spacious halls, verandas and terraced gardens. The land it was originally built on was an island in Galle Harbour. Captain Francis Bayley who was an agent of P & O bought the island in 1860 and built what was then his mansion, it was acquired in

1889 by the family which still own it today. It stands on the highest bit of ground in Galle which is why it survived the Tsunami of December 2004. We both had a brief but very pleasant stay, Audrey got her bath and I got a day and night away from maintenance work.

Audrey

Tony surprised me with a night in the nearby hotel on Saturday, I think he was feeling a bit guilty bringing me to this basically military base, it was not through choice, it just happened to be a stopping place before the rest of the Indian Ocean. At night and sometimes during the day, the harbour was sealed off with a barrier across the entrance, this was due to an assault by the rebels earlier in the year when they had attacked the harbour in small fast gunboats and caused a lot of trouble, in reality, the authorities were only trying to protect us.

I lazed luxuriously in the bath before I found out Tony had gone round all the rooms with the manager to find one with a good deep bath, an old colonial double bed and a balcony looking over the terraced gardens, he also arranged to have an internet link with our sons back in UK which I enjoyed. I was pampered and spoiled for the day and evening, we went out for a meal and a bottle of wine and returned to the hotel for coffee and liqueurs, it wasn't much in the scheme of things but it re-charged both our batteries.

Although the day off was enjoyable, it was back to reality and good to get back on board Cayuco the next afternoon, pity about that wobbly pontoon though, it was the bane of my life and I hated it.

It was getting near time to leave, on the 19th January we had our last briefing before heading towards the Gulf of Aden, everyone was concerned about the escalation of pirate activity in the area and we were all taking it very seriously. It was around this time that we consolidated the groups we were going to be in for the pirate alley section and discussed the tactics we would use to discourage unwanted advances from craft we didn't recognize. It was also very important that we all knew the arrival time in

Salalah, the procedure was to be closely controlled and the timing was crucial for the success of our transit through the troubled area, we also kept very quiet about our plans.

Due to our previous stay in the hotel at the weekend we skipped the rally party after the briefing and took a tuk-tuk to a little restaurant on the beach nearby. It was a stunning location courtesy of Edward the tuk-tuk driver, probably run by his family or friends, the meal was superb, a delicate blend of local herbs and spices combined together, we ate while listening to the waves roll along the sandy beach.

On the 21st January we attended a charity performance laid on by our friendly drivers, their wives and a number of friends were all involved. It was their way of thanking us and the Blue Water Rally team for the help and support given to them since the Boxing Day Tsunami in 2004. The dancing was impressive, but yet aggressive, it depicted the history and the struggle the Sri Lankan people have endured in their fight for survival throughout the ages. The whole show was very well put together and displayed the passion they felt for their country and heritage, they are truly a proud people.

While talking to one of the young drivers I learned that he had lost his entire family in the tragedy, he had been called away for the day to assist driving a group of tourists on a safari through the mountains. When he returned in the evening, his wife, children, parents, house and everything he possessed had gone, he'd had the misfortune of living right on the beach which took the full force of the violent waves.

We picked up the last of the fresh vegetables, greens and salad stuff we required, got ripped off by the store holder and couldn't argue as our driver was not with us. I took some more photos of the cows and other wildlife roaming through the streets and it was nearly time to leave.

I stayed on board that night while Tony went ashore with some other rally friends, while walking alone back to Cayuco, already safely inside the security fence and in the pitch dark, there were no lights on our bit of harbour, he heard a rifle cock ready for firing and an unseen voice, out of the blackness demanded him to stop.

Tony is not one to panic, he assesses quickly and stays calm in difficult situations, he admitted afterwards that the hairs on the back of his neck stood up and bristled. As he could see very little and his senses told him that the rifle was raised to fire, the circumstances were delicate to say the least; he had "been here before" in a previous life and instinctively backed off. What natural light there was came from behind his challenger putting him at a disadvantage, waiting for the next request he assessed his options while slowly moving to the left of where he thought the barrel of the rifle was pointing and out of the firing line. The voice turned out to be a new young overzealous recruit on his first night duty alone who had not seen Tony before; he had over reacted to the situation in the dark as he had not expected anyone to return through the base at this late hour. Tony calmly chatted to him, explaining about Cayuco, offered him a packet of cigarettes from his stash of bribe material and all was well with the world again.

Tony

All checked out and off again, no 24 hour pass before you leave here, when you check out, the Naval Personnel come back to the boat with you, undo your lines, cast you off and watch while you leave. Depending on who accompanies them, they may also ask if you have anything left that they have not already relieved you of. In the meantime a small boat appears and accompanies you out of the harbour to ensure you depart immediately. The personnel on here also check if you have anything left, cigarettes, beer, clothing, especially your hat, which they seem to prize above all else. This is a shame as not only is this practise against the custom of the majority of Sri Lankan's traditions; it is also against the authority's directive clearly marked in the entrance to the Naval Base. I pointed out that according to the directive we would be guilty as well if I complied with their requests, so we smiled, waved them away and thankfully sailed off into the opening arms of the bay.

Slowly motoring out to sea, I went forward to pull up the rest of the anchor, as we had exited Galle Harbour I'd left it dangling in the water to wash it off, it had surfaced covered with thick black evil smelling mud which stuck like glue. Rather than use the deck brush to clean it off I had hung it in the water and just proceeded slowly out so that the natural motion of the boat would clean it for me, it took much longer than I thought but eventually I was happy to have it back aboard. I lashed it down into its sea going mode and ruefully thought, oh well, at least that's the end of that.

Chapter 16

On to the Maldives and Oman

Tony

As we sailed out of Galle Harbour waving goodbye to the disgruntled marine crew, neither of us were too disappointed to see the back of them, the activities of the very people who you would expect to be monitored and above such tactics had tarnished our visit. The whole time we were there was only marred by the people you have to see to complete the entry and exit requirements. Don't let our experience put you off visiting though, the authorities are clamping down hard on these practises and Sri Lanka with its friendly and happy people is well worth a visit.

When ashore, it's best to trust the tuk-tuk drivers for most things, they generally have a code of conduct between themselves, then monitor and berate anyone who lets the standard drop. A driver will nominate himself to each yacht so they become your driver for the duration of your stay. Although he will also work for others, if you let him know your requirements he will look after your needs first to the best of his ability, he will ensure you get to your destination and pick you up after you've finished whatever the time of day or night. What one of them doesn't know about, another will, if he has made arrangements with you and can't make it, he will arrange for someone else to pick you up, that's the code. To us it's an odd system, it probably goes back a long way, but in their occupation it works well. They take it on themselves to look after you; don't even consider going shopping without one. In our culture it may seem an imposition, but they know all the best places and ensure you are not short changed, get the freshest produce and the best price.

Back to the rally, our actual day to leave Sri Lanka was up to the individual crews, we decided to go early on the 22nd January, the important date for us was to get to Salalah by the 10th February so that arrangements could be finalised for our departure to Djibouti. It was now too late to alter the timetable unless in dire emergency and we all had a duty to try and make the deadline for our arrival in Oman.

Once clear of the bay and headland we were sailing well, a good force 3 and all sail set, our plan was to head for Uligamu, one of the most northerly of the Maldive islands in the Indian Ocean. Our route from Sri Lanka was across the wide end of the Palk Strait between the land masses of Sri Lanka and India. The wind funnels down between these two countries and can generate some lively sailing conditions. This turned out to be true, we lowered the mizzen at dusk as we normally do unless it's very settled and the wind was already showing signs of increasing. By 22-30 we were well reefed down in 35 knots of wind on the beam rising to above gale force in the gusts, we were charging along at 7 to 8½ knots over the ground, it was hairy sailing on a pitch black night with no horizon, doesn't give you the most comfortable or relaxed sleep either. While I nodded below on my off watch, I heard Audrey on the radio calling up a ship that she was concerned about, it must have been OK because I didn't hear any more regarding it and dozed off to a fitful sleep.

The passage to Uligamu was about 470 miles in a westerly direction, we reckoned about four days and a bit would do it, notice the glib use of technicalities here, could be we were getting blasé. The first 24 hours we sailed 126 miles helped by the strong northerly during the night, afterwards it settled down into a more regular pattern. We still kept sailing well and the second night was a great improvement in the weather, a steady 5 knots on the log but even better still, a nice horizon with plenty of starlight. A lot of rally yachts reported the same conditions across the Palk Strait on the first night after leaving Sri Lanka which would indicate it is the norm.

Audrey

It was good to be on our way again, I enjoyed most of Sri Lanka when ashore, however, berthed on that unstable pontoon, coupled with the long and dirty walk through the docks, then the constant doubt as to what you would be invited to part with next on the walk through the compound took the edge off our visit.

The first night out across the strait was a bit wild and we were sailing fast, Tony tried to sleep with the help of the fitted lee cloths while I was on watch. There was a lot of shipping around as we were on the main route from south of India to south of Sri Lanka. About midnight just after Tony had gone down below, I saw the lights of a ship and the AIS alarm went off, the ships track appeared to be heading straight for us and because of the conditions I was unsure if he had seen us. His red and green navigation lights were alternating from one colour to the other as he yawed his way through the seas, always a bad sign when you are sailing a reciprocal course. I called him up on the VHF channel 16, I already had the ships name from the AIS, (wonderful bit of kit and best value for money we ever bought); the ship answered straight away and said he would check his radar. After a few seconds he came back to me and said he would alter course to starboard, I replied that I would do the same until he was abeam. It seemed only a few minutes later that he slipped by close to port; I was left wondering whether or not he had seen me but it appeared that he didn't, Tony stirred and slept on.

I'm glad to say the second night was much more comfortable, still sailing well but with a clear sky, I had the Plough (Big Dipper) to the north and I could still just make out the Southern Cross to the south, well, we were still only six degrees north so as we would soon lose it for good, I wanted to see it while I could. There was no moon at this time, only a thin slither of it this morning, we would gradually get more moon each night for the next few days so it was a good omen for the rest of the voyage, for now, we had to manage with just the starlight.

Some yachts who had left earlier and were ahead of us reported a windless area from 76° east, that was another day's sailing ahead of us or 120 miles as the crow flies. Luckily, by the time we got there we held the wind until 74° east, another 120 miles, we were sailing relatively slowly but because we had left early we had time to spare so it didn't matter.

By the third day, the wind was light and astern of us so it was back to the poled out genoas on each side, although we were only doing 2.5 knots over the ground at least it was in the right direction and free. We had also worked our way out of the shipping lanes so had no more big boats to contend with just yet, nearer Uligamu there is another lane where the ships take advantage of a short cut through the channels between the main islands so it was only a temporary reprieve.

During the final night of this voyage Tony had a near miss, at the time there was no moon, little starlight and the horizon was barely visible, he heard the throb of the engines at first and realising it sounded close, he quickly scanned all round Cayuco, he checked our lights were working and tried to pin point the direction of the sound. What looked like a large fishing boat, without lights of any description, steamed past and at speed less than 100 metres astern of us, Tony only picked out the shape in the last few seconds and heard as it thundered by. A point to remember; at the moment, the regulations do not require fishing boats to carry an AIS transmitter. As we don't usually use radar when sailing in good weather due to our limited battery capacity... say no more!

Tony

First light on the 26th January we were approaching the Maldive Island of Uligamu, as the islands are all coral atolls sitting on a reef system we took down the sails and motored in to the anchorage, we needed to charge the batteries again anyway. In general, apart from the first night, the four day passage had gone peacefully enough, it felt good to know we had sailed most of the way and saved our diesel fuel. The little petrol generator was earning its keep and was an economical answer to our battery charging needs, especially in cloudy or light wind conditions when the solar panels, wind and water generators were inefficient.

Our first impression on seeing the Maldives were of an idyllic group of atolls in a ring formation, Uligamu was the northernmost habitable one in the group, as we slowly negotiated around the south side of the island and turned north up in to the anchorage it looked prettier than ever. There was plenty of space for us all around but it was better to anchor just off the reef about 400 metres from the landing area in about 20 metres of water.

There was an anchorage for 3 to 4 vessels inside the reef in a pool of water with 5 to 10 metres depth, we thought it was a bit restricted if you wanted to leave quickly or at night so decided on the outside anchorage. In all there must have been room for 50 to 70 yachts in the large area and while we were there about 30 yachts came and went, it was a very popular stop over for a few days. There is a reef around nearly the whole group of islands so if the wind changed direction it would be possible to move to a more protected spot, with the seasonal calm weather while we were there, nobody had any anchoring problems.

According to Uligamu by-laws we were allowed to stay for the first three days free, after that there is a modest charge. On arrival you radio the Customs and Excise Officers and they come out in a small fast launch to assist in completing the paperwork, then you have to go ashore to the Island Office to register into the island, after that, you can roam almost anywhere unhindered. When the officers had completed the formalities, I removed our dinghy from its lashings, blew it up, fitted the outboard and we went ashore. In February 2009 we had to pull our dinghy up onto the beach and secure it to a handy coconut tree, security is not a problem; we were told there is a small jetty in the planning stage for the future.

A word of warning, the island is very lay back and is not run on the lines that we may be used to, the Island Office is only open till 2pm for example. Shops may be open but there could be no-one in the actual shop serving customers, sometimes you have to knock on the door alongside or even find out where the proprietor lives, they then open up and serve you. It's just that with so few people and trade; they only open if you actually want something.

One of the main grocery shops may not open at all during the day, the owner is the main supplier of diesel on the island and once a week takes off in his boat to get fuel from a neighbouring island, all in cans I might add. It is also possible they may decide to go out for a day's fishing or diving especially if someone from one of the yachts wants local knowledge and a trip out. Having said that the local people are marvellous, they will volunteer to help in any way they can, when we checked in to the Island Office it was near closing time so the manager offered to show us round the island. It is not that big but he walked us to all the shops, introduced us and told us what they sold. We then walked down to the south end where a new rather up market looking resort is nearly completed. The individual chalets, main reception areas and the entertainment sections look very exclusive. It will be an added attraction to the island and should bring some much needed work for the locals. We were told that a new pier and landing jetty is under construction for the resort and that this will be open to yachtsmen who visit Uligamu. This would certainly be a bonus, at the moment there are no regular facilities at all for obtaining a meal or drinks ashore. We were told an Uligamu evening could be arranged in the garden of an islander's house run on the lines of a BBQ, this was arranged for the evening of the day we were due to leave so we missed a good night of local entertainment.

Figure 32: The beautiful coral Island of Uligamu in the Maldives, a truly idyllic and peaceful place.

Audrey

Uligamu must look like everyone's idea of a small desert island, the anchorage was calm and the island looked magnificent, I was also pleasantly surprised to find that I had a strong mobile phone signal. A few minutes later my phone rang and I was talking to our son in UK, for some reason when he used his phone it had rang my number by mistake, we had a welcome impromptu chat and I caught up on some news from home.

There looked to be a fairly large development going on towards the south end of the island, well, large in comparison to the size of the island. It gave the impression of being in keeping with the natural surroundings as the developers are keeping the height of the buildings below the natural tree line, all very plush.

On our stroll round the atoll with the Island Officer he introduced us to a local family who would organize a local meal for visitors. This was an offer not to be missed so we arranged to come back the next day for a meal with them, it is all very informal and because so few people visit it is best to give them time to prepare something for you. We already knew that we would miss the evening BBQ being organised by some of the other yachts.

That night on board we both had a nice bit of steak kept in the freezer since Sri Lanka, we'd purchased some local tomatoes and onions and had some mushrooms in our fridge already; it all went down well with a few boat chips. These boat chips are my own creation and are like small shallow fried sautéed diced potatoes, very handy as a substitute for chips on a yacht as all you need is a small saucepan with a bit of oil in the bottom. All this was washed down with a nice red wine specially kept for the steak. We sat and ate our meal in the cockpit while watching the sun set below the horizon, what more could anyone ask for, anchored just off a desert island with a panorama which would have been the envy of anyone anywhere, we felt like millionaires.

The next day at the appointed time and after we had another interesting walk round the island, we turned up for our local cooked lunch. The table was laid out in a small room tacked on to the main house and the food was prepared on an open stove in front of us. The first course was fish soup, ladled out of a large pot kept on the side of the stove, eaten with fresh homemade bread which you dipped into your soup, the bowl was topped up as many times as you desired. Second course was a whole fish laid on a platter in front of us, the idea was to take off as much fish as you wanted, then take the vegetables from the dishes alongside, these included potatoes, carrots, a local turnip like vegetable, probably chow chow, and some local beans. We finished off with a local desert made with pastry, coconut and a syrup type sweet topping, for drinking there was water or a local made lime squash, no alcohol as it was probably against their religion. It was a delicious meal and it was obvious they had made a special effort for us, it was also noticeable the amount of fish they used which must be part of a staple diet here.

We did not see much livestock around the island, just a few chickens and the occasional goat I expect a lot of their supplies must come from the mainland. When we tried to pay for the meal, they didn't know what to charge as it was the first time they had cooked a meal for anyone else, we estimated what we thought it had cost them which in fact was very little and then took an educated guess at what it would have cost if they had bought all the ingredients locally. This was more realistic, so doubled it and gave them the equivalent of about fifteen dollars. They looked surprised and thought it far too much, everything was probably grown or caught locally, eventually we convinced them to take the money and left. Another unique experience; even had to work out how much to pay for our own meal!

After the meal we tried to stock up with as much fresh fruit and vegetables as possible, we managed to get hold of some more potatoes, onions, bread and papayas. Also filled up six 5 litre bottles with lovely fresh drinking water, a real windfall, it wasn't a lot but it would help eek out our supplies purchased in Sri Lanka, in our situation you took every opportunity to keep fresh provisions topped up as much as possible.

While shopping around I thought it would be a good idea to send some postcards to family and friends, we purchased the postcards without any difficulty. The problem came obvious while trying to purchase the stamps to send them, when we eventually found the shop which doubled as a post office; it had run out of stamps. Our Island Office friend had a solution, if we left him the money for the stamps, as soon as they were available he would stick them on the postcards and post them for us. Sounded like a good idea so that is exactly what we did, to be honest, we weren't optimistic and never expected the cards to reach their destinations.

Figure 33: Audrey on her almost deserted island, the only footprints visible were hers, apart from mine.

Tony

Our new friend came out with us to Cayuco on the second day when he finished his work at 14-00 hours, for a few dollars more he cleaned Cayuco's waterline all round the boat for us. He then asked us to see if any of the other yachts wanted their waterlines cleaning. Oh well, strike while the iron's hot, I always say. We passed his offer round the rest of the anchored fleet on the radio when they returned from their day out diving and snorkelling amongst the outer reefs.

Every evening about 18-00 hours the shallow reef between us and the shore was visited by large manta rays, the water was 3 to 5 metres deep and these huge fish could clearly be seen just under the surface. They were probably feeding but every now and then one of them came to the surface and caused much agitation on the water. Some people from the yachts took the opportunity to swim over to the reef and swam along with the manta rays while filming and taking pictures of them. I was not as brave and quite content to view them from the safety of Cayuco's cockpit, I'm afraid our photos were taken from too far away and did not come out very well at all.

On our last afternoon we walked through the town, took some more photographs and ended up strolling along the beach round most of the island. The beaches are white coral sand, pristinely clean, with thousands of different kinds of shell lying scattered about all over the place, it was possible to walk along selecting the best ones to keep as a memento. To be here on this island was a phenomenal experience but I fear to live there permanently would be very restrictive, with our knowledge of the world and our exploits thus far; it all seemed a bit excessive compared to the peaceful life on Uligamu.

Our three free days were up, they had gone very quickly, even if we wanted to stay longer it was not possible, Salalah in Oman was over 1200 miles away and we had allowed twelve days for the passage. Winds this time of year in the north part of the Indian Ocean are notoriously light, our expectations were for a day's run of 100 miles or less, we had plenty of fuel for the engine and expected to have to motor for some fairly long periods. I had spent some time checking Cayuco and trying to finish off all the little jobs which keep cropping up. This stopover was no different to any other, whenever you get the chance you check engine, gearbox, rigging, sails, warps, lights, top up all hydraulic reservoirs and try to keep everything working correctly, it's a chore, but much easier to do in a calm anchorage than at sea.

As the Island Office is only open until 14-00 hours we went ashore after a leisurely breakfast to complete the paperwork, we signed out from Customs and obtained our release paper to hand over to the authorities in Salalah.

This document is important when you check in anywhere, all the authorities liked to see an official certificate of where you had come from. They are also interested in how long it took you to sail there, where your expected destination is and how long you intended to stay. I suppose it gives them an idea about your voyage, it's certainly getting more difficult to sail right round the world in this way. As far as I can remember, every country set a time limit on our visa and all have penalties if there are any transgressions. Some countries need you to complete documentation and get clearance for your visit before arrival; I suppose it's a sign of the times that governments are having to think more and more about security and safety.

Late morning after the 10-00 hour rally radio net, we lazily weighed anchor and eleven o 'clock saw us slowly moving out of the picturesque bay, again it was sad to leave, we were in no hurry. It was exchanging one idyllic place for unknown hazards on the open ocean, a last photo shoot as we sailed between Vagaaru and Wagaru Islands and we were off. The direct course passes quite close to Vagaaru Island and there is deep water fairly close to, an extensive reef stretches to the north east of Wagaru Island which is difficult to see unless the sea is breaking over it. As soon as Cayuco cleared the islands the wind became apparent, in less than an hour we were sailing nicely along on a broad reach under main, mizzen and genoa, granted we were only doing 4 to 5 knots over the ground but it was delightful and Cayuco sailed herself for the rest of the day.

On the radio net earlier, some yachts that had left the day before reported sighting small fishing boats, I'm sure they were innocent but everyone was becoming nervous. The recent escalation of pirate activity outside the Gulf of Aden area was worrying everyone even right out here in the Indian Ocean, nobody felt 100% safe. The boats ahead had reported suspicious fishing boat movements, the bigger and therefore faster yachts were able to increase speed and outrun the small boats. In reality I felt this was somewhat overkill but I understood their concern.

It was almost certain that these fishing boats were only after a bit of bartering, in any case, it would be impossible for us to outrun them so we made plans in case we were approached. In the event of an incident, we would fit our full cockpit screen and only keep one side open. We would arrange all our bartering items to hand and then discourage them from coming onboard; the idea was to persuade them to barter from the boat. We weren't completely sure our plan would work but in the circumstances, about the best we could achieve. I also noticed that all the reported incidences were directly on the rhumb line between Uligamu and Salalah, having spotted this I altered our tactics slightly, we changed course and sailed a little more northerly.

Within 24 hours we were approximately 12 miles east of the direct line between Uligamu and Salalah, plus, we were over the horizon from any boats lying in wait for a bartering opportunity on the rhumb line. Whether these precautions were justified or even necessary I have no idea, suffice to say we did not meet any small fishing boats for the rest of the voyage. However, we did meet two larger fishing boats travelling at night without lights, I spotted them on radar when they were some miles away, realised they were blacked out and turned our lights off as well. As our lights had a smaller range I was banking that they would not have picked them up yet. I then rolled up all our sails to make us as small and invisible as possible, Cayuco was now drifting without even the engine. Quietly, I woke Audrey to ensure she would not put on any internal lights, together we watched as both boats motored slowly by less than a mile away. We could see their silhouettes outlined faintly against the horizon, it was a very dark night and we hoped they would not notice us; again, it was more than likely unnecessary, I was just trying to keep as low a profile as possible, no point is wishing afterwards you had taken more care.

Figure 34: Camels on the road in Oman, they have right of way

Audrey

By the 1st February we had sailed only 240 miles in 3 days and still had 962 miles to go, it wasn't too important, we had a bit of spare time, the sailing had been comfortable but slow. We decided to motor for a while and try to find the wind, it took nearly 24 hours but eventually we were sailing again, during this time a large pod of dolphins appeared and did a passable example of synchronised swimming while on their early morning feeding frenzy.

It was also a much busier part of the ocean; several ships a day were spotted going to and from the Gulf area. The wind stayed with us and during the night we maintained over a 6 knot average speed, another yacht slowly overtook us during the night clearly on the same course. By the 4th February we were still sailing well and approaching 12° north. It is becoming increasingly evident we will soon need something that so far on this voyage we have done without ... clothes! It was the same for the next three days, we kept moving north-west at a steady 5 to 6 knots and by the evening of the 7th the wind started to die, shortly after nightfall we started the engine. We motored all night long; it was now getting chilly and we had the summer duvet out for the first time since Port Mackay in Australia. The last couple of days were a mixture of motoring and sailing, the wind became more fickle as we approached the land and the shipping increased considerably.

At 09-00 hours on the 10th February 2009 after 12 days at sea, we entered Salalah Harbour and anchored in the outer basin away from the main channel to await instructions. Salalah is a busy commercial port so we had to be given permission to enter the small inner yacht harbour; this is tucked away past the main port and in a little used part near the security base and the fishing vessels. It did not take long for the large commercial ship we were waiting for to dock, then with entry permission granted we preceded up to our very calm and secure inner basin mooring. This was stern to an old commercial quay which was not particularly small yacht friendly, never mind, drop anchor, stern to the wall, warps attached, blow up the dinghy, leave enough room to launch and pull across to the well used ladder.

Our rally support co-ordinator was already on station, he organised our paperwork, introduced us to our local contact for any assistance and by early afternoon we were checked in and sorted as far as possible. In the evening, another rally friend who had arrived earlier and organised himself a hire car, drove us up to the lovely "Oasis Club", I would have to say, oasis by name and oasis by nature, this club became the unofficial rally HQ during our stay. It is an ex-pat enclave complete with bar and restaurant and as Oman is almost a dry country, this club was a very welcome retreat.

The 12 day passage across the final part of the Indian Ocean was one of the most uneventful voyages of the whole circumnavigation, it was notable by its lack of any engine problems, inconveniences or breakages, we weren't complaining and decided boring was good, boring means "no problems".

We were not totally at ease though, we all knew where we had to go next and without exception, no-one was over anxious to get going. Pirate Alley was upon us, the next passage was going to be a completely different ball game.

Figure 35: An oasis in the middle of the desert miles from nowhere supports an abundance of wild life

Chapter 17

Pirates Ahoy – Salalah to Djibouti

Tony

Even before we started the rally we all knew of the pirate threat in the Gulf of Aden, to be honest in January 2007 when we finally decided to go round with the Blue Water Rally the pirate threat to small yachts was minimal. There had been few incidences and most of these had involved the more affluent members of the yachting fraternity with their super yachts and obvious wealth. It's true that small boats were approached and the occurrence of these were well known, mostly it involved real fishermen who would barter some of the fish they caught for cigarettes, beer or maybe a bag of rice. This was perfectly acceptable and both parties gained something, sometimes the exchange would be carried out by signs and gesticulations without either being able to speak a word of the others language.

The normal approach would be for the fishing boat to close in to the yacht to about 30 foot (10 metres) away, one of the fishermen would stand up in the boat and hold up some fish, if the exchange was acknowledged, the fishing boat would then come alongside and the barter would be transacted. From what I have been able to find out, around the middle of 2005, a fairly large but privately owned American yacht with a couple aboard was on passage westward along the Gulf when approached by a small fishing boat. While the boat was along the port side and a deal was being done, another fishing boat came up on the starboard side and two people jumped quickly aboard the yacht. These others were armed and threatening; they forced the woman below with one of the gunmen and held the man in the cockpit. Later on the one in the cockpit took the skipper up to the bow and held him on deck against his will. The one below searched the boat and found about $3000 in the saloon plus a quantity of saleable electronic goods, it's not even sure if the first boat was part of the attack. By all accounts the incident was over quite quickly and although very frightening, the yacht was allowed to carry on its way.

Since then the word has gone round among the fishing community that small yachts carry large quantities of money, most of us realise this is not true but compared to the fishermen's meagre existence, even a few dollars may tempt some of them and let's face it, they are not all fishermen anymore. There have been other accounts of this kind of robbery, one of which is documented on the internet "Noonsite" forum and is worth reading. These accounts should not put people off from extended sailing trips but serve as a caution on the safest way to transit this area.

We have even heard of people acting as scouts and watching yachts leave ports in this vicinity, these scouts are in touch with small boats who work up and down the gulf waiting for possible soft targets. Some incidences occurred within 30 miles off the coast of Yemen and also along the Gulf where it is fairly easy to escape back to Somalia and Yemen. The boats can be about 30 feet long, (10 metres), look like fishing boats and there is no obvious reason to suspect them. The real problem seems to come from the larger boats called mother ships, these have small fast runabouts with powerful outboards and can attain speeds of 25 knots or more but are usually associated with attacks on larger commercial vessels, crew can be from two to six people in each and come up fast on both sides. Others are sometimes longer, up to 60 feet (20 metres), have larger crews, are slower but can be just as threatening. Don't forget there are still innocent fishing boats who only want to barter for cigarettes, beer or a bag of rice, the trouble is, there's no way of knowing until it's too late.

The other intimidating element is that nearly all the fishing boats, even the innocent ones, carry weapons, powerful rifles and AK47 machine guns being the preferred choice. It is disconcerting to see these lying about the boat in full view, even when negotiating a genuine barter, remember, in this part of the world, it's just everyday life. These events are not a new trend in these waters, it has been happening on and off for years. The more recent attacks on large commercial ships where the crew are held for ransom have brought it all to the attention of the world and are most likely being carried out by professionally trained gangs; it does not look likely that it will get better in the short term.

Salalah in Oman was a welcome addition to our itinerary, being a much closer port to the Gulf gave us a better opportunity to regroup and plan our strategy. There had been many questions asked about increased pirate activity and we were all very much aware of the risks. Many discussions between ourselves and the organisers had taken place regarding this stretch of water, it would be fair to say, none of us were looking forward to it with much enthusiasm.

Salalah is a very different kind of stopover, the terrain is mostly dry desert, quite dusty and the port is not really geared up for too many yachts. The concrete quay is used by large ships so has iron piles and dangerous obstructions for small vessels, the first yachts to arrive all dropped their anchor and reversed onto the quay. We held ourselves off the wall by adjusting the anchor chain and left a gap at the rear to launch the dinghy so we could reach the slippery ladder. At least the inner basin is fairly calm so there was not a lot of movement. Even with this arrangement not all the yachts could get stern to the wall, further along, some were anchored off with a rope to the rocks and had to use the dinghy to get ashore in the usual manner.

The skippers, who had managed to moor their yachts on the wall, had to devise some unusual methods of re-fuelling and getting water aboard in jerry cans. The port itself is a mixture of military and commercial, because of this access was controlled by security guards, we were all given passes to enter and leave but the guards soon got to know us and mostly waved us through, occasionally stopping us to do a random check

Salalah itself is a pleasant enough town, the roads in Oman are good although hot and dusty, there are plenty of well stocked shops, a wide variety of restaurants but they are all 10 to 15 miles from the harbour. There is little or no public transport, fortunately we had the assistance of Ali, our local agent, he quickly and efficiently organised a fleet of fairly cheap cars to hire, we shared one with Hugh and Shan from Stargazer and it was extremely good value.

One of the highlights of being moored in the port area is the Oasis Club; this was situated about one kilometre outside the main gate and became a haven for rest and relaxation. Happily we were all granted honorary membership for the few days we were there.

Oman is basically a dry state with alcoholic drinks only available in a few licensed premises; the Oasis Club is one of these and is also a very reasonably priced restaurant with good quality pub grub. All of the rally social events took place in the Oasis Club, most evenings whatever we did; we started or finished off in the club, sometimes both.

This is where the rally update took place for the next leg to Djibouti, probably our most important briefing yet. When leaving Sri Lanka we had all been given a latest arrival date to be in Salalah, it was very important that we were all ready at the required time to leave for the transit of the Gulf. To ensure the safest passage possible the rally organisers had been working behind the scenes for many months, the next leg had been very carefully planned and we had all made it by the designated time. To prepare our vessels it was important that we filled up with a maximum of fuel, maintaining a fixed average speed may require a lot of engine work and it was important to ensure we were all ready.

The easiest way to obtain fuel was in our jerry cans, as we wanted 500 litres and could only get 5 x 20 litre cans in the car, it meant doing five separate journeys until the tanks were full. This in itself was bad news, when we got the cans back to the boat we had the worse problem of getting the fuel out across the gap to the boat, one way would be to use the dinghy but it was very messy. The problem was neatly solved by using a line and pulley system rigged from the top of Cayuco's mizzen mast; tie the line to a can ashore while another line tied onto the can controlled the descent. Our next door neighbour was Rob, the American who was sailing Mani, he assisted by taking the strain on the masthead line while I lifted the can over the side of the quay and then slowly let my controlling line out as the can of fuel descended down to Cayuco's stern deck. Once all the cans were on deck, I went down and siphoned the fuel into the boat tanks, empty cans went back up using the reverse procedure, it was then refill them and start all over again. After the fuel tanks were full we used the same system to fill all the water tanks, as a bonus, after we had finished with Cayuco, we started on Mani which needed the same method to fill all their tanks, it was a hard couple of days.

Our time in Salalah was limited, arriving on the 10th February we were only there eight days and left on Wednesday 18th, all our preparations were completed early which left us a bit of time to explore inland and along the coast. On the 13th a joint birthday party was held at the Oasis Club as there were six of us who all had birthdays around the same time. On subsequent evenings we tried a Turkish restaurant, then a Lebanese and Chinese one in the main shopping area of Salalah. On one of our shopping forays, we found a nice out of the way store where pork sausages and bacon were available, they were in a freezer tucked away behind a partition and you had to ask specifically for them, not a bad find in Oman but at horrendous prices.

The Oasis club had good internet facilities and we managed to connect and chat to family, this was always a bonus, it cheered us up and took our mind off the pirate threat for a while. Imagine our surprise to find out that the postcards we had sent from Uligamu in the Maldives a couple of weeks before had arrived, oh ye of little faith! After our good news we stayed on for the weekly Oasis Club BBQ and had a really excellent evening.

A briefing on the Sunday sorted out the final arrangements for the passage to Djibouti, there were to be five groups each containing five or six yachts, the groups would leave over a two day period during the hours of daylight and a few hours after each other. The groups were also arranged in order of speed with the fastest group leaving first. Our group being the slowest and therefore the last to go consisted of five yachts. Cayuco being the slowest boat of the group was picked as flotilla leader; this meant all the other yachts should be able to keep up with us. Hugh on Stargazer would be the group communications man and had responsibility for all emergency exchanges involving safety. All of us had handheld VHF sets which have a limited range when on low power so excellent for conversation within ½ to 1 mile, and we all had the usual fixed VHF and SSB sets, some of our group also had sat phones.

We were almost ready to go, I helped Hugh with a little problem on his engine and it was time for some tourism before we left. Over the next two days we went out to the desert, up onto the mountain plateau known as Jabel Izzin and visited Job's Tomb (pronounced Jobe) of biblical fame, i.e. somebody who has the patience of Jobe, the small road sign identifies it as "El Nabi Ayoob" The Prophet Job. On the journey we saw many camels, went to a frankincense tree plantation and generally took in the outstanding views from the top of the mountain. The next day saw us visiting a wonderful oasis right out in the desert, these are truly outstanding places, in the middle of the dry dusty landscape where it is surprising to see anything living you suddenly come across a lake with green grass, bushes, trees and wildlife; maybe some small caves in the rocks and fish swimming in the cool water, it is an amazing sight. The question to ask really is, how did the small animal wildlife get right out here and how long has it been there? Birds, no problem, I can understand, but those funny little furry four legged, big eyed, nocturnal, marmoset type creatures, who we saw in the caves, no way would they survive a couple of miles in the desert, it just doesn't make sense.

Back in the Oasis Club the night before we left we accidently bumped into the crew of a Portsmouth, UK, destroyer which was part of the Coalition Force protecting the Gulf waters, they were leaving Salalah the next day to resume their patrol, it was re-assuring to see they were there and leaving with us.

Up early next morning and everything was ready, our small group consisted of Cayuco, UK, (Lead Boat), Stargazer, UK, (Communications), Penelope 3, UK, Shaula 3, (Italian) and Jupiter, (French), by 08-00 hours, we were all on our way. Leaving the relative safety of Salalah Port everyone had a mixture of emotions, we had been gearing ourselves up for this since leaving Phuket and not without some trepidation did we set off. Our plan was to motor-sail to a point near the International Recommended Transit Corridor (IRTC) within the Maritime Security Patrols Area (MSPA). This area is set up and coordinated by the Maritime Liaison Office in Bahrain,

(MARLO), and is being patrolled by the coalition force vessels trying to protect the commercial shipping. Yachts are asked to contact UKMTO or MARLO for the latest guidance and form convoys well before reaching the Gulf. There is an internet site covering all aspects of safety for commercial and small sailing craft, it's on "Gulf of Aden – Pirate Corridor Waypoints" there is also a lot of information on the yachting website "Noonsite", on these two sites are phone numbers and names to contact, at sea of course, you will need a sat phone.

On the way to the form up point we practised staying in formation, closing up and all turning away together in case of attack and using our low power handheld VHF sets for communication. We had all decided to motor sail with our speed regulated at 5 knots or maybe slightly more if we were fortunate with the current, our starting point for the passage was about 150 miles from Salalah, we expected to be able to enter the corridor before nightfall the next day.

Figure 36: An unusual way of winching fuel and water aboard in Salalah

Audrey

During the night dolphins came to play, two, like a couple of missiles, shot towards our hull leaving phosphorous wakes, they sped underneath ,and along the sides leaving zig-zag patterns behind them, it is a truly marvellous sight at night when dolphins do this. The other odd thing we saw on this trip, at least 100 miles offshore, were lots of baby turtles, they only looked about 6 inches (150 mm) across; it was the amount and size of them which attracted our attention. We had certainly never seen turtles of this small size at sea and certainly not in the numbers we encountered, that is what is so interesting about long distance sailing, you just never know what you are going to see next.

Tony

Our first apprehension came before we even got to our rendezvous, over 100 miles from the shore a lone fast open boat approached our convoy, there was nothing else in view and it was suspicious, why would a small open boat like that be right out here, safety's sake demanded I order a close up instruction for our little fleet and also an immediate turn away from the suspicious craft. The boat appeared to turn and move away from us, speeding across close to our bows, the sole occupant waved an arm, apparently in friendship, we waved back and he continued on his way. Resuming our course the encounter did not seem to be threatening and we did not want to radio in every incident, there was no benefit in crying wolf too often, the authorities would soon dismiss us as nervous nuisances.

 A short time later a dhow appeared from the same direction the small open boat had been heading, we watched as it slowly overtook us, it was towing five small open skiffs just like the one we had seen earlier, our entire group watched it closely but it just kept going and slowly disappeared over the horizon. This was almost certainly a genuine fishing boat, they tow the skiffs and when spotting a school of tuna, all take to the skiffs to catch the fish, unfortunately, pirates also use the same tactics to harass and then attack other ships and by all accounts they are not too fussy about which ships they attack.

Audrey

We entered the security corridor between the shipping lanes shortly after sundown on the 19th; there was a reassuring presence of Naval Vessels cruising slowly in the area. Next morning we had a fly over by helicopter, this had obviously come from one of the security force ships and was carrying out a routine reconnoitre of the area. Before leaving Salalah, we had arranged to proceed through the corridor at a steady speed, we left when we did because our passage through the area had been pre-planned, the security forces had been informed to expect us at certain points each 24 hour interval. That would give them a fair chance of knowing where we were at any point during our transit, to back this up, the information they held was updated daily by our communications man, Hugh, thus ensuring they had a running position for our group.

Tony

Our suggested box formation for the passage was two yachts in the front row, two yachts in the second row and one yacht in the last row, this yacht was positioned in the centre of the third line and behind the two yachts in the second row. When we practised the close up manoeuvre on the way to the corridor, it seemed to take a long time before the yachts were close together. Because of this delay, I suggested we try another configuration, three yachts in the front line and two yachts in the row behind but in the middle position between the three boats in front, this Delta arrangement gave us much quicker close up times. With this configuration of the group, Cayuco in the centre of the first row slowed down, the two boats on either side could close in quickly and the two boats behind speeded up coming in at a slight angle. The recommended distance apart was 400 metres, nearly a quarter of a mile, this was OK in daylight but at night we tended to close up a bit, we never discussed this as such, it just seemed to happen. The real problem with this group sailing is trying to stay a regulated distance apart, in practise our little assembly worked well together and we all kept an eye on each other. It's difficult to maintain a well ordered group collectively at sea, to be honest, it flies in the face of the reason most of us go sailing in the first place.

The corridor between the lanes is only 2 miles wide and the front row of yachts together was half a mile across so navigation had to be quite accurate. Fortunately, we all had chart plotters, so it was relatively simple to put in the waypoints given to us by MARLO. Then again, if we all went for the same waypoint, the group would eventually close up on each other, to counteract that, the two outside vessels put in a position a few hundred yards either side of the waypoint, don't you just love it when a plan comes together. Another minor problem is the given waypoints appear to get closer and closer to the shipping lanes such that it gets risky to follow them from one end of the corridor to the other. We solved this by putting in waypoints approximating to a normal 24 hour run and then sailed from one to the other, updating to the next waypoint as required. The passage is about 700 miles from Salalah to Djibouti and took us just over 6 days, 500 miles of this is in the corridor orientated along a straight line course of 252° T; it may be the curvature of the earth which causes this gradual progression to one side of the track over this distance.

Saturday the 21st February dawned and we all had to wish Hugh a Happy Birthday, we're sure he would have preferred a more exotic location for this occasion but then, not many people have the opportunity to have a birthday in Pirate Alley. My birthday was on the 25th February, by which time we all hoped to be in Djibouti, Hugh and I with Audrey and Shan, agreed to celebrate the event in style together on arrival.

Small Somali and Yemeni fishing boats kept appearing randomly, some alone, some in groups and some towing fishing skiffs. They were all watched with interest but nothing else caused us any concern until the afternoon when we heard a confrontation on channel 16 which sounded suspicious. Shortly after that, another sailing yacht was seen motoring across the eastbound shipping lane from the northerly direction, this yacht which was unknown to us steamed up at an angle across the lane and took up position behind our second row. In our second row were "Stargazer" (Hugh and Shan) and the French yacht "Jupiter" (Pascal and his two brothers). After a short conversation between the five yachts in our group, it was agreed that I, as lead boat, should talk to the skipper of the new yacht and explain our situation.

Establishing contact with the yacht by VHF, I discovered they were a male and female couple, the yacht's name was "Magnolia" and they were on passage to Massawa in Eritrea. They had left with another yacht but had got separated and then had an unpleasant experience with fishermen, at the same time they had spotted our little flotilla and decided to see if they could join us for added protection. I explained our situation, speed and direction etc., and told them we had no problem with them tagging on astern of us but asked them to maintain radio silence unless it was urgent and to only use deck lights at night, we did not want to advertise our presence in these waters. To be honest, we couldn't have done anything about them following on behind anyway and no-one in our group would have suggested they did anything else.

In the evening about 18-00 hours we heard a commercial vessel, the MV Suldanha calling for assistance, the master thought there was a possibility they were under threat of a pirate attack. A coalition ship answered immediately and advised them to steam at full speed and carry out evasive manoeuvres. After a few minutes, it transpired that the skiffs speeding round the stern were fishing for tuna and the emergency was stood down. We know now that this is a tactic used by the fishermen to catch tuna, the movement of large vessels through the water sometimes disturbs the shoals of fish that the tuna feed on, the fishermen capitalise on this occurrence by quickly scooping up as many tuna as possible. Of course this method of speeding round the stern of vessels is also used by the pirates before and during boarding the ships to capture them, so it is easy to see where the confusion comes in. The emergency was stood down and the MV

Suldanha carried on its way, we estimated later that it must have been travelling at around 14/15 knots. At this point in time, the vessel was entering the west going lane on the north side of the corridor and was probably around 70 miles behind us. One of the abnormalities of this area is the distance VHF radio waves travel; it is quite usual to hear ships over 100 miles away.

Our little flotilla maintained 5 knots throughout the night and we entered one of the intensive fishing areas designated on the chart, this is a place where a lot more fishing vessels congregate and traditionally it is a much busier fishing area.

Around 08-00 hours the next morning on the 22nd February, we heard a mayday on channel 16, it was the same ship as the previous night, the MV Suldanha, the Captain was transmitting a mayday of a pirate attack on his vessel and stated that the pirates were attempting to climb up the stern of the ship, we all listened intently and then contacted each other on a different channel with our handheld sets. A check on the reported position of the ship confirmed it had passed us during the night and was now about 30 miles ahead of us. We continued to monitor the radio, only a few minutes later, the Captain reported that the pirates had gained access to his vessel, were firing weapons and making their way along the deck to the bridge. Our entire group heard the sound of weapons being discharged during this broadcast on our radios. We were obviously concerned for them but also for us, the ship was less than 30 miles ahead and if captured would almost certainly be ordered to change course to the south, this would put it going across somewhere in front of us. A little while later, we heard another transmission from the Captain stating that the ship had been captured and 22 crew were being held hostage on the bridge, the ship had been ordered to alter course to the south and all coalition warships were being warned to keep more than two miles away as the crew were being taken as hostages.

A short chat amongst ourselves to discuss our situation resulted in us agreeing to keep going at the same speed and keep a watchful eye and ear for any updates, as a precaution we closed up together about half way in case we spotted anything untoward. We saw and heard very little over the next five to six hours, at our average speed this amount of time would put us at the point where the ship was captured, by now all was quiet and we saw nothing. We were left wondering if the apparent fishing incident the previous night was carried out by the same group of people. The first contact which appeared to be innocent fishing may in fact have been a softening up procedure. The consensus of opinion amongst us on our situation was that it seemed unlikely the pirates would be interested in our flotilla, the attack was obviously a professional and well planned operation and we agreed they were after much bigger fish; no pun intended.

Audrey

We chugged along happily motor sailing, the wind was generally light but we had the main up as a steadying sail and used it and the jib when the wind became useable. The next morning, Monday 23rd February around 06-00 just after dawn, Tony was sleeping while I was on watch, the radio once again burst into life, a tanker steaming east in the lane south of us, reported sighting 5 or 6 targets closing in on him from ahead, he gave out his position and the position of the suspect vessels, then requested advice from any coalition warship in the area. An almost instant answer from a warship ordered the tanker to immediately initiate a 180° turn and increase speed to the maximum, the warship also reported that they were nearby and would launch their helicopter without delay. By this time Tony was awake and came up to the cockpit, listening, he had already calculated that the position the tanker gave was very near ours. Another broadcast from the tanker a few minutes later confirmed it was only about five miles ahead of our position and the targets he was talking about were most likely us. A chat amongst our little fleet on low power radio confirmed we had all come to the same conclusions i.e.

(1) The "pirates" the officers on the tanker suspected they were watching on radar were in fact probably us in our little flotilla, the position they were reporting was almost exactly where we were.

(2) Because the threat to the tanker may have been genuine, we would have to maintain radio silence.

(3) Although tempting for us to use our radios to contact the tanker, it would risk informing anyone else in the area of our proximity, including any opportunistic elements in the vicinity.

(4) It was in our interests to remain unnoticed, if there was a genuine attack, it was too close for comfort.

We decided to keep a low profile and continue on our course and speed, in the meantime, the tanker had turned to port and increased speed, this meant it was now leaving the east bound lane and heading across the corridor towards the west bound lane in front of us. The tanker looked to be a large vessel, we saw it ahead going across our bows and reckoned it was over 100,000 tons, the problem being that it was now heading straight across the west bound lane instead of along it.

The next interesting development was the approach of a helicopter, it came in fast and low right over the top of us, then, the radio crackled into life again as the crew of the helicopter realised the case of mistaken identity. The crew informed our communications man, Hugh on Stargazer that:

"Ops were normal" which we assumed to be military jargon for "carry on" he then informed the tanker watch officer that we were not pirates, but a harmless fleet of small sailing vessels proceeding along the corridor and minding their own business, they asked the tanker officer to continue on with their voyage.

It now got more interesting than ever, the emergency over, the tanker, having got through the west bound lane continued its circle to get back on course and return to the eastbound lane. It had been lucky on its first run across the west bound lane and had managed to slot between other ships steaming west along the marked channel. Not so on its way back, what went wrong we will never know, but the tanker misjudged its route across the lane while trying to resume its original track.

Large ships started to alter their course to avoid the tanker, this had a domino effect on all other traffic in the area, we watched as ships big and small tried to miss each other all initiating changes in their track, when one altered course he invariably caused another one to have to change direction. It was a tense few minutes before it was clear that everyone had managed to steer clear of each other. The radio conversations between each of the ships concerned were a different matter however, they conducted themselves in a very controlled and professional manner but it was undeniably embarrassing for the watch officer on board the tanker. His parentage was brought into question on several occasions. It would not be fair of me to divulge the name of the tanker involved in the incident, it remains incognito in my log. "They", always say, there are 'worse troubles at sea', on this day there very nearly was. This incident highlights just how nervous professional and amateur sailors are while navigating through this area; passages should not be taken lightly. I joked to our little group, that this was,

"The Blue Water Rally Pirate fleet, a bit strapped for cash after our round the world sailing trip".

This wasn't quite the end of the saga, just then a warship was spotted steaming up quickly to the scene of the misdemeanour and having established everything was OK, stayed with us for a few hours, probably didn't want us to upset anyone else.

During the day, Magnolia peeled off to resume their voyage to Eritrea; they called us up on the radio and thanked us for all our assistance. We had been constantly shepherded and over flown by planes and helicopters from the coalition forces all the way down the corridor, we never did find out what they thought about our security modus operandi.

Only just dawn and already too much excitement, maybe this could be marketed as one of those adventure breaks? Forget paint balling, hang gliding and grand prix cars, take a week's cruise through the Gulf of Aden in a small yacht, - much more of a buzz!!

Little did we know, there was still more excitement to come?

Tony

We left the protection of the corridor just before 18-00 hrs the next day, our group threaded themselves between the procession of commercial ships coming down from the Red Sea and then changing course to enter the east going lane. An E U warship, watching the start of the corridor, steamed very slowly astern and to starboard of us.

From the end of the corridor to Djibouti is about 100 miles so most of another good day's run before we arrive, I had always believed this final section to be the most dangerous element of the passage. On the previous rally in 2007 an incident occurred about 20 miles from Djibouti with the final group of yachts arriving. There were parallels to our group and I warned our team not to let their guard down just because we only had 100 miles to go, we were still off the Somalia coast and as you approach Djibouti the shoreline gets closer.

The E U warship continued his course and very slowly overtook us about 2 miles off our starboard beam during the hours of darkness, it was re-assuring to see him there, he was in view most of the night and slipped over the horizon ahead of us just before dawn.

However, from about 03-00 hours, I had been watching two small suspicious blips on the radar screen; they were some miles behind us and travelling at the same speed. No sooner had the warship disappeared than I noticed the blips started to close in on us, I was not the only one to spot them, both Hugh and Gianfranco on Shaula 3 had seen them, all our group agreed to watch their movements closely. Over the next few hours of darkness the two dots on the screen gradually closed the distance between us. Around 07-00 hours just after dawn, the two blips came into visual range and we spotted two fishing vessels a couple of miles astern, one was slightly ahead of the other on our starboard quarter. They continued to close the gap and by 08-00 hours were only half a mile off our starboard beam. At this stage they did not pose a threat and appeared to be heading for Djibouti the same as us, we all watched them and monitored their course and speed.

The two boats were about 50 feet long, (15 metres), the worrying thing was they looked like Somali fishing boats and if so, were travelling in the wrong direction, we knew that Somali fishing boats used Djibouti Port, it was just one more fact to consider. We had been supplied with pictures of the Somali fishing boats which differ from their Yemeni counterparts in several ways; this additional knowledge did not ease our apprehension.

At this time we were about 25 miles from our destination but unfortunately, due to the angle we were approaching, we were only about 15 miles off the Somalia Coast and technically still in their waters, we carried on albeit a bit nervously. By 09-00 hours, the first vessel had slowly worked his way across in front and a couple of miles forward of our port bow, he then turned his boat to face towards us and came to a stop in this position. At the same time the second one had moved to a position half a mile forward of our starboard bow but continued to move at the same speed and direction as us. We watched; the air was charged with suspense; everyone in our group was now expecting some kind of confrontation. A check with our binoculars showed that there were 9 to 10 men on each boat, most of which seemed to have some sort of weapon slung around their shoulders, some of these looked alarmingly like automatics.

The situation was looking highly suspicious and as lead vessel I issued a general alert to the entire group to be ready for a close up move. I voiced my concern with Hugh on low power VHF radio and with everyone in the group, continued to assess the situation.

Hugh prepared to issue a pan pan emergency call if necessary, I then ordered a close up of the group, but to do it gradually so as not to alert them, this manoeuvre was completed as per our practise runs. Our location was now approximately 22 miles from Djibouti; we were out of sight of land and only about 3 miles from the theoretical maritime border of the Somali/Djibouti boundary, this stretches from the coast to some miles out in the Gulf.

Motoring at our steady five knots had brought us nearly level with the first boat on our port side which by now was less than half a mile away; the second boat had stopped directly in front of us.

It was 09-45 and you could cut the tension with a knife, we all watched and expected something to happen, the anxiety had increased due to the odd movements of the suspect vessels. The fishing vessel on our port side started an approach, we observed an increase in the smoke from his exhaust and he started to move quickly straight towards our port side, his bow wave grew larger as his speed increased.

Hugh on Stargazer instantly issued a pan pan emergency on channel 16, he relayed our group designation, possible pirate attack and our latitude and longitude position, this call was answered instantly by an E U warship who stated very clearly that he was changing course and would be with us as soon as possible. I then ordered a further close up of the group, an increase in speed and a 30° turn to starboard away from the boat coming towards us.

The suspected fishing (pirate) vessel, who probably monitored the same radio channel and may have heard the E U warship broadcast, continued coming straight at us for a few minutes. He then slowed down and although on the same course, maintained his distance from us, by now he was uncomfortably close. We watched intently as they appeared to be discussing what to do next. By this time we could clearly see with our naked eye the automatic weapons that most of them seemed to be carrying slung around their shoulders, all doubts about their intentions ceased.

It was about ten minutes since this incident had started and it seemed as if it had all the hallmarks of a temporary stalemate. It was around this time that the second fishing vessel, now on our port side because of our change of course decided to approach us at speed, our predicament was escalating rapidly. I tried to contact Hugh to raise the level of emergency but I was too late, Hugh was already broadcasting a full Mayday, Mayday, Mayday, pirate attack message and that we were now being threatened by two vessels. The response from the E U warship which turned out to be French was immediate and he replied that he would be with us in twenty minutes.

Our group included the French yacht "Jupiter" with Pascal as the skipper and his two brothers, he asked me if it would be possible to talk to the warship, he thought as he was French it would be easier for him to converse with them. I agreed and told him to go ahead, there was no point in observing radio silence now and it would let the French Warship crew know that three of their fellow countrymen were in our group.

As we were so close to Djibouti our radio transmissions had been picked up by the rally yachts that had already arrived, some attempted to contact us on VHF channel 73 and others in the group started chatting amongst themselves about the emergency. One of them contacted a British Warship that was in port, (in fact the one we saw in Salalah), only to discover that a helicopter had already been scrambled. The other consequence was to create a flurry of radio chatter which meant any talk between us was interrupted; our group was forced to choose another radio channel in which to communicate with each other.

John on Penelope 3 reported a loss of engine power which he assumed to be caused by partially blocked fuel filters, although he was still OK for now and steaming at five knots it changed our tactics slightly, I gave instruction to the group to close up further on John's vessel and continue at the best speed Penelope 3 could make, at the same time I ordered another 30° turn to port because of the second pirate vessel now coming in on our port side.

French is a common language in these parts and there is always a possibility that the pirate vessels, for by now we were convinced that they were pirates, had monitored the conversation between Jupiter and the French Warship. The Warship radioed and stated again that they were only twenty minutes away, almost at the same time we saw smoke from the funnel on the horizon. Both crews on the pirate vessels must have seen it as well because they stopped motoring towards us and held station in the water. We were still moving away from them and at this time there was less than 150 metres separating us, we all watched each other.

Within a few minutes a grey shape started to take shape steaming quickly towards our position, the pirates were clearly undecided about their next move, the longer they delayed, the better for us.

The people on the two pirate craft continued to observe us for some minutes while the warship closed in on our position, it started to grow visually. The closest one of the alien craft turned and started to move away from our group heading back towards Somalia; the second hesitated a few more seconds, but then he too swung round and headed after his companion. We watched them move away, the sense of relief was immense, all of us probably reflecting on what might have been and there was not much doubt in any of our minds that we had been extremely lucky. The time was 10-18, it was only thirty three minutes from start to finish of our ordeal but it had seemed a lot longer. A few minutes later the warship steamed passed us, he radioed to ask if the emergency was still active, Hugh replied that,

"As far as we were concerned, the emergency was still active" we had no intention of standing the emergency down until we were a lot further away than this, we watched the warship chase after the pirates who were still in view and resumed our course for Djibouti, we never did see the helicopter.

In a discussion between ourselves afterwards, it was agreed that our tactics had done a lot to confuse and irritate the pirate vessels, closing up and keeping together had been our most defensive ploy. We were all fairly convinced that if any yacht had got separated from the group, it would almost certainly have been picked off by the two pirate vessels. The fact that an E U warship was close by and available is down to the meticulous planning and organisation of our team at Blue Water Rallies. OK, there was an element of luck and we were all very appreciative of that, I for one would not traverse this area in a small ship any other way.

Audrey

Three hours later at 13-15 hours, five very relieved crews rounded the point to approach Djibouti Harbour; on the way in I suggested we all raise our Blue Water battle flags. As we entered the anchorage with battle flags flying, the foghorns from the other anchored boats started blowing. Amidst cheers, radio chatter and us returning the foghorn as much as our lungs could stand, we moved slowly through the yachts and dropped anchor in the calm and peaceful waters just off the yacht club. Of course everyone wanted to know about all the details so gradually the tale unfolded. A few hours rest allowed us all to immerse in the security of our surroundings and relax properly for the first time in the last few days.

For the second year running, completely unplanned, Tony had arrived at a destination the day before his birthday, last year it was in the Galapagos Islands, this year it was in Djibouti, both were significant, but arriving here safely was a major achievement and the relief was evident.

The incident with the pirates and the passage through the gulf warranted another poem. Although there was an element of danger at various points of the circumnavigation the pirate threat was a very specific one. The hazards of weather, rig failure and navigational problems just have to be dealt with and we always felt we would be OK. The scariest thing about the pirate threat was that we were not in control and felt helpless; we did everything feasible as per our rally briefings, after that it was mostly in the lap of the gods.

Freedom

There's no such thing as pirates,
They tell me with conviction.
They're stuff of films and story books,
Not fact, but purely fiction.

As we set sail from Salalah,
We wished that this was true.
We kept a wary vigil,
In case they came in view.

A nasty feeling in my gut,
Indicated, I was scared.
With many expert briefings,
We hoped we were prepared.

Preparation was our safest bet,
We could not face this alone.
Teamwork, the key to our salvation,
Our senses finely honed.

As we ventured on the Gulf,

Our nerves were frayed, by many a false alarm.
Through hell and high water, our keen wits and wisdom,
Had kept our small ships from harm.

But this was a different kind of threat,
No sailor should endure.
A threat to personal freedom,
Too vital to ignore.

For the draw of the sea is in our blood,
Exploration is our right.
Though the perils of entrapment,
Are a real and serious plight.

Our small platoon victorious,
Escaped to tell the tale.
Regaining rule of destiny,
To continue on life's trail.

Tony

There is no doubt in the minds of any of the yachts involved in this incident that it was anything but a serious attempt on our group, if the fishing boats had continued to come in on us, the outcome could have been very different, there was no way any of us could have taken on that number of men armed with automatic weapons. One of the known tactics used by the pirates on a single vessel, is to have one of them come alongside with the pretence of barter, while you are distracted, the other one comes up on the other side, quickly boards your vessel and you are then helpless.

The strategy outlined to us by the rally organisers had worked. To our credit we followed the directives rigidly. We stayed together, operated as a team, had practised the manoeuvres and had made ourselves what they called a hard target. Our discipline in keeping the group close together and then closing up even further when they made a dash for us may have given them second thoughts, if one of us had panicked and tried to break away, the result could have been very different. In our view, it was the single mindedness of the group that confused and delayed the pirates long enough for us to contact the coalition force warship and obtain assistance.

Entry formalities in Djibouti were completed and we returned to Cayuco with fresh food. In honour of Tony's eminent birthday and Hugh's belated "big day" during the voyage from Salalah, we invited them both to join us on board for the evening meal, over a bottle of wine and a few beers we all reminisced regarding our close call. Destiny, fate, whatever you want to call it, was on our side that day.

Soon our onward journey would be giving us other battles to overcome, the 1400 miles up the Red Sea to Egypt is notorious. Strong northerly winds blow almost all year round normally making for a very long and hard beat to windward. There are few windows in the weather that the small boat sailor can take advantage of to ease his journey north. One thing for certain, if you are lucky enough to catch one of the southerly blows at the right time, you take it with open arms, use it for as long as you can and cover as much distance as possible, in the meantime we all tried to enjoy Djibouti.

Chapter 18

Up the Red Sea

Tony

Djibouti used to be called French Somaliland and it became an independent nation in June 1977 when it was granted sovereignty from France. It borders Ethiopia, Eritrea and Somalia, still includes a French military presence and a body of French Legionnaires.

Being an ex French controlled country, the entry and exit formalities are uncomplicated, the administrative centre is in the harbour and they request that you use your dinghy to go over to the steps on the quayside, then walk up to the Harbour Offices to complete the formalities. This arrangement means you can clear in without going ashore outside the restricted area; all the staff are in one building complex so it is very straightforward and only takes a few minutes.

Audrey

My Djibouti diary starts, "It's the 25th February, Tony's birthday, he's still sleeping and we are safely anchored off the old Yacht Club buildings, don't know what kind of birthday it will be but I'm glad we made it through the Gulf of Aden safely.

It was a very comfortable night, I think we both caught up on some lost sleep and recovered from the nightmare of the last few days, it feels a bit unreal looking back but we know it happened and we are relieved to be here.

Tony

After obtaining our clearance the easiest route to town was through the military base which used to be the Djibouti Yacht Club. From here all stores fuel and supplies can be arranged, although the base is run on military security lines there is no problem coming and going at any time of the day or night.

Outside of the main gate it is a 250 metre walk to the roundabout along the built up harbour wall, it gets a bit depressing walking along here. Beside the road there are families living rough, all they have is a cardboard shelter erected from what they can salvage. A row of old disintegrating fishing boats, way past their working life, form accommodation for other unfortunates, there seems to be a lot of them. Most are probably refugees of one sort or another, it is a sad fact of life in modern Djibouti, as we walked by, their hollow eyes watched us, their children played in the dirt and it all looked very hopeless. As you cross the road and carry on walking into town, it leads you past the Royal Palace, guards in smart uniforms are everywhere, such poverty and opulence within 400 metres is an eye opener. Other routes were through the commercial docks and the market quay, both were not as convenient and there also appeared to be a security problem, especially when leaving dinghies tied to the jetty.

Djibouti is generally a very underprivileged town and has many problems with immigrants legal and otherwise, the neighbouring countries are not renowned for their stability and Djibouti has become a sanctuary for many different people. We personally witnessed no problems from this situation but some other yachts did have unwelcome visitors, usually at night and even with occupants sleeping on board. It is an ongoing problem and care is needed to protect you from the undesirable elements, valuables are best kept on your person or safely locked away. We never felt worried or intimidated while ashore during the day or evening, a Djibouti man we got friendly with said there were never any problems with the local people, it was always what he called outsiders. With no social services to speak of for the illegal's and little or no work for them to do, they scraped an existence as best they could, usually begging. Some of the refugees are stateless persons and had nowhere else to go, it was not easy to witness their plight and yet be able to do nothing about it.

Audrey

It was a shock walking up the road outside of the military base, the poverty was as bad as we had seen anywhere, but these people did not have choices, this was all they could ever aspire to, it was dreadful.

After our initial shock the first full day went quite well, we found a cafe with a good internet connection, topped up my mobile phone, then found a nice bar for a spot of lunch, even met up with a few rally friends and had a beer to celebrate, everyone of us were alarmed at the sights we'd seen as we left the base.

That night for Tony's birthday meal and a rally get together, we all went to an Ethiopian restaurant, everyone had to eat with their fingers, tearing off bits of unleavened bread and then using it to pick up a strange assortment of communal grub. This was followed by a local dancing group who entertained us with their many different styles and costumes; all in all it was a very absorbing evening finishing off with us all on the dance floor. It was certainly a birthday not to be forgotten. Then to get back to Cayuco we had to walk past the homeless families sleeping rough on the side of the road, we all felt a bit guilty.

The next day I started to clean up the boat and began cooking to stock up the freezer, the next leg is up the Red Sea to Port Ghalib in Egypt. Port Ghalib at the moment is the first port of entry and because of the prevailing northerly winds the approximate 900 mile passage can take quite a few days. Of course that is the straight line distance, by the time you add the extra miles due to the amount of tacking needed against the prevailing wind, the distance sailed can be considerably further.

That evening all available rally participants were invited to the Governors residence for dinner at the British Consulate, when we arrived he turned out to be a Frenchman, very fitting we supposed for Djibouti. An extremely pleasant and informal evening was had by all, another advantage one supposes of being in an organised rally. We were all given an opportunity to explain our voyage so far, I for one, tried not to elucidate too graphically.

Tony

While Audrey prepared her meals for the freezer and did her best to clean up the boat, I was doing the same with my tasks, the fuel was ordered and started to be delivered the same day, it all had to be carried from the base, down to the dinghy and ferried out to Cayuco. Again, we needed 460 litres of fuel; we had motored almost all the way from Salalah in the light conditions to maintain our 5 knot average speed. Fuelling up in this piecemeal way is a messy job, however hard you try it is almost impossible not to spill diesel. Our siphon tube helps but having to use it with a Baha Filter/funnel arrangement and then with a nylon stocking over the top, it wasn't conducive to keeping everything clean. Once again we had to use our 20 litre jerry cans, five of these equals 100 litres so we needed 23 of them to fill the tanks. This process took three days to and fro between Cayuco and the pontoon with no respite during the hottest part of the day; at least we got a break while they took the cans away for refilling.

Water was collected in the same way, this time of course in our two 20 litre water containers. In Djibouti, the same as many other places, you have to pay for water, we used up a few favours filling the cans clandestinely in order to save a bit of cash. Every time we went ashore for a meal or a drink, we took our small 5 litre water bottles with us and asked the waiters if they could fill them up for us. Just in case you think we were getting things too easy, don't forget the two 20 litre petrol cans have to be filled up as well, for this we used our little two wheeled collapsible trolley and hauled it to the petrol station and back again. As a bonus, while trying to complete all the refilling, I also fell victim to the Djibouti tummy bug, I wasn't the only one; most of the rally was affected as well.

Our briefing for the Red Sea was on the evening of 27th, once again there were many questions, the passage north up the Red Sea is not an easy one and we would sooner or later have to tack into 25 to 35 knots of wind, maybe more. It is also a very busy shipping area with commercial traffic heading to and coming from the Suez Canal. There was an interesting discussion on the still possible pirate threat, there had been fairly recent attacks in the western gulf and even north of the straits of Mendab at the southern end of the Red Sea, this was something we had not given a lot of thought to until now. Most of the rally made their own decisions to keep in the same groups where convenient until a long way past the danger area.

By the 28th February we were almost ready to leave, just a last run for fuel, water and some stores, this was the last day of the month and clearly none of us intended hanging about in Djibouti. We prepared as best we could for a long hard flog up to Port Ghalib, there were places we could stop so had pencilled in Massawa in Eritrea and Port Sudan as likely rest places. A better option in Sudan is Suakin south of Port Sudan and much more peaceful, so I'm told. Just before we sailed Eritrea and Ethiopia started bombing each other again, it was declared out of bounds, unless we were in trouble, Massawa looked out of the frame.

Last preparations on the first of March, we returned to our friendly French restaurant for a last meal taking with us our 5 litre water bottles, they were kind enough to fill them up for us, where else would you go out for a meal and go begging for tap water as well. Have to say, we were looking forward to getting on the way again.

Audrey

Woke up on the 2nd March and had a quick breakfast, on the radio we heard that two more boats had been broken into during the night while the crew slept, not a lot was stolen, just a few dollars left over from a shopping trip. One of the crew members actually stepped into a pool of water on the saloon floor left by the burglar, whoever it was must have swam across from the shore and climbed aboard, it was another yacht with a sugar scoop stern.

Everyone took their dinghies over to the offices to clear out of Djibouti, nobody said very much but it was obvious we were all eager to leave, enough was enough. There is an element in Djibouti that are prepared to take high risks to get what they want, they and their families are probably starving, one of our skippers said to me, he would rather have given the money if only the burglar had asked. I was reminded of Captain Slocum's solution in 1894/95 when he sailed along the Magellan Straits of South America, to dissuade the local natives coming aboard at night he put tin tacks on the deck, he soon heard their approach when bare feet found the tacks. Once again we appreciated the merits of owning an older boat that resembled Steptoe's scrap yard; when swimming, Cayuco was an extremely difficult boat to climb back onboard if the ladder was not down. Being a 1960's design, it did not have the spoon stern of the modern yachts; these are very useful in assisting boarding and bathing, but also useful for people in the water, whether friendly or not.

The day before, our original group of five boats from Salalah and two other yachts about the same size had agreed to stay with us to go north for the first 150 miles or so, this would put us all through the Straits of Mendab and past the Hannish island group at the southern end of the Red Sea. Again, sailing in this area you have to take in all the information you can from a number of sources, there's not a lot of point arriving somewhere that's in the grip of a coup or some other disaster. Don't laugh, it has happened before and probably will again.

Tony

By the time we had checked out, returned and packed our dinghies away, it was late morning of the 2nd March before we left, midday saw us all motoring out towards the west side of the Maskali and Moucha Islands about eight miles offshore. Two of our little flotilla had left Djibouti the night before and spent the night at anchor in amongst the reefs of the islands, we had arranged to radio them when approaching so that they could rejoin our group. The reason they wanted to spend the night there, apart from it being a much nicer anchorage than the harbour, was to give their waterlines a scrub off in nice clean water. Not many people wanted to swim in the murky waters of the Djibouti Port. As we sailed by, the other two came out from the reef and our now expanded group of seven yachts continued on our way, conditions were calm and sunny but what wind we had was coming from ahead so the iron topsails stayed on.

Another group of rally yachts that had left earlier in the morning radioed to say they were experiencing very rough conditions, a strong wind right on the nose was slowing their progress as they sailed towards the Straits of Mendab, they were only 35 miles ahead of us but in very different conditions, such is the way of the sailing yacht anywhere in the world.

Continuing on our way towards the Straits where the headwind was reported to be, it was obvious that if the bigger boats ahead of us were having difficulties making way over the ground, then we would be in an even worse position. They say that great minds think alike and this scenario is no different, without any discussion between us, all the skippers in our group started looking on the chart for somewhere to anchor, just in case we decided to find a bolt hole for the night. The long distance sailing boat skippers thinking is, wherever possible find an anchorage without giving up hard won ground, this mind set was to stand us in good stead for the next few weeks. We had about 30 miles to go before rounding the Phare de Ras-Bir lighthouse where the rough conditions being reported seemed to start. This lighthouse sits on the headland just after the small village of Obock, an ideal evening anchorage if ever there was one. Almost without any radio contact we had all come to the conclusion that Obock was as far as we were going to get today. With no argument and after a short radio chat we all altered course slightly to head in for the anchorage, at the same time we heard that the group ahead of us had turned back and decided to anchor up for the night, Obock being the obvious choice for them to head for as well. We all arrived at virtually the same time and settled down for the evening, a radio chat amongst all of us later, established that the forecast tomorrow was for much better weather. The prediction was for a calm initial start to the day with a south easterly breeze coming in towards late afternoon. This was the news we had all been waiting for, what a bonus, an extra comfortable night at anchor, nearer to the straits and without having to do a night sail, plus the promise of a fair wind on the morrow, sometimes you can be forgiven for thinking somebody is on your side after all.

Next day, a fine morning and we were off again, not much wind but everyone enjoyed reasonable motor sailing conditions.

A yacht from the group ahead radioed that they had picked up a net round the propeller, sounded serious but a few minutes over the side with a sharp knife solved the problem and they were soon on their way again, something we are all aware of and hope it never happens.

The weather remained calm and the engines stayed on, there was no point wasting time around here, we all wanted to press on for the Straits. Around lunch time Audrey came up with a little tasty salad, cheese, ham, boiled egg and a bit of rabbit food, we were tucking in nicely when I received a radio call, could I contact another yacht which had left a couple of days before on the SSB radio, he was waiting on our dedicated rally SSB channel to talk to me. Wondering what this was all about I left the salad and went to the radio, it takes a few minutes to warm up so I grabbed a drink while waiting. When the radio was ready I found myself talking to Roy, one of our friends on the Australian yacht Evelyn, he had been in the other group of yachts that had left Djibouti two days earlier. After suffering a complete engine breakdown and because of the distance to go to Port Ghalib in Egypt, he had turned back to Djibouti for repairs. At the time they were all motor sailing and tacking north against the strong headwind, due to the engine failure it was easier for him to sail back south. He was heading our way and would shortly be in the same area as us. He kindly invited me to come aboard for afternoon tea and cakes as he sailed by and then, would it be possible for me to have a look at his engine at the same time. I said I would try but wasn't hopeful, I didn't even know if it would be possible to get onboard, rafting up or boarding another small yacht at sea is a risky business and both yachts could be badly damaged.

Anyway, that was the problem we were faced with and it would be interesting to see what could be done, the first thing was to arrange a meet up at sea. A quick look at the chart and estimating both our combined speeds suggested a possible waypoint about twenty miles ahead of our current position, we also arranged to contact each other on VHF radio when closer together.

About 14-00 hours our VHF crackled into life, it was our friend with the engine problem, again he invited me to come aboard for afternoon tea as he sailed by, I replied in the affirmative and said I would love a cup of tea. I also said I would bring some spanners and try to assist if possible. We spent the best part of the next hour on the radio while he tried all the things I suggested and explained what else he had done. It started to look as if I would have to go aboard and check the engine, at this stage I was at a loss as to what else I could do. Perhaps I could get a cup of tea and a biscuit as well.

I was not happy about rafting up in the open sea but it was still fairly calm and looked like it would stay that way for a while. By now our two yachts were about 20 miles away from each other and with our combined speeds we should be together in a couple of hours. I had discussed his engine make and type plus what kind of fuel system it was, it was a layout I was familiar with so that should make it easier. In the meantime I arranged all the spanners which would be the most likely ones to use and put them securely in a bag.

Monitoring the position of each other we gradually closed up until at 16-00 hours we were in visual range, then when about half a mile distant, Roy lowered Evelyn's sails and allowed her to drift. We were still motoring anyway so I slowly closed the gap and stopped alongside with about one metre space between us. The trick with rafting up at sea is to use lots of fenders and get the springs on quickly. Even a small swell causes the two vessels to behave differently, you have to be aware of the masts and rigging as an incorrect position or snag here can seriously damage the rigging as well.

Both of us had discussed the manoeuvre and prepared all the warps beforehand, we winched the spring warps up tight and left the breast warps loose, this keeps the boats aligned and slightly apart. Audrey and Liz (Roy's wife) were in charge of keeping the fenders in position between the two vessels and possibly drinking tea as well.

Having succeeded with the first objective and got the two boats to behave themselves while tied together and not ripping each other's decking off, I hopped aboard and went below to the engine compartment. A quick assessment of the system was good, a fairly large engine room with plenty of space to work. I removed my spanners from their bag and started checking all the usual suspects on the tick list in my head, battery, starter, filters, fuel etc.

Audrey

Both of the yachts involved in this were husband and wife teams, when Tony disappeared below with Roy, Liz and myself were left to fend for ourselves as best we could, no pun intended, because the main job was keeping the fenders in place, the two vessels needed constant attention to keep from closing up and damaging each other. We chatted together while ruminating on the possibility of them having to sail all the way back to Djibouti, it was not a prospect either of them wanted to think about, apart from the waste of valuable time, it was also finding a diesel engineer that could be trusted. Previous work carried out on some of the yachts in various places by local engineers had sometimes left a lot to be desired.

We waited on tender hooks while Tony got to grips with the problem, it seemed like after only a few minutes we heard the engine turning over. It didn't start but this wasn't a problem for me, I know how Tony works and the fact that he was turning the engine over on the starter told me he had probably found something. Liz looked concerned that it still wasn't starting, this was how the engine had been since it stopped, just turning over with the starter motor but not running. I tried to re-assure her that it was a good sign; I explained that I recognised Tony's method of working and told her that I'd reckoned he'd found something, that's what he does with Cayuco's engine when he's investigating a problem.

With that we heard them trying the starter again, it turned the engine over and it tried to fire up but cut out again straight away, I looked at her and said, "Don't worry, that's a good sign, he's going to crack it." After a few more minutes the starter whirred the engine over again, with a cloud of black smoke out of the exhaust the engine burst into life and revved up, this time it didn't cut out and kept running, the engine was working again, Tony left it going and after giving the engine a few more revs up and down and checking the tick over speed he was satisfied that the problem was over and they could carry on up to Port Ghalib. What a relief for them not to have to go back to Djibouti, they were ecstatic!

Our entire little flotilla had stayed with us sailing in circles while Tony attempted to help the other yachts engine problem. Some of them were keeping in touch by radio with the yachts that had left with us this morning, plus, the group of yachts which Evelyn had left the day before, these were all spread out up the southern part of the Red Sea. I leapt over to our radio and announced that,

"We have lift off, the engine is going", the radio erupted with screams of delight from all the other vessels on VHF and SSB, Tony had become the hero of the fleet, he was elevated to Demigod status, all the women wanted to have his babies, (in theory of course). It seemed the whole operation had only taken minutes, I joked that it had taken longer than that to find the phone box in order to change into his cape and tight fitting trousers with the underpants on the outside.

Tony scrambled out from below and onto the deck clutching his trusty spanners, with a brief goodbye to Roy and Liz he was back on board Cayuco, started our engine and quickly removed the warps, by 17-00 hours we were back on course again. Roy and Liz decided it would be a good idea to stay with our group, so for the next few days we numbered eight yachts all heading north.

Tony

As I replaced my spanners back into their allotted quick grab sea going positions, I found a nice bottle of Australian red wine at the bottom of the bag with a little present to enjoy a meal ashore when we arrived, that's a nice thought I said to Audrey, I'm sure that will come in handy later on.

Our little service job had slowed us down and we were still 30 miles from Bab El Mendab, (Straights of Mendab). We continued to motor sail for the rest of the daylight hours while the wind continued to rise from the south east, this was just what the doctor ordered. As soon as we could I turned off the engine, no point in using fuel when you can sail. There was a long way to go and not too many places to stop for fuel, anyway, it's "greener", to sail.

As darkness fell, the wind continued to increase; it's a natural wind acceleration zone between the land masses on both sides of the entrance to the Red Sea.

By nightfall we were still 15 to 20 miles away from our waypoint at the start of the channel through the Mendab Strait. I had always wanted to approach this point just after nightfall; my thinking was, if we could slip through the danger area at night, with a bit of luck we could be well on our way by daylight. This was working out perfectly, not only had we got the timing about right, but we had a strengthening southerly wind from our starboard quarter, also, the pirates, if they were about, don't usually like to attack when its rough, it's safer for them in more settled conditions.

There is no entry in my log of when we actually entered the main shipping channel, at 18-00 hours I recorded our normal radio net and after that it all got a bit hectic.

Our choices were to sail up the west side of the strait in the half mile gap between the sparse channel buoys and the rocks, or cross both lanes and sail up the east side of the passage. Both options had their own problems, in the end we opted to cross the TSS at right angles and sail on the eastern edge of the northbound lane, this would give us more room in the channel, plus, we would be going the correct way as per international maritime law. We all crossed the TSS safely and kept well out of the way of the shipping. It's not only difficult for sailing boats in these situations but also for commercial vessels, even if they pick you up on radar, they can't always determine who you are or what you're doing. As we'd already seen, a group of blips on a radar screen, in front or behind of you looks very suspicious if it's impossible to eyeball them and now we were eight blips in the dark. There is always the radio of course and sometimes it can be beneficial to inform them of your intentions. One thing for sure, in that channel at night, commercial ships can't deviate very much from their course, there just isn't enough room to start taking evasive action.

There was an increase in shipping, the wind came in with a vengeance at 30/35 knots and we all took off like scalded cats. The current was flowing our way at 3 knots in the narrows and we were sailing at 7 to 8 knots through the water, it all got very hairy and it was a very dark night. The game plan was to cruise sedately at 5 knots and keep in formation as much as possible, this soon went out of the window and it became every man for himself. Technically I think the group was still acting as though I was the group leader, a yacht called me up on the radio about 19-30 hours and asked what I thought we should do about the plan to stay together; I took the hint and replied,

"We can't afford to miss these conditions, just go for it and get as far as you can, if necessary we'll catch you up".

It was a pitch black night with no moon, there were a lot of yachts and shipping about, the visibility was poor and the sea conditions meant you kept losing the other yachts navigation lights. Another problem was the room to manoeuvre; the whole strait is only 6 miles wide here and has two main shipping lanes north and south, each of these is two miles wide and there is a one mile separation lane in the middle. This gave us about half a mile of safe sailing zone on either side of the channels, now add the TSS, (Traffic Separation Scheme) to the equation and you can imagine the difficulties, remember, it's very dark, we're sailing fast, there was no moon and the channel buoyage leaves a lot to be desired.

We tore through the straits in pitch black conditions, not even a horizon, we kept just outside of the TSS but our speed over the ground was 8 to 11 knots, it was a very scary night, I don't think anyone slept but none of us were prepared to ease off, we had to use this heaven sent wind for all it was worth. There was heavy shipping traffic, in a way they helped us, we could see their lights behind and ahead of us. We had to stay on the eastern edge of the channel and ensure we stayed out of their way. You also have to contend with small islands and rocks, some of them unlit due to the lack of service teams for the lights or just not lit at all. Your navigation has to be accurate and at the speed we were travelling, there was not a lot of room for error.

By dawn we were all starting to breathe a sigh of relief; most of the strait was behind us, we had another 12 hours of daylight and at our current speed we would be past the uncertain area of the Hannish Islands by nightfall. The wind had eased slightly as we were also north of the acceleration zone between Djibouti and Yemen; in fact we were now only about ten miles off the coastline of Eritrea. A radio check confirmed we were all still more or less together and only a few miles separated our group of yachts, this was a surprise for Audrey and I, it just showed how hard we had pushed Cayuco all through the night. The sleep patterns and watches had been forgotten during the wild night, it was more important to keep maximum visual check on the boats around us. Now, it was time to start catching up on our lost sleep.

I have already made the point that the Red Sea is a notoriously difficult place to go north in a sailing boat, this is because the wind blows hard from the Mediterranean nearly all year round. Very occasionally the wind changes and blows from the south or south east for a few days, this happens more frequently down at the Gulf of Aden region but rarely at the Suez Canal end. If you are lucky enough and the gods give you one of these southerly winds you don't squander it, you ride it all the way as far as possible, you know the wind will change back to northerly within a few days, sometimes after only hours, just keep going, it will get harder soon enough.

Our welcoming south easterly wind held fair and we continued north at well over 100 miles a day. The options to call in at Massawa, Eritrea and Suakin in Sudan evaporated as the conditions remained the same, this was marvellous, nobody expected a free wind for as long as this going up here. Everyone without exception agreed to continue as far as we could and nobody wanted to stop until the wind went against us, we all knew it would, it was only a matter of time. By and large, to sail as far as Port Sudan with a southerly wind is good, to get further north is better, but you also have to appreciate that you have now run out of refuelling options. After Port Sudan there is no fuel until Port Ghalib and the weather prediction was not good, we knew it was going to change just weren't sure when, we still kept going north.

Another scare early morning on the 5th March, we heard the MV Nautic broadcasting a mayday pirate attack, just the right time when the pirates like to hit. The position of the ship was only 25 miles ahead of us, all the yachts still in our group which had heard the broadcast closed up again, we turned 25° to port in order to move as far away as possible from their position while still holding a mainly northerly course. The mayday was cancelled an hour later, we wondered whether another nervous watch officer had seen our group on radar and panicked, no other radio contact was received.

For six days and nights we kept tramping north carrying all the sail we could and keeping up as much speed as possible, every evening at dusk we had the spectacular red and gold sunset as the sun set over the thousands of miles of desert, the next morning we had the same from the opposite side at sunrise, what a display.

Knowing the weather change was imminent, we started discussing amongst ourselves the possible bolt holes to hide, by Sunday the 8th March 2009, we'd had a good run; six days nonstop with a southerly wind behind us is fantastic for these parts. The forecast was predicting 40 knots of north east wind by the next morning, it was only a matter of how much further we could push our luck, no one fancied struggling against a 40 knot headwind.

As I said earlier, after Port Sudan there are no towns or even villages that are recognised stopping places, also, we were still in Sudanese waters and had not officially entered, so care was going to be needed.

Nearly all the way up the Red Sea on the west side there are reefs and inlets in the desert, these are called Marsas. The sea is also a relatively shallow area; anywhere you look there are islands, reefs and atoll like anchoring places even in the middle. The east side with Yemen and Saudi Arabia is virtually a no go area. It's possible to take shelter among the reefs and Marsas when a north wind starts blowing, after a few days the wind eases off and you can head north again. It will probably be 20 to 25 knots on the nose but that's better than 35 to 40. The general pattern here is for the wind to blow strongly from the north at 35 to 40 knots for 3 or 4 days and then ease off to 20/25 knots for a few days before back to 40 again; having used the southerly wind as far as possible, it was now going to get a lot more difficult.

We searched the chart for these bolt holes in the desert and preferably one with an easy entrance through the reef and a good deep channel up to a safe anchorage. As none of us had been here before, everyone searched the charts and then we had an open discussion using the radio. A few places looked better and a short list was drawn up, the one which seemed to fit the bill was called Kor Shinab, it is a natural lagoon indentation in a barren region reached by a winding channel over a mile long, there was plenty of depth and lots of room for a number of boats. That was the one we voted as best for entry, plus, we would be there about 10-00 hours tomorrow morning when the wind was forecast to change. That was our first choice; we then discussed other alternatives and these depended on whether we had to seek shelter earlier or managed to get further than we thought.

The evening before was calm with little wind so we all started motoring to maintain our 5 knot average, by daybreak the wind had started to blow from the north, not very strong at first but it was rising slowly. We arrived off Kor Shinab around 10-00 hours, the sun was behind us, perfect conditions to pick our way through the reef entrance, the first one to arrive carried on in and called back the depth, we all followed. What a strange place, after negotiating the reef passage you have to head for the shore and try to pick out the way in, it all looks the same, it's difficult to actually see the entrance. We all had our chart plotters on but it made no difference, all you can see is sand and the chart plotter directions are only an approximation, it's there somewhere, you've just got to find it. Shortly someone spotted the channel, there're no buoys or any kind of marker, not even any shore signs or transits, it's all just desert and sand is the same colour everywhere along these shores.

Slowly we picked our way up the meandering channel, surprise surprise, two French sailing boats were coming out; we waved and carried on in, after about a mile and a half we entered a large lagoon with other channels branching off, we decided here was far enough. By this time the wind had increased dramatically, it was amazing how it had risen so fast, the sand was blowing off the desert, all I wanted to do was anchor and get down behind the wheelhouse out of the way; the wind was touching 40 knots already. Everyone chose their anchoring spot and within minutes we were all on the radio chatting about this weird place, we had got in safely after six days of fair winds and within minutes of a new gale starting from the north, how lucky was that.

Now we had time to look around our surroundings it was very different than what we had been used to, it looked very barren, miles of sandy desert disappearing as far as the eye could see, a few bushes, some stunted trees and a little hill, as we watched, a military vehicle trundled along the desert, we then realised that there was a road all the way along the shoreline. Of course we were not allowed to go ashore, don't know if my adventurous spirit would even stretch that far anyway, this did not look like a place to start pushing your luck with the local military police.

A check of the log revealed we had sailed nearly 700 miles from Djibouti and we were 295 miles away from Port Ghalib, not bad at all for the Red Sea. A couple of the yachts left the Marsa after two days to try and make some more miles north, after 6 very rough and wet hours at sea and not getting very far, they put in to another Marsa only 15 miles further up, later in the evening on SSB they said conditions were appalling and it would be better to wait a bit longer. The interesting thing was, they said the two French yachts that left as we entered Kor Shinab were also sheltering in the same Marsa as them.

Figure 37: Bartering with the Sudanese fishermen while anchored in Kor Shinab Marsa

Audrey

The day before we got in to Kor Shinab was the 8th March, that was the anniversary of the day Tony and I met on a blind date 39 years ago, little did I know then what I would be doing all these years later. A year ago on the 8th March we were on our way to the Marquesas Islands in Polynesia, the longest passage on the circumnavigation; according to my diary we had strong winds and lots of rain, not quite the same this year anchored here, blowing 40 knots but at least there isn't any rain, only red sand.

As we left Djibouti I was glad we had stopped for the night at Obock, when I talked to the ladies on the yachts that had left before us and continued through the Straits of Mandeb, they told me what a horrible night it had been. They had a strong headwind and motor sailed while tacking nearly all the way in awful conditions, it seemed terribly dangerous and all in all they had a worse night than we did. Most of our trip after that first scary night up the entrance to the Red Sea became quite routine, while sitting at anchor in Kor Shinab we had time to reflect on our lucky break with the conditions. We caught up on our sleep, prepared for the next leg and I took some nice evening sunset photos over the desert. There was a sloping hill ashore which according to the chart was called Quoin Hill, apparently the shape of the hill resembles the tapered wedge (quoin) used on the old sailing ship cannons. The quoin gave the slope (rake) to the cannon's barrel so that the range could be adjusted when firing. The hill was named by the old sailors on the ships of the past, they sheltered here from the wind while trying to sail north, exactly the same as we were, how they ever sailed those ships into and out of this lagoon beggars belief, they probably had to pull them in with longboats.

One of the other yachts started a quiz in the evening to relieve the boredom, not that Tony and I were bored for there was always something to do; we were quite enjoying the strange experience. It carried on with us all chatting on the radio until someone told a joke, after that the floodgates opened and everyone was joining in, they were not complicated jokes but the silly ones like, elephant jokes, doctor jokes and the like. It ended up with saying goodnight the same as in The Walton's on TV, goodnight Grandpa, Goodnight Jim Bob, Goodnight Grandma, etc.

We had an unusual visit this morning, saw a small open boat moving through the anchored yachts, when Tony checked them out with the binoculars they had brown loose clothing on, neither of us knew who they were so when they left one yacht to go to another, Tony called up the first yacht to find out what it was all about. They were a bunch of local fishermen and were going from yacht to yacht bartering the fish they had caught for anything useful. Sooner or later it would be our turn so Tony quickly went through his boson's store gear, and the lockers which never get opened except in emergency, there were some things he hadn't used in 10 years and probably never would. He collected some rolls of twine, old coils of rope, strong litre plastic bottles with tight fitting screw lids, some fishing gear and line and the piece de resistance a stainless steel hurricane lamp. By the time the fishermen came alongside, Tony had collected an assortment of bits; he bartered with them as you do and negotiated for a couple of nice bream type looking fish. He had kept the hurricane lamp to the end, then, as an afterthought he produced the lamp from under the bulkhead, the fishermen saw it and there was a mass rush forward in the small dinghy. The first one to reach grabbed the lamp and retreated into the boat clutching his prize while the others looked on, we hope it became a communal asset but it looked as if he'd claimed it for himself. The evening meal of fresh fish, a can of new potatoes in butter, petit poi and a tomato went down very well indeed.

I had a go at baking some bread to eke out our supplies, turned out not too bad, Tony made a great spaghetti bolognaise and I froze the rest for later. We sat in the cockpit, had a glass of wine and listened to some CDs. After three days anchored it looked like we could be on our way again, the forecast was probably the best we could hope for this far north.

Tony

It was four days before the wind dropped; the forecast was for 25 to 30 knots on the nose, it would have to do, some of our numbers were getting restless. Next stop looked likely to be Port Berenice 140 miles away to the north, there is an anchorage in the large bay outside the port and this would be our first stop in Egyptian waters. We would not be able to clear in there though, it's a military base and visitors are discouraged, it's right on the border of the disputed territory between Egypt and Sudan, anchoring in the large bay about two miles away amongst all the fishing boats was tolerated. Anyway, there was only a small weather window;

it was a bit doubtful whether it was worth attempting it, by the time we got anywhere near there, it was forecast to be blowing a hooly again so we were expecting a rough trip

That proved to be correct, at first light we left the anchorage, could see why it's called the Red Sea, after a blow everything is covered in red sand, it gets everywhere. We set the sails and beat out into the open sea, it was clear we were in for a rough couple of days, there was not a lot of point going back or waiting, this was normal weather in the Red Sea. The state of the sea was not too bad so we just kept thumping into it, Cayuco is not so good at beating and we fell a few miles behind the other yachts. It made little difference; all of us were following the same agenda and had decided to make for Port Berenice. If the weather improved, which was unlikely, we'd all carry on as far as possible, in fact the opposite happened, the weather deteriorated badly. After two days of punishment we put Cayuco's head pointing towards the shore and entered the channel up to the anchorage at Port Berenice.

Again we were entering an unknown channel in the dark, the way through to the anchorage is best tackled in daylight, there are lots of rocks and shoal patches around the bay. Nothing around here is easy, some bends on the way in and few guiding lights, it was a difficult night. Eventually we dropped our anchor at daft o clock just before daylight right in amongst the fishing boats, these of course had no lights why doesn't that surprise me anymore. I sat in the cockpit and waited for dawn to check the anchor was holding and that our position was not impeding anyone else and then I slept for a long time, I had been awake for most of the last two days.

Audrey

Our 4 am arrival meant it was nearer 5 am by the time we had settled, sitting in the cockpit all I wanted to do was go to sleep, it had been a very tiring two and a half days. I had to wait in case Tony had to move the boat again, it's just one of those things, Cayuco is our home, it has to be safeguarded at all times.

As the sun came up, it was beautiful, the increasing light turned the colour of the rocks in the channel from a vibrant red gradually to a vivid violet, the sea became progressively brighter until it was a stunning light blue. Cayuco was tucked in behind a long sand spit, behind that was the inside lagoon and the high mountains further inland in Egypt.

The violent wind was whipping the sand off the spit and over the top of us; we were sheltered from the wind and anchored close to the shore in flat calm water. Looking around, we were not the only ones here, there were many other sailing boats taking refuge, even rally yachts which had left earlier than us were here waiting to leave, chatting later, they said it had been like this for days, many independent yachts had also anchored up away from the onslaught, one independent yacht said he had been there for nine days.

Tony

The wind increased further, two rally yachts with us yesterday which had tried to continue rather than come in here, had been forced to put in to another Marsa further up the coast. These boisterous conditions continued and yachts kept arriving. In the end there were 9 rally yachts sheltering and a lot of independents, we were all a captive audience, could not go ashore and yet could not continue. The jokes and the Walton's goodnight thing continued, getting up to epic proportions before dying a natural, think most people were getting bored sitting here, some of them were also starting to worry about stores and fuel reserves. So far we had been trying to get up the Red Sea for fifteen days and hadn't touched land; several yachts had crossed the oceans in less time. Audrey was still preparing our meals from the stores in the freezer and because we had sailed most of the way, we still had plenty of fuel.

Not a lot to say about Port Berenice, we waited five days before the wind decreased enough to venture out. When eventually a window in the weather appeared it was a mad rush into 25/30 knots of headwind for another 120 miles into Port Ghalib.

Leaving at 08-00 hours on Wednesday 18th March this leg took us 39 hours, it was a hard wet sail, arriving at 23-00 hours the next day meant it was another night entry. On the radio we were advised that the entrance through the reef was not clearly marked and should not be attempted until morning, a yacht trying this some months before was still stuck on the reef and starting to break up. However, what they didn't know was that I had already allowed for this and earlier had radioed a rally yacht which was arriving in daylight; I'd asked him to take the waypoint co-ordinates on the way in and radio them back to me.

Armed with this information I was quite prepared to risk it, we dropped the sails, started the engine and went in slowly, near the coast the wind had died considerably. The entrance was very small and narrow with a turn to port half way in, it was not marked on the chart, in fact it was not marked on anything, it was a new marina and so far it had not even been added to our chart plotter information. As far as navigation was concerned this place didn't exist yet, to make entry worse many lights from the resort on shore completely hid all the tiny inefficient navigation buoys. Gradually we worked our way down the channel from waypoint to waypoint using the echo sounder as a backup, the last 200 metres we gently slid past a ghostly image close by on our port side, it was the sailing yacht we had been told about sitting high and dry on the reef, talk about a wakeup call.

Once inside all our rally friends were waving to us from the quayside to attract our attention, tying up on the quay, they were all surprised to see us come in at night, except of course, the one who had supplied me with the waypoints.

An efficient officer was waiting for us; our paperwork was taken away and returned within the hour, simple, all done and we were legal. It had taken nineteen days to sail from Djibouti, although nine of them had been spent on anchor, Port Ghalib is the first place going north that you can clear into Egypt but I'm told it is much better to do the paperwork here than in Hurghada, the formalities are quite a bit cheaper as well.

Port Ghalib is a privately owned diving resort; it is really beautiful and has all the facilities. It was an ordinary Marsa and has been carved out of the desert, most of the marina part was excavated and expansion work is still going on. It is built with different lagoons for the various types of boats; it has restaurants, bars and very good hotels for all the guests and even a nearby airport.

Next morning the harbourmaster allocated our berth and after fuelling up we moved along to a stern to mooring near the bar/restaurant complex, it was the first time since Salalah that all the rally boats had been ranked up against a quayside. There were places to order fresh salad, vegetables and various meats but as the passage to Hurghada was only 140 miles we did not need to purchase very much, we also found a small village shop about 2 miles walk away selling most of what we wanted.

Nobody was staying here very long, the timetable for the Suez Canal transit was getting closer and no one wanted to miss that, within a few days it would be time for the off again.

Chapter 19

Egypt and through the Suez Canal to Crete

Audrey

When we arrived at Port Ghalib there were about five rally boats already on the quay, they had all got in before nightfall but had to wait till the morning to be allocated a berth in the marina. It looked like a lovely place, although it was dark and late there were still a few places open, we turned down the offer to walk round and check the place out, just sat in the cockpit, had a glass of wine and turned in. It had been a rough trip and neither of us had slept much since leaving Port Berenice, tomorrow would be good enough to see the rest of the resort. While sitting I checked the phone and was happy to find a signal, I sent a text to family as normal but didn't get a reply, it didn't matter, it was great to be in the calm marina and we had a few days rest before the next leg up to Hurghada. To be honest, this was not something to look forward to; we were now right up near the top of the Red Sea and the conditions showed no signs of improving.

Next day we had a nice comfortable stern to berth near to a restaurant and bar complex, think we will be eating on board though, it's an expensive place and even just a beer is pricey by Egyptian standards. Although the amenities were costly the marina wasn't, only $10 a night about £7, we were impressed with that, we looked around and found the cheapest bar but still more than you'd expect, After a two mile walk into another village-like complex, we found a little local supermarket a lot cheaper than in the resort. Our time in Ghalib was limited, it was only a couple of days rest and on again, I ordered some fruit and vegetables from a nearby store but disciplined myself to get only the bare essentials

Even though food and drink were pricey, it was our first marina since Phuket nearly three months ago and I was determined to enjoy it. We treated ourselves one night to a steak and a bottle of red wine with other rally members at TGI Fridays, also got a chance to use their free internet service so it wasn't all bad. Because the marina is so big we had to take an internal ferry to another part of the complex, as this is a free service it doesn't matter so mustn't complain. As yet there was no way to walk round to the other side, the marina is still being built and some of the roads and bridges have not been constructed.

It was a shame we couldn't stay here for longer, our schedule was to get to Port Tewfik at the southern end of the Suez Canal for the arranged canal transit; this had already been paid for so it was all systems go until we were within safe arrival range.

Hurghada, was the next stopover, unless you get a fair wind there is an advantage to taking short legs between stops this far north in the Red Sea, at Hurghada it was planned to have another briefing and commence the paper chase for the Suez Canal. We were all waiting for a decent forecast to make the 120 mile jump and it looked like the 25th March was as good as it was going to get, four days rest and the preparations to leave commenced.

Tony

This was always going to be a quick turnaround, fuel, store and water up, get all the rest and relaxation you can, enjoy the facilities and off again.

It's a beautiful place and geared up as a diving and training resort, boats are on hand to deliver the guests to a whole range of sites from novice to deep water, having said that, there's plenty of scope for tours and other experiences if members of the party want to enjoy a range of activities.

The 25th March saw a group of us leaving Port Ghalib late in the day, we had planned to leave earlier but as one of the yachts leaving motored past us, his engine cut out and he was left drifting across the marina. All hands to the ropes, we pulled him in to the bank and once again I was up to my armpits in diesel engine fuel system.

His fuel system, pipes and filters were blocked solid with a black jellylike substance; it looked like diesel fuel bug which starts with receiving contaminated dirty fuel and then actually grows within the tank. It's a serious problem and takes a lot of work to clean the system properly. It took me the rest of the morning and most of the afternoon to clean out all the lines and filters before the engine was running again. Fortunately I had a quantity of Biocide which I treat my system with regularly, once cleaned out I dosed up his fuel tank with a level relating to a scorched earth policy (i.e. overkill) and told him to hope for the best, there were no guarantees with what I was able to do in the time frame. The main quandary with this fuel bug is that it is very difficult to get rid of, the Biocide might prevent it from growing but it still leaves all the black jelly in the tank, the only real cure is to clean the whole system out.

So, much later than planned we had to leave, our paperwork had been completed in the morning to depart and the marina was pushing us to make a decision, in Egypt they like you to check out and then in again to the next harbourmaster, probably to keep an eye on you.

We were now in a rush to leave harbour and clear the reef system before nightfall, our yachts only just got through the reef passage and into clear water before dark so laid a course out to sea to give us a bit of room. This was not a problem, as we cleared the shelter of the land it was obvious the forecast was way out, the wind was right on the nose, setting the reefed main and jib Cayuco again thundered out offshore and into the big seas.

At night, it's just not safe trying to hug the coast and keep in calmer water; there is absolutely no warning of where the reefs are, it's not too clever in daylight either. All night long we beat our way north into the increasingly heavier sea; this was de jà vu all over again. We ended up further out to sea than anticipated and before long were mixing it with the shipping lanes again.

In this area there is a wind shift from day to night time, if you get it right, it's possible to get a lift of about $20°$, I tried to work the system and stay on the good tack longer during the different times of day. I'm not sure whether the wind always knew the rules, sometimes it seemed to work, other times it didn't. In the end it made little difference, it was just a horrible passage, waves continually broke over us, everything was wet again and it was difficult to relax, sleep was out of the question, thank god they were short passages.

Just after midday on the 26th a radio call from Stargazer explained that they had an engine overheating problem, I talked him through the potential causes but it became clear he had checked out all the straightforward possibilities. He was ahead of us so I asked him to give us his position and told him we would try to close up on him. From then on we motor sailed and started to cover the ground a bit better than before, I don't like motor sailing when we have a good wind, as I've said before Cayuco is not good to windward but she holds her canvas well in a strong blow.

All went well until about 04-00 on the 27th, we were sailing with the auto pilot working when it started making funny noises, it was still steering the boat OK, but it was obvious I would have to have a look at it in daylight. I had fitted our spare electric motor earlier in the voyage so was not too happy with this occurrence.

When daylight came, I discovered that the noise was from the casing which had cracked, I still had the old casing stored below but to fit it I would have to dismantle and remove the steering wheel. Never mind, we set Cayuco up with the main slackened off slightly and the jib hardened in as normal, she balances quite well like this when on the wind but you do lose a bit of ground; then, satisfied that she would continue to sail by herself for a while, I took the steering wheel off; very odd watching her sail by herself without the wheel.

I'd done this job before but only in a marina and workshop, at sea it was a completely different ball game, not the least of the problem was trying to keep all the bits in the same place without disappearing into the bilges. A quick dismantle, swop over the damaged parts with the old casing, rebuild the unit, refit the wheel, connect up the electrics and we're back in business. Cayuco sailed along as good as gold all by herself during this time and actually made up a couple of miles towards our destination, wasn't as efficient but it kept us moving, the whole process was over in about an hour and we were on our way again.

Stargazers overheating problem continued and further conversations by radio looked likely that it was their raw water pump itself which was the cause; this was not something to tackle at sea .without specialist knowledge. Fortunately our conversations were picked up by Roy and Liz on Evelyn, the yacht I had assisted earlier with the engine problem at the beginning of the Red Sea passage, being a larger yacht they had arrived at Hurghada earlier. As we were fairly near our destination, they volunteered to come out and tow Hugh and Shan in the last few miles, this enabled us to remain on course. The weather improved dramatically as we closed the shore, I picked a line between the reefs and arrived at Hurghada just after 16-30 hours, hurrah; at last we'd got in somewhere in daylight.

Arriving at Hurghada was important as there was a rally briefing the next day referring to the Suez Canal transit, Audrey and Shan went to the meeting while Hugh and I investigated Stargazers overheating problem. After a fairly lengthy diagnosis it did indeed look as if the raw water pump was faulty, Hugh had a spare onboard so another hour and it was fitted; a good test and it appeared to be OK. While fitting this pump we also managed to purchase some new hoses and replaced all the old rubber ones which looked as if they might be decomposing, always a warning to replace them if there is any doubt.

It's not always easy to replace equipment or technical bits in Egypt, it's possible to order from some retailers in the marina or it can be a long walk around town trying to find what you want, the latter is what we had to do. Alcoholic drinks are not available through normal channels either but have to be ordered from wholesalers supplying the complex, the process is fairly simple, you order from the list and they deliver straight to the yacht, it's very reasonable in price too.

It was still nearly 200 miles to the south end of the Suez Canal, when we departed here it was going to be out through the reefs and up the Gulf of Suez, our transit dates were approaching but the wind just continued blowing strongly from the north. I serviced the engine again and fuelled up using our cans once more, Audrey spoke to our family on Wi-Fi and had a brilliant signal, the laundry was finished, she sewed up more of our spray cover which was coming apart and Cayuco got all the salt washed off her and a bottom clean. We all waited ready to go but the wind still kept blowing, there is a bigger reef system off

Hurghada, it was possible to creep up inside almost to the Gulf of Suez and it was tempting to see how far you could get, but no one tried it.

Figure 38: Cayuco sailing up the Red Sea.

Audrey

For three more days we waited, Tony and I took a walk into Hurghada proper, immediately outside the security gates the plush surroundings changed; it was all very different from the lavish buildings and the wide open spaces inside the marina. Hurghada had clearly been around a long time, the streets were made for horse and cart, or in this case maybe camels and donkeys. Houses, shops, garages, industrial premises all looked jumbled together as if it had just happened rather than being planned. If you knew where to look it could well have been possible to buy anything you wanted, I'm sure it was all there somewhere. It wasn't a pleasurable place to walk about; it was dirty and unkempt, goats, donkeys and chickens just roamed about all over the place. Everyone was very polite; we even found a pork butcher surprisingly and topped up our supplies. It was suggested that we all find a local restaurant for tonight to see what it was like, the idea fell on stony ground, I don't think many were overjoyed about walking around these streets after dark; we ended up in a Thai restaurant inside the marina which turned out to be disappointing.

One evening sitting outside a bar waiting for others to arrive, a voice said,

"Well hello again" it was Dave and Ricki, the Australians we had met in Antigua and Phuket, once more we had accidently bumped into them, after the initial amazement we had a natter and agreed to meet later for a beer. It was astonishing that our paths had crossed yet again, all round the world, both on different agendas and here we all were again; it was clear there was some catching up to do.

April fool's day came and went followed by the second and the third, at last the weather showed signs of easing off; we prepared to leave on the fourth. Mid morning a large group of yachts all left Hurghada Marina together, the intention was to stay inside the reef system as long as possible and keep in the relatively calm water as far as we could. We even discussed anchoring for the night behind the reef and making an early start in the morning, it did not look that inviting outside in the open sea. One of the boats with us suffered complete electrical failure in most of his systems and decided to anchor behind the reef anyway; he sorted out his problems and carried on the next day.

Tony

Audrey and I looked at each other, our feeling was, the sooner we start, the sooner we get there, it had all the hallmarks of another unpleasant trip, so we just kept going, all the boats behind except one, followed. A radio message from a group of yachts that had left before us predicted appalling conditions; they had hit very short steep seas just as they entered the Gulf of Suez. A strong wind against current situation had caused the waves to become very short and steep, rising up to 5 metres and every yachtsman knows what that means. One wave larger than the rest had swept completely over one of the bigger yachts, this sometimes happens when waves are steep and close together, the yacht lifts to the first couple of waves but can't rise fast enough to lift over the third, the result is a wave riding over the bows which rushes back over the decks and can be very dangerous.

As in everything to do with sailing small yachts, you pay your money and take your chances, I was gambling that the strong wind of the afternoon would reduce some hours after the sun had set. This is sometimes a natural phenomena, when the sun stops heating up the land, the wind fades considerably, I had no idea if my plan would work in this location but we would be getting to the area where the problem was about 20-00 hours, just after sunset, all we could do was keep our fingers crossed. We had similar phenomena as in the bottom of the Red Sea, wind acceleration from the north between the land mass on each side and a narrowing of the channel which causes the current to speed up coming from the south, a typical wind against current situation, never a good combination.

Shortly after dark while continuing towards the start of the Gulf of Suez we noticed a drop in wind strength, a good sign. As the Gulf of Suez is a fairly narrow waterway, only 15 to 20 miles wide, the seas tend to decrease much quicker when the wind drops, it all looked right for my theory to be put to the test. Of course we still had the very busy shipping lane to contend with but everything went well, all through the night we pushed north and by morning our group of yachts were well out of the potentially rough part at the start. It is an unusual place to travel at night, not only do you have ships moving about, but have to contend with static oil rigs as well, at least they are very well lit up and can be seen for miles, naked flames reach out burning off the excess gases produced during production.

The trouble free run wasn't to last, now Cayuco decided it was her turn to start playing up again, we'd used the engine a lot in the last few months, just before 10-00 hours the next morning the engine gave a little cough and stopped. This is always annoying but even more so at the moment, I'd just serviced the filters and I had fitted a brand new unit in the line from the tank. It's fairly easy to bleed the fuel system so that's what I did, within a few minutes we were off again. The reason for all the motoring now was because we wanted to get to Port Tewfik and complete the paperwork for the canal, plus, the wind was still on the nose. It was difficult to sail because of the headwind and all the commercial traffic, we didn't feel like tacking backwards and forwards across the shipping lanes. The weather had improved, wind had decreased and therefore the sea state was quite reasonable.

The engine fuel problem got worse throughout the day and night, I bled it another three times trying to coax it along as far as possible; I intended to have a look at it properly when we got in. Unfortunately that was not to be, just before dawn the engine stopped again and refused to restart, nothing for it but to refit the old line filter and try once more. I completed the job fairly quickly in the dark with Audrey holding the torch, again Cayuco looked after herself under sail, would you believe the old filter was OK and the engine ran without a problem. Later on, checking the new filter unit, I found a tiny crack which was letting air into the casing, simple to rectify with a bit of araldite, but not what you expect on a brand new component.

During the second night the wind returned from abeam, we were able to sail for a couple of hours before it veered northerly then it was back to engine again. When we arrived the plan was to anchor off Green Island, a holding area, while awaiting instructions to enter the Yacht Club at Port Tewfik. The Canal Authorities prefer to escort you in with their small pilot boats during the break between the south and northbound convoys. We arrived at 08-00 hours, just in time to join the queue to enter, slowing down during the night and timing our arrival had worked well, all the yachts who had arrived the night before said they'd had a distressing night and rolled badly all the time. Shipping traverses the canal in six hour periods, so in any one day there will be two northbound and two southbound convoys. Having said that, the commercial ships move in almost immediately the outbound ones are through so there's little time in-between transits. The first yachts to move managed to reach their destination at the Yacht Club pontoons before the commercial vessels entered the canal, the later ones like us, had to wait until a ship had passed before heading across the canal and into the yacht club. There is plenty of room between the commercial ships, canal regulations call for a one mile gap between each of them for safety reasons so crossing is not too much of a problem, it's just the authorities don't like you doing it without someone from their office in charge of yacht movements.

The Yacht Club is nothing special, just a couple of pontoons, with stern to berthing and with water and electric, security could be a problem normally but our team had arranged for security guards to control the entry and exit gate 24 hours a day, it worked well.

I rechecked our fuel system in an attempt to ensure it would keep running throughout the whole canal transit, a yacht with engine problems is treated very severely and will be towed out of the system, the cost is prohibitive. I also took the opportunity to check Stargazers system as well, it had been showing worrying signs and we all wanted to get through the canal in one go.

Audrey

In the evening we all went out to the Red Sea Hotel just outside the Yacht Club for a meal and to relax, we discussed the transit and went over the information we'd been given, the barter system works overtime in Egypt and we were concerned about some of the stories doing the rounds in our group, we wondered if our barter store would be enough.

The Yacht Club put on a rally party on the evening of the 7th April which we all subscribed to, it was good fun and we all had permission to supply our own drinks. BWR organised the music but we never did find out what happened to the whirling dervishes or the curry we had paid for, whatever, the kebabs were tasty, after all, it was Egypt.

The next day was a quiet one, just messing about on board and waiting for more instructions, the big day for us was the ninth when we were due to visit Cairo, the Egyptian Museum and the Pyramids

An early start saw us on the coach at 07-00 hours with a two hour drive to Cairo and the museum. I was impressed with the "mask of the Boy King" and other artefacts from the Tomb of Tutankhamun. The labelling and description about some of the display is basic but apparently there is only room to show a portion of all the possible exhibits, the curator and his assistants try to show the artefacts on a rota basis and attempt to describe the items as best they can, it is a mammoth task. To see the entire museum and its treasures in the time we had was impossible, but what we did see left an everlasting memory.

The next stop was for an Egyptian style buffet lunch and then across the River Nile to Giza and the Pyramids, it was a thrill to actually be there and see these ancient wonders of the world but the hassling of the traders spoilt the experience. Their persistence was rude and annoying, it must be worse in the peak season but for us it was one memory we could have done without. We managed to enter the second pyramid, an uncanny experience, very claustrophobic through low and narrow tunnels leading steeply downwards to the depths of the structure. At the bottom was a small room with a sepulchre, an oblong box structure supposedly for a burial of some kind, it is hot down there even in winter. We also visited the Sun Ship, this was found beneath the ground in 1954 alongside the pyramid and encased in concrete, it has been painstakingly restored, a marvellous achievement, it's housed in an air conditioned building to help preserve it, that's a bonus. Afterwards, to complete the experience, it was a short walk to the Sphinx, more touts, more hassle; I asked them what they didn't understand about the word "No".

Naturally, the whole place is a photo opportunity; everywhere you look there is another view, it's impossible not to wonder at the marvel of these structures.

It was getting late and the coach driver wanted us all back onboard for the trip home, the sun was setting behind the Sphinx and the Pyramids, I would have liked to linger longer but our schedule did not permit, a good day out marred only by the constant irritation of the pedlars, I appreciate the need to work, but there has to be common sense as well.

On the way back we all had the opportunity to pick up a few stores in the big supermarket, a good call, everyone was getting low on the essentials and we had another long voyage coming up soon. The Cairo traffic is quite crazy, a dual carriageway with four official and clearly marked lanes, except that everyone tries to make five or sometimes even six lanes while all trying to squeeze forward at the same time, glad I could just sit back and watch the antics.

Figure 39: The pyramids at Giza with the Sphinx in the foreground on a quiet day in winter

Tony

As the yachts cannot transit the canal all at the same time, the fleet was again divided into manageable groups, there was to be three sets of ten yachts passing through the canal on three separate days. Originally we were all going to take two days to transit the canal, anchoring in Great Bitter Lake for the night half way through, a later pronouncement had us all going through in one day, not a good decision for Cayuco. Because of our fairly low speed, no matter how early we got away in the morning, it meant us all reaching Port Said late in the day and after dark, not a good time for anyone. For administrative purposes we were all clearing out of Egypt from Port Tewfik and therefore could not stop again in Egypt. This meant that after a long and heavy day getting through the Suez Canal, we would have to steer a course through the busy harbour in the dark and then continue on out to sea whatever the weather. It also meant Cayuco would probably be holding our group up through the canal, the convoy has to stay together so all had to go at the speed of the slowest yacht, i.e. Cayuco. Audrey and I contemplated trying to revert to a two day transit but were talked out of it by the rest who all said it would be OK, Oh well; we'll just have to go for it and keep our fingers crossed.

The first two groups got away on their allotted days, passed through the canal and out into the Med. The weather was good for them and they mostly had a nice easterly breeze all the way, they made good time to Crete.

All we wanted to do now was leave, the forecast in the Mediterranean was favourable but only for the next day or two, another meeting, another delay, we had to wait for a warship to go through, that's when the canal is partially closed for safety reasons. Once more we waited, another aborted early morning start and another day lost, informed about 08-30 it was a no-go, this was really annoying all the crews ready but we have no choice, again we hang around all day and kill time.

On the evening of the 12th April we are told once again to be ready before daybreak tomorrow, the 13th, unlucky for some?

But not for us, although we have to hang around for what seems a long time after dawn, at 06-30 we're off, at least we don't have to have a pilot on board, that's a plus, he would try to force us to go faster and we both know Cayuco is just not up to it. We are really worried about our overheating engine, it's been OK for a while and we hope it stays that way. Our other worry is the air leak problem on the fuel system, I hope what I found is the cause but I won't be sure until the engine has run for some hours.

It was great to be in the canal heading for the Mediterranean, just hope everything keeps running, half way through we reach the Great Bitter Lakes and have to wait around for another pilot boat so we can continue, don't want to stop, must keep going.

It was a long gruelling nail biting day, but we made it with our heads held high, as predicted we did not arrive at Port Said until well after dark. The pilot boat guided us through the busy harbour but we kept losing sight of him in the glare of shore lights and the sheer volume of traffic, he was difficult to follow as he kept speeding up and shooting off ahead. Cayuco just kept plodding on while Audrey and I tried to ensure there were no buoys, boats or any hazards in front of us. After a pretty scary two hours in the blackness of night, we negotiated our way out of the entrance and past the two mile long barrier which lies to the north east of the entrance channel. At last we were through the worse bit, all we had to do now was negotiate our way around all the anchored ships waiting to go south down the canal and then we could settle down into our routine for the passage to Crete, what bliss, we thought, that however, was a bit premature.

Our plan during the first night was to get well offshore, the wind was almost certainly going to blow strongly from the west to north-west within twelve hours and that believe it or not, was just the way we wanted to go. By daylight the benevolent easterly wind had pushed us 25 miles out into the Med. we were making good time while possible, by midday the nice friendly easterly had become a hostile north westerly and started to increase, our holiday was over. Three hours later it was 30 knots and the waves had increased accordingly; it was time to batten down again and start fighting for every inch of ground.

18-00 hours saw us well reefed down and heading west, the rally radio net at the same time confirmed that all the boats that left with us had the same conditions and were beating into the strong wind, even some of the yachts that had left two days before us, although closer to Crete, were still battling it out. As the forecasted wind was stronger to the north we decided to stay to the south and work our way along the African coast, albeit about 30 to 50 miles off.

Figure 40: In the Suez Canal being overtaken by a large container ship

Audrey

The conditions were typical early season Mediterranean, cold, wet and windy, the shipping was heavy and every half an hour we had a broadcast from the Active Endeavour fleet on protection patrol in the area. During the night we motor sailed because it was easier, then during the day it was back to sailing, this conserved fuel but it was still going to be an epic slog to windward. Tony tried to take every advantage of the diurnal wind shifts to make as much west as possible but Cayuco does not do hard to windward, it's better to sail full and bye about 45/50° off the wind and keep sailing faster.

Cayuco bravely soldered on for the next three days, thrashing into the sea and taking water onto the foredeck, throwing it disdainfully back when she was able. Sometimes, if she caught a wave wrong, it would ride up and over the bow, a wall of water would cascade along the decks and smash into the wheelhouse. Occasionally a wave would go straight over the top and come crashing down onto the stern deck before rushing off back where it belonged. We left the auto pilot to get on with it but intermittently we would take over and hand-steer it ourselves for a while, first to give us something to do, all we wanted was to get there and also because hand steering kept a better course to windward as long as we concentrated. For four days and nights we battled, on one tack it would take us hours to get 5 miles closer to Crete but the other tack would be better. By the 17th April our position was 180 miles south west of Crete, nearly four days of constant windward work averaging 50 to 60 miles a day had taken its toll and we were tired. It had been slow going but the wind was now showing signs of abating, still the wrong direction but it became easier and Cayuco sailed faster because the waves did not keep knocking our speed off.

While motor sailing last night, the engine stopped again just as Tony had gone down for some sleep, we were both weary and I felt sorry for him, he had to get up and dressed then crawl into the engine compartment. In the dark with me holding the torch he tried to bleed the fuel system, it was difficult to clear the air from the fuel lines and he suspected there was another problem developing due to the battering we had been taking. There was plenty of fuel in the tank and it had worked OK in worse weather than this so he didn't think it was a fuel surge problem.

Tony

As per our tactics on this passage we started motoring after the 18-00 hour radio schedule, it was the 17th April and there were still a few other yachts trying to get to Crete the same as us, about five of our group had already arrived and one had diverted to Cyprus. During the night the engine again cut out and it became more and more difficult to bleed the air out of the fuel lines, there was obviously a very tiny crack or pin prick somewhere in the pipe, it would be difficult to trace it out here. The weather had improved, wind still on the nose but we had heard on our radio net that it was about to go easterly at 12 to 15 knots, that would be perfect to finish the rally at Crete. I bled the fuel system each time the engine stopped which was every couple of hours and we motor sailed as best we could tacking to the north west.

This arrangement continued until 05-00 hours when the engine stopped and that was it, air continually bled through the pipe, I couldn't clear it enough and the engine just refused to start. There was nothing for it but to sail as best we could until daylight, the suspicions I had went through my mind, somewhere on the fuel system a problem had been developing for quite a while, now, something had broken, all I had to do was find it and repair it.

Everything is easier in daylight, but first I had to sleep, we had been hammering into the seas for nearly five days now, Cayuco and ourselves had taken a beating, I needed a couple of hours to recharge the batteries, Audrey took over sailing, I went below and instantly fell asleep.

Audrey

Tony was at a low ebb, he'd been fighting Cayuco ever since the beginning of the rally, everything that had broken he'd repaired, everything that had gone wrong, he'd found a solution, the sheer determination to keep going had worn him down. I've never seen him give up on anything, but he was dejected, so close yet so far, he was still struggling to achieve his dream, could anything be as unkind as this and the weather had not eased off very much yet.

I told him to sleep, I would steer the boat by hand for a couple of hours and then he could have another go at the engine in daylight. About 07-30 he woke up and immediately started again, whatever was causing the problem, it took some time to find it, we had a cup of tea and a bit of breakfast, the hours went by and it still deluded him.

At 10-00 hours we had our radio net, as the engine wasn't running Tony started the generator and turned on the radio, he managed to talk to a couple of boats who had nearly arrived in Crete and they promised to pass on the message that we were delayed. Our ETA had changed and we said it was unlikely that we would be able to get there before Monday the 20th April, another two days at least. The wind was still north-west and although we were sailing faster, it was still a beat to windward; the only good news was that the wind was forecast to turn easterly some time tomorrow on Sunday the nineteenth.

I set Cayuco up to sail herself for a few minutes while I went below to put the kettle on, Tony had disappeared down in the engine compartment again, having made the tea I told him to take a rest and we sat in the cockpit with one of our last nibbles from the biscuit box.

Figure 41: On Spinalonga Island, an ex Leper colony off the coast of Crete.

Tony

During the time I was enjoying my tea and biscuit and ruminating on the vagaries of diesel engines and fuel systems, my mind wandered between sailing the last few miles and the possibility of finding the fault. I had checked just about everything on the fuel system to no avail, all there was left to check was the fuel pipe inside the tank, very unlikely but what else was there.

We were still sailing well although still tacking and were about 130 miles from completing a voyage that started in August 2007. For nearly 30,000 miles we'd had breakages of major equipment, storms that threatened to overwhelm us, pirates trying to attack us, it seemed we had fought all the way for every mile. I was muttering gibberish, how could it do this after everything else that had gone wrong and when we were so close, I was pretty much incandescent, my mind was in turmoil, I had to relax and look at the problem logically, I tried to calm down and compose myself.

Finishing off my tea I reluctantly disappeared down below again and started undoing the fittings surrounding the pickup pipe in the fuel tank, almost before I withdrew the pipe the answer was staring at me, there was no pipe, it had gone and I just looked at it in bemusement. Finding the problem was only half of the answer, what could I do about it out here well over a hundred miles away from our destination? I told Audrey about my discovery, we sat in the cockpit while going through in my mind possible remedies and mumbling quietly as I do when working through a problem.

After some minutes, I thought, if I cut a length of fuel pipe off from the good bit of pipe, replace it with a bit of reinforce plastic tube and a couple of clips which I've got, I would have another length of pipe to refit into the tank. So that is what I did, unfortunately, the top fitting was damaged in the process and I couldn't seal it, air was still bleeding into the system, Cayuco carries a lot of handy bits in her bosun's locker but we would need a main dealer for the bits I wanted, it was back to the drawing board.

The starboard fuel tank was still half full and we had some cans of diesel on deck, let's face it, the weather had not been conducive for emptying cans of fuel into the filler on the deck. An idea started to form, if I tipped the remaining fuel into the starboard tank, I could use that, the only trouble was that the fuel leak off pipe from the injectors went back to the port tank which was now out of commission. The leak off pipe takes the excess fuel delivered to the injectors for lubrication and cooling purposes back to a fuel tank to be used again; unfortunately, it was going back to the wrong tank. Using only the starboard tank would mean rerouting the leak off pipe to feed back into it, this idea was just not practical. More thoughts and idea's flowed through my brain, all I had to do, was empty the spare fuel cans into the starboard tank and then use one of them, suitably tied into the engine compartment, to catch the fuel from the leak off pipe. After a few hours when the can was nearly full, I could change the can over for an empty one and siphon the full one back into the starboard tank, viola, a workable solution. I estimated how much useable fuel we had left and although a bit tight there was enough to get us in even if we had to use the engine all the way.

Audrey

So that is how we finished the voyage to Crete, we sailed for the rest of the day and motor sailed during the night. Every few hours Tony would disappear below, change over the fuel can and pour the other one back into the starboard tank; this was recycling on an unlikely scale.

In the early hours of Sunday the 19th April before dawn, we could see the lights on the east coast of Crete, it was such a welcome sight, by daylight the island was just visible in the mist, we still had some miles to go around the north east corner to Aghios Nicholas Marina but we were ecstatic to be this close.

Tony

All the other yachts had arrived, although we tried the SSB at the allotted time there was no answer, I went back on deck after the 10-00 hour radio schedule to find a wind coming from the north east, I stopped the engine, pulled out the jib, adjusted the main and we were sailing again, this time straight for the headland we wanted.

Throughout the day the wind kept up a steady 12 to 15 knots and gradually veered more easterly, this was a grand wind to finish on. By noon we had rounded Cape Sidheros on the north east corner of Crete and were sailing past the Islands of

Dragonada and Gianysada to starboard. There was only 23 miles to go; it was now clear we would be in before dark.

Audrey

I tried the VHF radio but we were still too far out, my mobile phone gave that familiar little ping that says "I've logged on and ready" but I wanted to wait until we were right in before I notified family.

About ten miles out I tried again and this time got Hugh and Shan on Stargazer, they were amazed we had made such good time, nobody was expecting us until tomorrow morning. As we hadn't been able to raise anyone on our scheduled radio times it was not possible to tell them we had sorted the problem. I said we would be in about 17-00 and were looking forward to being back on dry land. Shan said there would be a few people waiting to share our joy and shake our hand etc.

Nothing could have prepared us for the reception we received; as we sailed closer the happiness was obvious especially in the organiser's voices on the radio. Approaching the marina we dragged out our ancient horn to blow into should there be any friendly "tooting" from the other yachts, my goodness; the marina erupted!! All the boats were still dressed overall for the official end of rally visit by the Mayor, plus it was the Greek Easter weekend celebrations. There was a cacophony of noise, horns blowing, people waving and cheering, the radio was calling nonstop; from our vantage point it looked very intimidating. Cayuco made her slow steady way to the finishing post as only a proud old lady of her stature could, she was battle weary but our little ship had made it. We motored up to our allotted berth, turned to go in stern first and with every one watching, all Tony wanted was to moor up without making any mistakes.

Every one of the rally members gathered on the pontoon waiting to congratulate us and hear our story, it's a wonder the pontoon didn't sink. Tony was glad he had taken the time to have a shave and put on a clean shirt; with so many kisses bestowed on him he looked decidedly embarrassed. In fact we were both inundated with kindness, cans of beer and a goody bag were thrust at us, plus a bottle of wine intended for the Crete welcoming ceremony which we had missed. As there was a spare goody bag up for grabs, we got that too, we were informed that we deserved it. To sum up the last two years, it's just what I've always believed; sailing is just a mixture of shite and delight!

We learned that we were in time for the rally trip to Spinalonga Island the following day which included lunch. This was marvellous, as it was one of the trips we really wanted to go on and at least we would be going by coach (no more boats.) Spinalonga Island is an old Leper Colony of which a very interesting book was written, a lot of people on the rally including us had read the book on our way round the world. It would be odd to eventually walk round the now famous tourist attraction, Spinalonga ceased to be used as a Leper Colony in 1953 when a cure for leprosy was finally discovered.

Of course, that night we had to go ashore for a meal with a few others, as you can imagine, we all had plenty to say. The trip and lunch the next day was fantastic, the island itself is an interesting place, we also noticed it had a fairly shallow and calm anchorage between itself and the shore; we put that in the memory banks for future use. The seafood lunch was an island special with all courses being a different type of dish; prawns, calamari and sea bream, it was all delicious. The "as much as you can drink" wine truly flowed freely, waiting staff running backwards and forwards attempted to keep all the carafes filled; even by rally standards an extremely well oiled group of individuals boarded the bus to head back for the marina.

The next day was 21st of April 2009, it was the official end of rally party, there was a good attempt at making it a joyous event but we all knew it was probably the last time we would all be together, after today we were all going our separate ways. The usual dancers, this time Greek, a meal and we all had to wear an item of clothing purchased on our way around the world. Some of our number had produced songs to sing, Audrey had made up one of her poems but this time we put it to music and both of us performed to the gathered assembly, as far as we know, it went down very well but by the time we sung it, everyone was again pretty merry.

For your entertainment we give you the words to our leaving song at the last rally party, sung to the tune of "Bless 'Em All". Believe me, we were actually asked all these questions before we left UK so we have no apologies in repeating them.

Questions and Answers by Audrey Walter

Bless "Em All", Bless "Em All",
Our friends they don't get it at all,
All of our workmates, And those down the Pub
They think we are having such fun on this tub,
And they say they would like to be here,
But we don't think that they'd persevere

Chorus.
They haven't a notion
Of life on the ocean
But never mind lads, Bless "Em All"

Bless "Em All", Bless "Em All"
The questions they ask can be droll
Why do we travel so slowly this way?
When Ellen Macarthur's much faster they'll say
But the media here is to blame
And of course we can't do it the same,

They haven't a notion
Of life on the ocean
But never mind lads
Bless "Em All"

Bless "Em All", Bless "Em All",
They haven't an inkling at all
Why do we have to take watches at night?

If we'd just drop the hook
Then we both could sleep tight.
But then how do you answer a friend
When you really don't want to offend,
Say "Don't be a wanker",
"Of course we can't anchor",
I don't think you'd see them again.

Bless "Em All", Bless "Em All",
Our friends they don't get it at all,
They don't have a notion,
Of life on the ocean
But never mind lads
Bless "Em All"

And when you retire for a piss
It is vital you comprehend this
One hand for the boat
And one hand for the Skipper
While your member is poised
In the base of your zipper
And you're trying like hell not to miss.

Bless "Em All", Bless "Em All"
Our friends they don't get it at all,
They don't have a notion,
Of life on the Ocean
But never mind lads
Bless "Em All"

`This rendition was accepted with much amusement from our fellow ralliers; it touched many a familiar chord.

As the party finished, there was that sad feeling that comes over you when you know it's all ended, that was another emotion to deal with.

Of the original 30 yachts that had started the rally in Gibraltar, only 18 had made it all the way round to Crete, most had left of their own accord to spend more time in the various places. Other cruisers had joined us in the Caribbean, Pacific, Australia, and Thailand so at the end we still numbered around 30 vessels, it made no difference to us, we were still the oldest and slowest boat and the last one to complete the 2007 – 2009 Blue Water Rally.

In the marina we met the people from two new yachts who were signed up for the next BWR start in October 2009, they were heading for Gibraltar so were very interested in our experiences.

We had enjoyed the ups and downs of the last two years, even the thought of the awful, scary bits will fade with time, the one enduring question has got to be,

"Would we do it again?" The nearest answer I can give to that is.

"Well, if it wasn't for the Blue Water Rally team, we may not even have done it this time, but I'm sure Tony would give you a different answer".

I'm proud to have completed the circumnavigation with him; maybe I didn't set out with the idea of doing the whole round the world thing, but it definitely became my challenge as well as his in the end.

Epilogue

Tying the Knot

Tony

The Blue Water Rally was over for us, some yachts that started in Gibraltar were sailing through the Mediterranean back to Marina Bay for the official finish there on the 20th June 2009.

We had originally started from the Greek Island of Kos in 2003 and then sailed back to UK to fit out Cayuco for the circumnavigation. All we had to do from Crete was to head north for 130 miles and sail across our 2003 outbound track west of Kos. Crossing this imaginary line would complete our personal round the world voyage, Audrey and I could then say we had truly "tied the knot". We had lived aboard for almost six years and a lot of water, nearly 33,000 miles of it in fact, had flowed under Cayuco's keel during this time.

As with all major achievements in life, afterwards it can be a bit of an anti climax, we now had to face up to our financial situation and go back to work, all dreams have a price tag attached.

Our last few days in Crete were spent with friends; we toured the island and readied Cayuco for our sail north. It has to be commented that it felt a bit tame after the previous few years.

Audrey

The 23rd of April was St Georges Day so another excuse for a few drinks and a meal ashore with some new friends we had met on the pontoon.

Some priorities that we had already committed ourselves too, was a family get together in Turkey, both our sons, their wives and children were going to be in Marmaris for a week in June, as they had already booked a room for us as well it was imperative we got there on time. I was looking forward so much to seeing them again; we had not been together since we left UK in August 2007. I was particularly eager to see my three grandsons, when we left one was 2½ years old and the other two were only a couple of months, they were now two years older and I could hardly contain myself knowing I would be with them again soon.

During our time away, as we have remarked, occasionally we managed to link up with all of them on the computer. When the camera worked we spoke to them and they could see us while on the small screen. We had become known as "Nanny and Granddad Boat." they came to believe we were miniature "TV sized people," as that was the only way they had seen us! It was quite a surprise for them when they eventually saw us in real life.

The other pre-arranged engagement was for a BBQ at a country park near our home arranged by our son, there was to be as much family present as possible, this was for early August in England and we had already booked our flights.

What happened after that for the moment was up in the air, somehow we would have to come to terms with our bank manager and it was certainly back to work.

The 25th was a therapeutic day, getting boat cleaned up and ensuring everything would be ready when we wanted to leave. In the evening we had a meal onboard and then met Hugh and Shan from Stargazer for a drink ashore, they were leaving the next day. Two other rally members we met came back for a drink onboard Cayuco, they were all leaving soon and it really would be all over.

Tony

We made a decision to stay at Aghios Nicholas Marina for a while, the time would enable me to get a few necessary jobs done on Cayuco and a couple of rally members wanted some assistance with some difficult jobs before they left as well. There was no hurry to leave now, it was good not having to keep to a timetable anymore. We both enjoyed the lack of pressure and joined in with the social life of the liveaboards on the marina; they came from many nations and most had over wintered in the port.

The days rolled by and drifted into each other, we went to the BYO Sunday BBQ run every week by all the crews on the yachts, watched the start of the snooker final in the local sports bar, it was all very lay-back. On Audrey's birthday in early May, I cooked her a breakfast, celebrated with Buck's Fizz and later on in the day went for a meal with the fourteen ralliers who were still left in the marina.

I then got a phone call from an acquaintance who ran a 60 foot catamaran in Turkey as a charter boat, he had been let down by someone and was looking for a relief skipper and hostess for the last week in May. A quick word with Audrey and we had a job for a week, now we would have to make a move and head for Turkey, at least the money he was offering would help our sorry bank account.

As we had a few days left on the marina we continued with the clean up, Audrey did her best with all the accumulated rust stains, I sorted the CVs and qualifications needed for the charter job, fitted a new stern light and we both enjoyed the social life, if we weren't careful, we could get used to this. The 19th May came round fast, we said goodbye to the few rally friends still in Aghios Nikolas and left for Turkey, the weather was calm, a gale that was blowing a few days before had passed by and even the sea just had a pleasant little roll to it.

For us this was a short trip, only 130 miles, just an overnighter, Crete dropped behind us, we had enjoyed it there, we made a promise to come back and visit again one day. It was a very pleasant night's sail; the hours of darkness did not yet have that Mediterranean balmy air feel about it, just a bit early and slightly chilly.

The next morning the sun popped its head up over the Greek Island of Kos, the last time we had seen this was as it disappeared behind us when we left in 2003. Our outward bound track was just a few miles ahead; soon we would cross that imaginary line that indicated the end of our voyage round the world.

At 11-30 in the morning on 20th May 2009 in position 36° 56′ north and 27° 12′ east we crossed our outward path, the point that signified our circumnavigation was over and we had officially "tied the knot". A few hours later we moored up in the new Turgutreis Marina near Bodrum in Turkey, when we left in 2003, the marina had not even been built.

It was over, all the struggles we had faced around the globe faded, all the nights at sea in the inky blackness were finished, gales we'd battled through for days in various parts of the world were behind us, the memories of gear breakages at sea while trying to keep calm and sailing became distant recollections. Together we had made it as we had set out to do, there was not a lot of celebration or merriment, we were the only ones there and just gave each other a hug, we thought about all the different experiences, emotions and personnel mountains we'd had to climb. It had taken a tremendous leap of faith, which had eventually paid off. Now it was time to return to normality, whatever that used to be.

Best wishes to you all, fair winds and calm seas.

Audrey and Tony Walter.

Figure 42: All the family came out for a holiday in Turkey to welcome us back from our voyage.

www.ingramcontent.com/pod-product-compliance
Lightning Source LLC
Chambersburg PA
CBHW020828160426
43192CB00007B/562